CLASSIFICATION LIBRARY MATERIALS

Current and Future
Potential for
Providing Access

EDITED BY
BETTY G. BENGTSON and JANET SWAN HILL

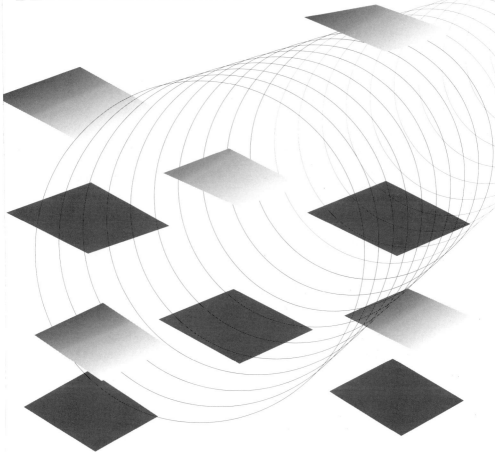

Neal-Schuman Publishers, Inc.
New York   London

Classification of Library Materials is based on a series of regional institutes sponsored by the Resources and Technical Services Division, Cataloging and Classification Section, American Library Association.

Published by Neal-Schuman Publishers, Inc.
23 Leonard Street
New York, NY 10013

Printed and bound in the United States of America.
This book is printed on acid-free paper which meets the standard established by the American National Standard Institute Committee for Information Science—Permanence of Paper for Printed Library Materials. (Z–39–48, 1984.)

Library of Congress Cataloging-in-Publication Data

Classification of library materials : current and future potential for
   providing access / edited by Betty G. Bengtson and Janet Swan Hill.
      p.   cm.
   ISBN 1-55570-027-6
   1. Classification--Books.   2. Classification--Nonbook materials.
   3. Library materials--Classification.   I. Bengtson, Betty G.
   II. Hill, Janet Swan.
   Z696.A4C69   1990
   025.4'2--dc20
                               90-8054
                                 CIP

Contents

Introduction

Now, after a period of relative neglect, the application and mechanics of classification and the role classification will play in the future are receiving attention. The use of the machine to manipulate records, to provide additional access points more easily, and to provide through Boolean operators access heretofore unavailable has led to renewed interest in classification for information storage and retrieval. The study of the use of online catalogs sponsored by the Council on Library Resources in 1981 revealed the strength of the demand for subject access.

In the past few years, there has been considerable study and discussion about descriptive cataloging, authority control, and subject headings with regional institutes offered on each by the Association for Library Collections & Technical Services (formerly Resources and Technical Services Division). However, there has not been an American Library Association conference on classification since the Institute on the Use of the Library of Congress Classification held in New York in July, 1966. In an attempt to rectify that situation, ALCTS sponsored a preconference institute designed to be a state-of-the-art review and a series of regional institutes designed to give more practical training in the use of the two major classification systems used in the U.S.—Dewey and the Library of Congress. The preconference was held July 4-5, 1985 at the ALA Annual Conference in Chicago. The fact that 130 people gave up their July 4th holiday to attend the meetings attests to the strength of interest in classification.

The chapters in *Classification of Library Materials* have been assembled from various sources. Most reflect presentations given originally at the preconference in July, 1985. Some were repeated at the regional wokshops between 1986 and 1988. The Nichols paper was not given at the preconference, but was presented at the regional institutes. The Younger paper was written for this volume. Papers read from prepared text appear essentially as they were submitted by the authors. The presentations of Liz Bishoff, John Comaromi, Mary Ghikas, Mary Kay Pietris, and Arnold Wajenberg were given as workshops, without a prepared text. In these cases the text has been edited from a tape transcription of one of the workshop sessions. For both types of presentations, substantive questions from the audience and their answers as recorded during the preconference have been incorporated into the text wherever possible. Where appropriate, the papers have been updated to reflect developments since their original presentation.

In his chapter, based on his keynote address at the preconference, Hugh Atkinson reaffirms the importance of classification and calls for even more rigor in its application as decentralization increasingly removes the user from the materials and substitutes browsing in the online catalog for browsing on the shelf. Phyllis Richmond's review of general classification theory provides a background for the remainder of the papers.

Nancy Williamson reports the results of a survey of graduate schools of library and information science instruction in classification and of employer needs and expectations in the area of classification knowledge.

Russell Sweeney discusses the Atlantic divide in classification—the different attitudes towards classification in North America and in Europe.

John Comaromi and Mary Kay Pietris briefly review the Dewey and LC classification schemes, highlighting history, current developments, and recurring problems. Classification in copy cataloging is explored by Arlene Taylor.

Karen Markey reports on the Dewey Classification Online Project, an experiment designed to test the use of classification to enrich subject access in the online environment. Mary Ghikas and Lizbeth Bishoff present the administrator's viewpoint in separate sessions on setting and implementing classification policy.

Elizabeth Nichols presents the results of a survey of classification usage and decision-making patterns among California libraries. Jennifer Younger discusses known item searching, shelf browsing, and classification policies. Arnold Wajenberg's delightful wrap-up summarizes significant themes from throughout the conference presentations. The importance of classification, its potential role in online catalogs to enhance information retrieval, and the problems of dealing with changes in classification schemes were the recurrent themes addressed by the contributors to *Classification of Library Materials*.

Betty Bengtson

1

Classification in an Unclassified World

Hugh C. Atkinson

When talking about classification, at least in this country, working librarians must approach it from a practical point of view, even though understanding the theoretical bases is necessary before committing to a useful, practical approach. Classification is, after all, as Maltby points out, "the systematic arrangement of library material in a manner which is useful to those who use it"[1] (those who use a library or those who seek a particular piece of information). The important thing to remember about this definition is that it refers not only to an arrangement, but to a useful arrangement.

Classification is necessary not just because it puts something in a particular place in the library but also because it demonstrates to the user a relationship of one kind or another. This relationship is usually with materials classified in the same area, and, if it is a good classification system, with materials scattered throughout the collection. This is where the notation as a retrieval device can demonstrate a relationship that is not clear from the notation as shelf placement. The most familiar example in the United States is the system for mnemonics found in the Dewey classification.

When we talk about classification in the U.S. library world, we do not mean Bliss or Ranganathan or some of the fancier schemes. In the United States there are really only two classification systems in general use, plus some that are homemade. The two major ones are, of course, Dewey and Library of Congress. The information contained in this chapter should be interpreted in the light of those two classification systems, not in terms of such radical schemes as Colon classification or even the Universal Decimal Classification, which is so popular in Europe. While Pauline Atherton (afterwards Cochrane), as we catalogers so fondly call her (based on the old form of entry for George Eliot) and Karen Markey have made a fairly cogent argument[2] that the

Library of Congress is not truly a classification system, since it has relatively little ability to demonstrate the relationship of one item to another. Nevertheless, we will consider it a classification scheme and recognize that in academic libraries it is perhaps the one most commonly used.

I come from an academic library that does not use LC. The University of Illinois has always used the Dewey Decimal Classification and we are not planning to change. There are two reasons for this attitude. The flippant response evokes Stephen Dedalus's comment to Cranly in *Portrait of the Artist as a Young Man*. When Stephen had stopped being a Catholic, Cranly asked if he was going to become a member of the Church of Ireland, Stephen asked in turn why he should ". . . forsake an absurdity which is logical and coherent . . . to embrace one which is illogical and incoherent."[3] For a more practical response I point out that the disruption to users would be so great, and would last so long that changing from Dewey to LC is an option that is simply not available to a library that is committed to decent service. Switching from Dewey to LC is not going from one absurdity to another with a loss of logic. Neither system is absurd, but at UIUC (University of Illinois at Urbana-Champaign) we prefer the more complex Dewey with its clearer emphasis on relationships, its attempts (albeit occasionally unsuccessful ones) to provide a consistent approach to both information and library materials. Yet both Dewey and the ever popular alternative provided by the Library of Congress are far from absurdities. They are necessities. The larger a library grows the more difficult it is to find material, and to double that complexity by using two classification schemes would be an unpardonable act as far as I am concerned.

BROWSING

One of the problems that besets us as librarians is that our patrons do not always act in the manner that we would prefer. They do not always use the tools we so laboriously provide; they do not value the things that we value; they place a premium on things that we see to be less essential; and they have a habit of ignoring those things that we consider to be more essential. For instance, getting the building open seems to be valued far more by our patrons than high quality reference service or high quality cataloging. The one thing we can agree on is that whether we like it or not, whether we think it is the best way to approach the literature that we so carefully acquire, store and provide access to, browsing—whether done on the shelf or in the catalog—is one of the primary ways of finding library material and of satisfying library needs. That is the fundamental reason that I think classification is so important for libraries and librarians, and why I believe that off-site storage facilities and other devices in library systems that do not allow browsing take a very high toll in library use and patron satisfaction. The same principle, by the way, may well be true for those systems that will come upon us, machine-based information systems and machine-readable library materials. If the browsing function is not somehow provided we will be unable to provide library service to the extent that it is really needed. Nor will we be able to convince our patrons that the service they are getting is that which provides for their information needs. Whether it is academic libraries as Fussler and Simon[4] noted, or in technical libraries as Slater and Fisher[5] demonstrated, the browsing function is an essential part of the strategy for retrieval of material. This is true whether the patron is seeking known items or is seeking library materials by subject. Browsing is the primary retrieval system for a very large portion of our patrons' library searches. Therefore, the work of classification is as fundamentally important as any task in librarianship.

ONLINE CATALOGS

It is quite clear that the age of the online catalog and of machine-readable access to a library's holdings is here. The question is not whether we are going to provide such catalogs, but when and in what form we will make that provision. We will have to decide whether the online catalog will be designed cooperatively with other libraries or whether we will do it alone, whether we will provide it through a utility, whether we will buy a stand-alone system, and so forth. The question of whether we will move to a machine-readable catalog has already been answered in the affirmative, and there is general consensus in the library world that that is the appropriate response. It is the future of the library's bibliographic control.

The move toward automation has two aspects that are of interest. First of all, one should note that in the very near future cataloging is likely to be fully automated or at least semi-automated. For instance, if a Kurzweil machine can read a book to a blind patron, it can just as easily read the title page and perhaps the verso of the title page and match the data captured to data in a large bibliographic file. In fact, if the machine does not find a record, it can probably be programmed eventually to perform most of the tasks outlined in the current catalog codes. For the vast majority of literature, the information found on the title page plus some physical measurement is enough for descriptive cataloging. A machine can measure the size of a book. A machine can read the last page number. A machine can transcribe the title page form of the author's name.

It is not hard to imagine connection of a Kurzweil machine or something like it to a personal computer or to OCLC, and then to an inputting device for use when a matching record is found. In fact, it is not hard to imagine developing cataloging codes that make such activity the standard. What is much harder to imagine is that same machine being able to perform the function of analyzing the item as to what it is about, or performing the kinds of analyses and notation that demonstrate the relationship of that item and what it is about to the other books, journals, films, videotapes, and the like, which are in the library—in short, the activity of classifying the material. From a very practical standpoint, it is clear that such a machine may well take away the job of the descriptive cataloger, but it is much further in the future that a machine will usurp the job of the classifier.

As we look at the decentralized and other systems, which are helping libraries make more productive use of professional librarians' time and more efficient use of support staff, it is also clear that even in non-automated systems the professional will probably be assigning the descriptive cataloging to the nonprofessional, reserving only the subject analysis and classification to herself or himself. Thus, classification will be far more likely to require our services in the future.

CLASSIFICATION FOR SUBJECT RETRIEVAL

In addition to self preservation, which is a strong motivation, as we look at ever more complex libraries, we can see the universal need for good classification. Whether material is found by browsing or whether indexes or catalogs are used to lead patrons to library material, it is very clear that one of the great problems in retrieval of library materials or information has changed. In many cases the major problem is no longer trying to find out all there is about a subject, but rather sorting through what there is in order to find material that answers specific needs; sorting out from the plethora of answers to our query those that are best suited to our use. It is not information scarcity that is a problem, but rather information overload. This is one of the places where classification comes into its own. A well applied, good classification system will show relationships of the item found to items that are broader and narrower in subject content. A well applied classification number provides the library patron with the ability, once having found one item, to assemble other items in the forms and amount that he or she needs.

One of the most striking examples of the use of classification for subject retrieval is found in the work of Karen Markey. In a 1985 issue of *Information Technology and Libraries* Ms. Markey and Pauline Cochrane had an interesting article on the use of online catalogs and online indexes for the classifier.[6] The University of Illinois at Urbana-

Champaign is one of the places where Ms. Markey tested theories about the usefulness of a machine-readable form of the Dewey index and schedules. She performed some experiments in our Mathematics Library, and it was clear to me as I watched other people using the catalog she constructed and when I used it myself that the alphabetical indexes—the A to Z approach to subjects—were immediately enhanced by the ability to move up and down the topical hierarchy from mathematics to algebra to Reinges integral and the like. It was clear that those relationships that were not present in the subject headings but were present in the classification notation enabled retrieval with far greater precision than anything I had seen before. In fact, I was so impressed with it, that if I had to choose between an A to Z alphabetical list of subject headings and the machine-readable Dewey index and a program to use it as a retrieval device, I suspect that I would use classification rather than subject headings. Of course, far greater retrievability results when one uses both. It is very likely that a combination of word searching in titles, subjects, and descriptive cataloging entries, coupled with classification and classification indexes will provide the most powerful approach to library materials. If that occurs, it may be that we will no longer be facing the phenomenon that we now see in so many academic libraries—that some 80 percent of the uses made of our collections are for known items. It is my suspicion that the present situation only exists because we have not provided adequate subject retrievability. The studies that demonstrate this alleged phenomenon are flawed because they ignore present physical browsing activity. When we do provide good subject access and retrievability to our holdings we may see an enormous rise in the use of that kind of access. It is clear in public libraries that a far smaller portion of catalog use is for individual known items, and that a very large amount of user interest is in general subject or author, not in a particular title or literary form.

It is often assumed that only large libraries, catering to those specializing in the esoteric, that require fine classification and precise subject analysis. I disagree. Let me give you an example that I came across in my own use of my local public library, the Urbana Free Library. I admit that libraries in university towns tend to have a different clientele and a different book selection policy, and perhaps even a different library administration from libraries in other kinds of cities and towns. However, the Urbana Free Library is not an atypical medium-sized public library. It is a good library for a town of 35,000. It is well administered and well supported by the town. The fact that the director teaches at the University of Illinois Library School and holds a Ph.D. from the University of Chicago does, of course, tend to set it apart from most other libraries in towns of 35,000. That, however, is not the point of this anecdote.

I was looking for books on Indian cooking, especially recipes for curry dishes. The practice in the Urbana Free Library, as it is in so many libraries of its size, is to carry the classification to as few places to the right of the decimal point as possible, seldom more than three. 641.591 is "Cookery characteristic of areas, regions and places," with area notations added. Now, if you simply use 641.591 or 641.592 and Cutter by author, the problem is clear. When one is looking for Indian cooking, one may well be interested, as I was, in the cooking of allied regions or cultures. Thus, a book on Bengali cookery, or cookery of the Kashmir or Bangladesh would be as important to the user as one about the cookery of India in general. The Urbana Free is a relatively small library, but nevertheless there were some two and a half sections of cookbooks in the 641.591s and 592s—fairly typical of a library of this size in this kind of community. Now by Cuttering after 591 or 592 one has Chinese cookery intermixed with Italian and the cookery of Canada intermixed with the cookery of India. Joyce Chen and Julia Child get shelved together. I really needed the demonstration of relationship that Dewey would have afforded if the classification had been carried out further. Indian cookery is 641.592411 and Bengali cookery is 641.592144. If these longer numbers had been used, instead of having to browse through three to five hundred volumes, I would have had a far more precise, and probably far more complete search result. Until I looked at the Dewey classification schedule I did not know that a book I could easily overlook would be one on the cookery of Kashmir. Thus, it is not the size of the library or the general rules of administration of classification that should have been applied in this case, but rather the needs of users. Long isn't always bad, and short isn't necessarily better. It depends on what the number tells the user.

The "arrangement for usefulness" that we defined as being what classification is really about is called for in all libraries. It is clear in this case that the classification had been used simply as a place to park the materials, and not as part of an information system for the user. This example illustrates clearly why the job of the classifier is truly one of intellectual analysis, which is not only analysis of the material, but also analysis of the potential reader. The job of classification does not end with the analysis of the book. If classification is ever complete, it is complete only after there is an analysis of the book as well as the uses to which it is likely to be put.

PATRONS USE PATTERNS

Just how books and other library materials are used by our patrons is one of the least understood aspects in all of librarianship. As Paul Metz notes in his admirable *The Landscape of Literature,*[7] it seems impossible that such complex systems as libraries have been designed to meet needs that are not understood, or are misunderstood, and about which we know so little. It might well be that the easy task of the classifier is to analyze the subject of a work, and the harder task is to analyze just how a patron is likely to use it.

One of the apparent but often ignored truths in librarianship is that there is not just *a* patron, or just *the* patron, but there are many patrons, each of whom brings to the library a unique set of needs and an equally unique way of using library materials. Of course, these unique ways and uses can be sorted into patterns, and that is the job of the classifier. Are we arranging materials for the specialist or the generalist? Are we providing access for those who use a particular subject as a primary resource or for those who regard it as a peripheral interest? Mr. Metz points out complexities in the use of academic libraries, but it is clear that what we do not know about the use of libraries of all kinds may well be greater than what we do know. That becomes a real challenge for the classifier. It requires the realization that good library service requires very rigorous classification and that classification must be done by someone who recognizes the limits and the ambiguities of the *inherent subject* of a work as well as the scope, limitations and ambiguities of the classification scheme. Most important, the classifier must recognize the range and differing needs of the patrons for whom that classification is performed and the library service provided.

The ability to strive simultaneously for perfection and to recognize the inability to reach it, all the while recognizing the anomalies of the task itself, requires an intellectual strength that I think classifiers have always demonstrated. That strength is required to an even greater degree now, since we are just beginning to adjust our librarianship to the theory that the best library service is that which is easiest for the library patron to use; that the best library access methods are those that provide for the strategies that our patrons want to employ; that the better library collections are those that are made up of materials that the patrons want or will want; and that the language of librarianship, of its service and its catalogs should be the language of our patrons. Sanford Berman's long campaign to have libraries provide a language of access that corresponds to the language used by patrons to formulate their requests is essentially correct. Sandy often reminds me of those prophets who wander through the pages of the Old Testament proclaiming the truth so accurately and so irritatingly that the rest of us, while recognizing the validity of the message, wish they would just go away and stop demanding such difficult reforms.

DECENTRALIZATION

There are good reasons to believe that we are moving into a world of decentralization. There are many examples of the decentralizing of the activities of our society. For instance, responsibilities that we have traditionally assigned to the federal government are moving from Washington to the individual states. Right or wrong, that kind of change is going on in our society. While we may not necessarily agree with each individual application of that change, the changes are occurring because we are part of a society that is demanding them. Society is requiring that the information, the decisions, the responsibilities, the authority and the need for information about things that affect our daily lives must move ever closer to the individual. That kind of decentralization requires a communications network that is broader and stronger, capable of higher volume than ever before.

We have heard a lot of talk about decentralizing libraries. As we decentralize, as we move to branch libraries, or as we move to greater use of interlibrary loan, not only can we no longer say we are independent agents, independent libraries, independent states, but we should also note that in the process of ever more independent decision making there is a requirement for ever more *inter*dependent communication. As soon as one moves to a "distance independent" communication world, as soon as one moves from a set of shelves that is nearby, or from a catalog that is at hand, to dependence on interlibrary loan, on library bibliographic and control systems, on multi-state processing centers and the like, as one moves to a network of various sized units, then the requirements of analysis and classification become ever more rigorous. One cannot just grub around on the shelves because the shelves are somewhere else. The patron has to be provided with the kinds of information that are necessary to make informed decisions. Do I want that piece of information? Shall I borrow that book? Does that periodical contain what I need? Does our state have the kinds of library materials and information necessary to support this kind of industry? As we get more sophisticated telecommunciations systems coupled with decentralized library activity and holdings, all situated within an interdependent network, the answers to those questions require fine and sophisticated classification. Classification has to be both precise and far more detailed than we have ever had before.

We are moving forward to a time when, without destroying our present library structures, we will add networks—whether local, state, regional or national, perhaps overlaying one network on another, and providing vastly expanded library service. We can see more decentralized library activity and more interconnected series of very small nodes. In such a network design, where we see increasing volume over the communication channels and decreasing total numbers at each of the nodes, precise, accurate, and complete analysis of individual biblio-graphic items is extraordinarily important for the full utilization of such schemes.

In the modern era, we have never had to use the catalog instead of the books on the shelves. Up until now, no matter what we said as theorists, the catalog was an aid to using the shelves, not a substitute for them. When we evolve a concept of "library" that encompasses all of the collections within a five-county area, however, or all of the holdings in a state or in a region such as the Pacific Northwest, we will not have the luxury of the shelf at hand. Without that nearby presence we will have to have a catalog and a system of classification that demonstrates the kinds of relationships we might see if we walked through the library stacks. Not only will the need for the local catalog be enhanced by the use of classification, as demonstrated by Karen Markey, but also classi-fication may become an essential tool for the decentralization and networking of library and information centers in this country.

Future catalogs and future information retrieval systems will require classification schemes that show relationships and deal with the hier-archy of subject relationships as expressed by useful mnemonic devices.

COLLECTION DEVELOPMENT

Another example of the use of classification as we move toward a changed world of librarianship is occurring right now in Illinois. The Illinois Board of Higher Education is sponsoring initiatives in the area of cooperative collection development among academic libraries. The State Library has been pursuing the same ideal within the public library community. The two approaches are being coordinated, and there is a lot of interaction between members of both working groups. The process is not only leading up to cooperative purchasing and selection, but is evolving a methodology by which such cooperative activity can be a rational process. Hopefully, it will be a process that will bring to the students and other researchers who reside within the state as compre-hensive and complete a library collection as possible. The technique being employed is a refinement of the conspectus developed by the Research Library Group (RLG) and adopted by the Association of Research Libraries for the analysis and description of library collections. Under the leadership of the collection development officers of the librar-ies, a fair number of the larger academic libraries in Illinois have cooperated in performing the kinds of shelflist counts that are required by the national shelflist count project. This group is building matrices by those subjects from the national shelflist count for the participating libraries. In addition, a number of other somewhat broader areas are being analyzed in terms of collection quality and quantity to supplement the analyses done by the national shelflist count. Those two factors, together with such factors as the date of the material, the age of the collection, and the languages of the materials housed in the collections are being used to provide profiles both of individual collections and of the state's holdings. It is from these profiles and analyses that future purchasing programs will be developed. We look forward to both expansion of the matrices and the building of appropriate online databases. The purchasing programs that will spring from and be based on this kind of analysis will, we hope, be a successful and responsive collection development effort. It is an attempt to establish a system by which the selection and purchasing programs are in the hands of the same bibliographers who direct the purchasing programs and selection in the various libraries, or at least a representative group of them. Thus, we are trying to move away from a simple and self-serving program of buying expensive items and are trying to avoid the political process of supplementing various libraries' book budgets. If we can develop a rational plan for library service for the patrons of academic libraries within the state, it will attract significant funding without interfering with the present levels of funding for state-supported libraries.

Most academic libraries in Illinois use the Library of Congress classification scheme. It is clear, as I look at the kinds of data and analyses that are going on in the process of trying to provide the best possible collection development program, that there would be great benefits if all the cooperating libraries applied a much finer and more precise classification scheme. It is not enough simply to provide the translation of LC into Dewey, or Dewey into LC (which heaven knows is problem enough), but rather, if we had all used better schemes in the first place, we would have been able to provide analyses that included the types of the hierarchical relationships that can provide guidance for purchase to collection development officers or book selectors in the same way that I, as a public library patron, needed guidance in the cookbook section of the Urbana Free Library.

An administrator or a participant in the library planning process would be much happier if he or she were able to perform the collection development function using a classification scheme that demonstrated both hierarchy and relationships and that was able to connect that information to particular bibliographic items in particular libraries. Thus, while I think we will in fact do a good job of cooperative collection development, I think that it would be a better job if we were able to perform some of the kinds of analyses for all libraries that we will be able to perform for some of the public libraries.

Cooperative programs are becoming widespread and are soon going to be active in all parts of the country. The Pacific Northwest, California, Alaska, Indiana, and many other areas are initiating similar projects. New York State, through its 3R program has long been a leader in this area. It is not simply the translation into purchases of bright ideas or perceived lacunae that will make these programs a success, but rather better programs that are dependent on approaching the statewide library collection activity with the same kinds of analyses with which we should have approached our own collections.

THE FUTURE OF CLASSIFICATION

For many years patrons could only search library records by the first word that appeared in a particular place or spot on a catalog card. With the advent of machine-readable systems catalogs can be searched by starting left or right of the decimal point and by combining various Boolean statements for both pre- and post-coordinate indexing. The user can start at the end as well as at the beginning of a call number, or even in the middle. We are now approaching a position, with advances in size, speed and data handling ability of computer-based systems, to be able to search the facets of Dewey numbers through millions of records in ways we could not dream of before. Not only the hierarchies in classification schemes such as Dewey, but the interrelationships demonstrated in the construction of the notations themselves will provide the user with the ability to bring together information about physically separated materials and to display that information. Portions of the collections separated by physical distance, and by the structure of the classification system itself, may thus be brought together. For instance, we will be able to use the geographic facet to bring together for the study of a culture materials that have been classified by discipline. That will be repeated over and over again through all of the mnemonics. With such techniques the problems of whether or not to invert a file of subject headings may well disappear with the increased searching power of computers.

As a parenthetical aside one should remember, of course, when speaking of classification, as B.C. Vickery and every writer on classification and analysis reminds us, that it is the understanding of the classification, not of the notation (the shorthand by which the classification is expressed), that is important.[8] In the education of classifiers, it is the understanding of the scheme, not the memorizing of schedules, that is of fundamental worth and value. Much of the theory that underlies classification is best found in that dean of all writers on the subject, A.C. Foskett, in *The Subject Approach to Literature and Information*[9] especially in the early chapters, "Features of an Information Retrieval System," his section on pre-coordinated indexing systems, and the companion chapter on pre-coordinated indexing languages.

Multiple Classification

The requirements of future catalogs and library systems seem to be leading us to want to provide multiple classification for single items. The application of classification in modern machine-based systems will require as many alternate classification numbers as are legitimate to the piece. By that, I do not mean that we should simply reverse the mnemonics and place the concept by which the original number is expanded as the base and reverse the notations, but rather that alternative class numbers should bring out additional subjects. Since so many books are about more than one subject, one should bring out those additional subjects, not just aspects of the main subject. If it is a good classification scheme, or even an imperfect one with a good theoretical basis, such as Dewey, the scheme itself will demonstrate some of the relationships inherent in the item. In the same way, future systems will require us to produce many more subject headings than are now found in the standard American catalog record. One of the most fascinating things about a reasonably good and well applied classification system is that it is partially self-explanatory, at least to the moderately inquisitive and intellectual user, who, while using a library, has previously unnoticed relationships brought to his or her attention by means of the classification scheme.

Delivery Systems

The library must be able to deliver books into the hands of library users, not just tell them about their existence; thus, the delivery system is an essential part of the library network. Self-service schemes that allow the patron to participate in library activity traditionally performed by library staff are being developed. At the University of Illinois our experience demonstrates that full interlibrary loan activity cannot occur without a basically self-service approach for most interlibrary loan operations, just as exists for most of the library's internal circulation activity. The library staff steps into local circulation activity only when something goes wrong, or when reference assistance is needed, or special handling is required. The same holds true for almost all interlibrary activity. At UIUC only about 30,000 volumes were borrowed per year so long as interlibrary loan activity required the traditional submission of a request to a professionally administered interlibrary loan service. Since we implemented a self-service activity well over 150,000 items are borrowed a year. Within two years, we expect to be near 200,000, or approximately ten percent of our local circulation. That level of activity demonstrates the importance of explicable self-service and patron-driven library systems. The same principles will operate with regard to the use of library classification. Classification schemes have to be built into the self-service retrieval devices available to the library's patrons in such a way that the almost limitless depths of library need begin to be satisfied.

CONCLUSION

One of the constant truths about library activity is "the better you do it, the more people want." I know of no library anywhere that truly satisfies the information needs of its clientele. Information needs are so broad and so complex, that even with great improvement we always seem to be in a situation where our patrons need, and sometimes demand, more. It is a comforting phenomenon viewed from one perspective. It does mean that we are both important and necessary in this society.

The history of professional librarianship is marked by a very long transition from activities performed by library staff to activities performed by library patrons. It is a shifting of both the record-keeping and the library activity from behind the library desk to in front of it. The shift is occurring in a direct parallel to the rise of our own professionalism. This transition has occurred not because we want to pass off to somebody else those tasks that rightfully belong to us. Rather, it is the only way for so few to provide the level of circulation and reference and other services that are demanded. The rise of programs for self-service searching of computer-based reference services, such as Chemical Abstracts and ERIC, are simply part of the latest aspects of this phenomenon. And the process continues. Our problem is similar to the problem faced by professionals in the field of mental health. There is far more need for their services than there are people to provide it, and so group therapy and other substitutes for the individual therapist-patient relationship are increasingly common.

As we look at a library future, which is increasingly self-service, which will be marked by networking and interlibrary activity and interlibrary dependence, we see a future of rapidly increasing complexity, both in the materials themselves and in the needs of the patrons. Librarianship must process an enormously increasing volume and complexity of information. The role and position of those who perform the necessary analyses of the literatures and information and who provide analyses to patrons in a useful, consistent, and accurate form, will be essential in the provision of the kinds of library services that are even now required.

In one sense, we keep re-inventing (and doing it rather poorly) forms of classification. We do so through user-friendly interfaces to online public catalogs and to online reference services. Here in Illinois, we are inventing classification schemes when we try to build matrices for cooperative collection development. We already have good schemes. It is too bad we do not use them better. The rise of such makeshift classification schemes are a sign of our failure both as administrators and as librarians to employ the classification schemes and analytical tools that we have. As an administrator, I do not believe that it is an appropriate role for librarians to redo the classification numbers already formulated by those classifying materials at the Library of Congress, but I do believe that it is an appropriate role for the professional librarian who is originally classifying material, whether at a local library or at a national one, to classify all material as completely and as accurately as possible. It is also appropriate to insist upon accurate and complete classification at all levels of librarianship. In this world of librarianship in transition, classification is not just the scholarly and theoretical discipline that the British are so fond of, nor is it simply the shelf arrangement that we administrators have so often mistakenly foisted off as classification. It is instead one of the essential tools for providing modern library service. It is one of the devices that will enable us to provide the kinds and levels of library service that we regard as ideal.

The study of classification is addictive. It is both fun and it is important. How well we employ intellectual rigor and to what extent we reflect through classification our commitment to the best in library services and to the free access of information, may well define the librarianship of the next three decades. Classification really does stand at the core not only of library theory, but also of library practice.

REFERENCES

1. Arthur Maltby, *Sayers' Manual of Classification for Librarians* (London: Andre Deutsch, 1975).
2. Pauline A. Cochrane and Karen Markey, "Preparing for the Use of Classification in Online Cataloging Systems and in Online Catalogs," *Information Technology and Libraries* 4 (1985): 91–111.
3. James Joyce, *A Portrait of the Artist as a Young Man* (New York: Modern Library, 1928), 287.
4. Herman H. Fussler and Julian L. Simon, *Patterns in the Use of Books in Large Research Libraries* (Chicago: University of Chicago Press), 1969.
5. Margaret Slater and Pamela Fisher, *Use Made of Technical Libraries*, Aslib Occasional Publication No. 2 (London: Aslib, 1969).
6. Cochrane and Markey, "Preparing for the Use of Classification," 91–111.
7. Paul Metz, *The Landscape of Literatures; Use of Subject Collections in a University Library*, ACRL Publications in Librarianship, 43 (Chicago: American Library Association, 1983).
8. B.C. Vickery, "Notational Symbols in Classification," *Journal of Documentation*, 8 (1952): 14–32. This fine paper is continued in the *Journal of Documentation* under the same title in two further parts, "Notation as an

Ordering Device" in vol. 12 (1956): 73–87 and ". . . Further Comparison of Brevity" in vol. 13 (1957): 72–77.
9. A.C. Foskett, *The Subject Approach to Information*, 4th ed. (Hamden, CT: Linnett Books, 1982).

2

General Theory of Classification

Phyllis A. Richmond

The subject matter, principles, and theory concerning classification are spelled out in works on philosophy, usually in the areas of logic, language, and scientific method.[1] The action involved in classifying, of course, goes way back and, in fact, it has been demonstrated that animals classify, at least to the point of determining what is edible and what is not. Operationally, classification is vital to survival.

Currently, the variety and ambiguity of classification systems are well-known facts. Organizations like the Classification Research Group in England[2] exist for the purpose of catching up with modern needs to fit new knowledge into the background of old knowledge. Knowledge itself is constantly defined and redefined, categorized and re-categorized in all of its fields by researchers who name classes, philosophers who fit them into the fabric of what is known, by librarians who make classification systems, and other librarians, who, in the process of using them, discover inadequacies in even the best systems.

The subject matter of the "general theory of classification" underlies all systems. Classificationists (those who design systems) have to have a pretty good idea of the general philosophy, not only of present organization of knowledge, but of past systems as well. It is surprising to young people entering the field to find out how much is owed to Aristotle, who flourished 23 centuries ago, and how often the wheel, so to speak, gets re-invented.

It is long recognized that classification of knowledge is largely made by people who create new knowledge. Much less well-defined, however, are the content and boundaries set by those who claim to be classifying and setting the boundaries of an amorphous content called *information*. The term *information*, which the late Fritz Machlup has shown to have about 30 distinct meanings,[3] has become very popular because of changes in the format, packaging, and distribution of knowledge. Knowledge was formerly packaged in codex book format, but now comes piecemeal in reports and articles as well, plus non-paper formats, which use a variety of equipment and media. Recently it seemed as if everyone would need a computer with a modem, a printer, and so forth in order to communicate directly with those who created knowledge. This rosy view, however, is meeting with a fate similar to that of the expectation 30 years ago that microtext would replace print on paper. When either of these potential replacements came to be tried out seriously, prediction of their success turned out to be somewhat premature. Copying by means of xerography proved to be much more useful than film, fiche and so on, while the computer is more successful as a word processor and statistics processor than as a computation machine, at least for our purposes. In both cases, an analogy to water finding its own way downhill is apropos. Statements to the effect that computers would deal with information at the individual level, replacing current organization of media, turned out to be similar to the views that two can live as cheaply as one, or that an automated library would save money. Love is equally blind in both cases.

Fritz Machlup's summary of the 30 distinct kinds of *information* clearly shows that the *information age*, like the "Tower of Babel" allegory, is going to be fragmented.[4] The possibility of general classification theory developing into a viable means of putting things in order becomes more and more remote.

General classification theory, as applied in the Dewey Decimal Classification, the Library of Congress system, the Universal Decimal Classification, the Bliss Bibliographic Classification, the Colon Classification of Ranganathan, the Faceted Bliss system now being developed by the Classification Research Group in London, the Rider Classification, and hundreds, if not thousands of systems developed for special collections, still functions. It is unlikely that alternatives such as indexing, or thesaurus-making in its twentieth century form, can replace systems of general classification, chiefly because the general systems are not language-dependent. Also, as imperfect as general classification systems are, it is very hard to make one. The Classification Research Group has been working on theirs for almost 40 years and finally could do no better than update Bliss in a faceted format.[5]

GENERAL CLASSIFICATION THEORY

With these generalities out of the way, what is General Classification Theory and why is it important? General Classification Theory is based on a few simple principles:

1. Every thing, object, notion, etc. has to have a distinct and unambiguous description of its unique qualities.
2. Principles involving likeness and distinctness must be used in creating classes.

3. Hierarchies and other relational methods are necessary in order to group fundamental characteristics and to identify fundamental differences clearly.
4. The final system should appear as a logical progression from general to particular.
5. The system must be hospitable to all knowledge, including things that never were, such as phlogiston; things that never shall be, like utopias; and things that are impossible, like the square root of minus one.
6. Since multiple relationships in different contexts are commonplace, each classification system must have means of covering every context, including future additions. Its hospitality has to be such that additions and changes can be made easily.
7. Each classification system must have cross-references and an index.
8. A method of constant updating is mandatory for adjusting the old and adding what is new.
9. A method must be found for automatic adjustment of class numbers to suit the needs of the system as it grows. This suggests adoption of hospitable computers as a necessity.
10. A concordance, in addition to tables, schedules and indexes, probably would be exceedingly valuable in keeping up with terminology.

In all subjects, dead or alive, there is a constant learning front. This research is where the new things to be classified appear. Granted there may be a need to wait for new terminology to settle down. In general, this happens by the time monographs, as opposed to journal articles, appear.

Usually there is a strong relationship with the past, even if only to refute it. Most professions can be characterized as "learning" professions —growth of their body of knowledge requires constant updating. Librarianship is definitely a learning profession. In fact, what we have had to absorb during the past 30 years is revolutionary rather than evolutionary. Librarians are learning a number of different ways of doing things and thinking about things. We are dedicated to searching for better ways of presenting new knowledge in the forms that can be used most readily by those who need it. Of necessity, it always seems as if we are behind and running to catch up, but we are fleet of foot.

We are constantly developing new knowledge in our own areas, which, while sometimes secondary to other subjects, is nevertheless of great value. With the aid of modern technology, we are beginning not only to identify and find what is needed, but also to deliver the goods. A 1,000-item online search is of great value only if it can be accompanied by the documents it revealed. Twenty years ago we could not even produce the list. But the dreams of the 1960s are the realities of today, and there is no reason to think that today's dreams cannot also materialize. We are in a much better situation now to experiment with systems like Smalltalk-80,[6] which is based on fundamental classification theory and yet is flexible enough to meet a variety of needs. To schedules, cross-references, and indexes, not to mention thesauri, we may yet add a relatively sophisticated means of getting a tough job done.

MAJOR CLASSIFICATION SYSTEMS

So what does all this mean for classification? As indicated, there are five major systems: The Dewey Decimal Classification, the Library of Congress Classification, the Universal Decimal Classification, the Bliss Bibliographic Classification (currently being reincarnated in faceted form), and the Colon Classification. All except the Library of Congress are based on classical logic division in one form or another. Of these, Bliss is by far the most logical, but it was completed, as was the case with Colon, so late that the others were too well entrenched for it to replace them. The same is true of the Rider International Classification,[7] which should not be overlooked for a small library, as its logic is excellent.

One nice thing about having computers as servants is that one can use more than one classification system at a time. The MARC system, in its fullest form, has the capability of allowing user access to a number of classification systems: Library of Congress, National Library of Medicine, National Agricultural Library, National Library of Canada, Dewey Decimal Classification, Universal Decimal Classification, and that of the U.S. Government Printing Office. More could be added as needed. When nothing but manual systems were available, it was a case of picking one and sticking to it. Changing systems was very difficult. Changing is still not easy, but it now is a little easier to live with a dual system than it was in the past.

Ranganathan's Colon Classification

From the point of view of classification theory, Ranganathan's Colon Classification has been the most interesting.[8] It can be manipulated to produce classes that delineate subjects very closely. It is especially useful for classification of a single subject or topic, as, for example, in a special library or collection. This kind of classification can be made to fit a subject like a glove, and also cover it in great depth. Some of its principles could be used to improve much of the Library of Congress system, because part of that system is made up of limited hierarchies. The basic methodology of the faceting process is re-invented (with another name) constantly.

The Library of Congress System

The Library of Congress system is only partly based on logic. In some places, it is impossible from looking at the coding, to figure out the basis for putting one class next to another. Obviously this has disadvantages for browsing, but has advantages for serendipity. On the other hand, the frequent use of A to Z listing as subclassification makes it almost impossible to run out of space for interpolating. The system still has huge unused areas, which gives it greater hospitality for adding new material than most other systems. It is best described as an enumerative system, and since it contains large numbers of little hierarchies, it is somewhat like a classified thesaurus. One may question whether *ordered* systems like this should even be called classifications or not. An order is definitely there, but the use of logical division is spotty. To repeat, the hospitality for new material in the Library of Congress Classification exceeds that of other systems. The fact that it survives without a general index suggests that the various parts stand alone quite well, and hospitality—which is quite hard to achieve when one has to cover all knowledge in one cohesive system—is better served by not having cohesiveness. The Library of Congress system could be considered as a set of individual classification systems, since, for practical purposes, each class can stand pretty much on its own. The system sprawls—in contrast to the Dewey Decimal Classification, which is comparatively economical and compact.

Faceted Systems

Faceted systems have existed since the late 1940s. In preparing these, one asks a set of questions regarding each subject:

What is it?
What is it made of?
What does it do?
What is done to it?
Where is/was it?
When is/was it?

Classification is done by selecting what is pertinent, fitting the data to the facets and presenting the result as a whole in the order:

THING - PART - ACTION - PLACE - TIME

as a bare minimum. The number of facets is dependent on the needs of the subject being classified and may include more than the above.[9]

RECLASSIFYING A LIBRARY

The feature that all existing library classifications have in common is that not one of them has collapsed, in the sense that the old Harris system used at Cornell University until 1948 collapsed. Reclassifying a library of any size is a long, tedious and expensive procedure. If a library has played fast and loose with parts of the system—that is, cutting, adding, rearranging and otherwise altering the basic system—then that library will one day regret it. If a library does not change when its classification system changes, or update when the system updates, it will regret that as well. In a computerized system especially, deviation means trouble. If the system is unsatisfactory, there are user groups available to help change what needs to be changed, modified, improved, or deleted. But making wholly individualized alteration to the computerized product means losing touch with other libraries. Classification systems are not models of perfection (except, perhaps, on the drawing board), but there is even less chance of using them successfully for any kind of searching if there are a lot of deviations.

In theory, making an ideal classification system looks like a splendid idea. In real life, you can make a fine system, as did Bliss and Ranganathan, and employ it in your library. However, as soon as you are dead and buried, the library will switch to a more standard system because it is much easier and less expensive to use pre-classified material than to try to classify everything in-house. The original Bliss for example, does not have anything new after 1952. As a rule, making a special system for a special collection may be necessary to make that collection usable, as many special libraries have found out, but devising a new general system is not very practical except as an intellectual exercise.

European libraries tend to have closed stacks, with access via a classified catalog. Our so-called mark-and-park syndrome is a product of the open stack system and the dictionary catalog. If you want to get rid of it, all you have to do is close your stacks and shelve by accession number. This would enable you to shelve by size, and pack the books without regard for topic. Since it would not be necessary to have room in each class for future publications, as has to be done with our present classified *shelves*, considerable space could be saved.

If new or revised knowledge in the future comes via some medium other than the codex book, then marking and parking is unnecessary, but the classified catalog will be vital. Currently the amount and expense of equipment needed for such a possibility makes it too expensive. Also, be sure you understand what you are getting into when you change to such a catalog, and weigh the trade-offs. One of the most interesting things in recent work on information is the revelation of Claude Shannon's insistence, from 1951 to date, that his famous theory does *not* define the *concept* of information, but of "mean statistical unexpectedness of an item of information selected from a given ensemble."[10] A considerable part of the fundamental theoretical basis for some areas of information science comes from this specific form of quicksand mistaken for solid ground, and misinterpreted.

DEDUCTIVE AND INDUCTIVE LOGIC

Before discussing what all of this might mean for the future, a bit more should be said about deductive logic and induction as they pertain to classification systems. The simplest illustration of the difference between the methodology of deductive logic and induction was made by William Whewell, a British philosopher, some 145 years ago. He wrote:

> Induction mounts by a leap which is out of the reach of method. She bounds to the top of the stair at once; then it is the business of Deduction, by trying each step in order, to establish the solidity of her companion's footing. [11]

The geometry of Euclid is a classic example of deductive logic. You prove a set of rules, step by step. Induction, on the other hand, is an explanation for something that actually happens. Every time it happens again, the explanation is confirmed once more. The first time it does not happen, or happens only as a result of some change, then the explanation is thrown out and a new one has to be developed. This happens constantly in science.

What is the difference whether our methodology is inductive or deductive? And who cares? Two things are important:

1. Deductive systems are always out of date.

This is why Bliss, though the best classification system, is not being used, and why the others all have to be updated regularly, but still never catch up with what is current in any field of knowledge.

2. Inductive systems, such as faceted ones, can be made and kept up-to-date for individual subjects, but these will fail to coalesce into one grand and glorious, up-to-the-minute system.

The Classification Research Group, therefore, tried to make the best of both worlds by creating a faceted system solidly grounded on the logic of Bliss.

INFORMATION

Another whole set of groups is concerned primarily with "information." While currently there is a terminological mess to be settled before any significant, serious research can begin, it is abundantly clear that this is an area of concern. The terms "library" and "library science" nowadays appear to be going out of style, largely because of an unfortunate stereotype dating back to the early part of this century. One cannot fail to notice that others are quite willing to involve themselves with the intellectual parts of what our profession has been doing, and doing well, for the past 90 years. Such stereotypes, as any member of a minority group can tell you, die hard.

But there are other problems equally difficult that it is possible to do something about. The specter of computer technology unnecessarily scared the living daylights out of our rank and file. The people who thought we were too stupid to automate our own work are long gone. In the days when computers were big, slow, and limited to what a good adding machine can do now, there may have been some justification for such fear, although the MARC Project got off the ground in spite of all impediments. Most microcomputers can do what seemed so difficult then. Would you believe that people seriously said it was impossible to automate the Library of Congress Classification? The user-friendly computers appearing now are opening new avenues for developing programs that can handle that kind of classification with ease and also cataloging, particularly for non-book materials. Smalltalk-80 and the program called "Methods," which is based on it, are examples of useful programming systems.[12]

Organizing Bibliographic Tools

We have every reason to be proud of our accomplishments so far in organizing our bibliographic tools, the catalog and major indexes. At this point, it is necessary to emphasize again that there is one factor to be kept in mind especially: in classification, we are dealing with subject material that has already been identified subject-wise—both named and categorized—by experts in the field. Our job is to provide the best possible access to this natural classification, keeping up to date as it changes and never ceasing to access it better. We are not classifying physics or philosophy; we are classifying material *about* physics or philosophy, and, as Robert Fairthorne has reminded us, it is the "aboutness" that is our mission.[13]

At this point, it is important to emphasize once more what we have accomplished so far in organizing our bibliographic tools and automating large parts of them, including the catalog and major indexing tools. Since this country is mainly monolingual, we have made more progress in indexing than in classification. We have not felt the urgency of developing classification systems that has motivated other countries. The fact that an ALA pre-conference could limit its workshops mainly to the Dewey Decimal and Library of Congress systems, and to problems chiefly arising from American practice is largely due to our monolingual approach. "Mark it and park it" has a different connotation in a closed-stack-and-classified-catalog situation.

We picked up the thesaurus approach quickly and improved it. We constantly re-invent the faceting process, which fits all media more exactly. Also we have justifiably ignored the unwieldy Broad System of Ordering.[14] With sufficient funds to build new libraries and/or new wings on old buildings, we have not had much incentive in the past to get the most out of existing space. So classification research has not been a vital necessity, and few have contributed to it.

Propositional Representation

There is, however, a possibility that may change this situation. Scholars working on many aspects of cognitive science and artificial intelligence are interested in classification. People remember in different ways. One method developed during research on human memory is propositional representation. Some people remember better verbally, others visually—whichever way, it appears that an abstract representation is remembered. For this, a method called a "propositional network" was devised. Such a network functions like a dictionary, as it defines concepts in terms of other concepts in a pattern that ultimately can be circular.[15] This is basically what a thesaurus does. It develops small but pertinent little networks. Much of the Library of Congress system operates the same way. One does not have a giant system of interrelated terms as is the case with the Dewey, Universal Decimal, or Bliss systems. The Library of Congress system may or may not be a classification system in the classic definition of the word, but it definitely is in the sense of a propositional network.

Computers, using methods based on Smalltalk-80, appear to have possibilities for improving visual representation of classification.[16] The Apple Macintosh functions in such a manner, as do other machines with greater storage capacity. The function of "windows" relies heavily on classification. Some of these new systems are based on cognitive science—a field worth watching as a possible means of presenting both the Dewey and the Library of Congress systems in a format easier to use than that employed at present.

CONCLUSION

Summing up, a number of possibilities for improving both the Dewey and the Library of Congress classification systems exist. One is that automation could improve the use of either one or both, as searching agents, by making it possible to use new methodology developed in the process of refining Smalltalk-80. Both classification systems are amenable to such a development. In other words, neither system is at a dead end.

Another possibility is that the revitalized Bliss, being developed by members of the Classification Research Group, could be added as an intermediary language for both.

Insofar as the "mark-and-park syndrome" is concerned, there is no particular reason to continue the use of classified shelving. Browsing can be done sitting at a terminal, *providing* that enough access points have been built into the system—plenty of *classification* points of access. Most of us are doing this now with indexing systems. Classification would permit better results because it would use what is essentially a tree structure, rather than guessing the way through whatever relational characteristics the indexer happened to think of, or that the accompanying cross-references provided. Remember that 39 years ago Julia Pettee pointed out that there is a concealed classification in subject headings.[17] The whole thesaurus process is an attempt to take care of this unfortunate situation. Why not do it right in the first place?

In conclusion, it should be pointed out that an either/or choice in terms of Dewey or Library of Congress no longer makes sense. We need both, because the two approaches are significantly different. Not only that, but we need the indexes to both, as well as the whole subject heading system, which complements both. Last but not least, we also need substantial thesauri. The whole idea is to make access as easy for the user as possible, and since we have a multiplicity of user points of view, we need a multiplicity of systems to cover all possible angles of approach. Therefore, let us think in terms of cooperation and complementation and of using all available systems. We have nothing to lose and everything to gain by such an approach.

REFERENCES

1. Max Black, *Critical Thinking, An Introduction to Logic and Scientific Method*, 2d ed. (Englewood Cliffs, NJ: Prentice-Hall, 1952).
2. Classification Research Group reports appear periodically in the *Journal of Documentation*.
3. Fritz Machlup (with Una Mansfield), "Cultural Diversity in Studies of Information," Fritz Machlup, "Semantic Quirks in Studies of Information,"

in *The Study of Information: Interdisciplinary Messages*, eds. Fritz Machlup and Una Mansfield (New York: Wiley, 1983), 3–56, 641–671.

4. Ibid.

5. Reports of the work of the Classification Research Group appear periodically in the *Journal of Documentation*. Cf. vol. 12 (December 1956): 227–230; vol. 14 (Sept. 1958): 136–143; vol. 15 (March 1959): 39–57; vol. 17 (Sept. 1961): 156–172; vol. 18 (June 1962): 65–88; vol. 20 (Sept. 1964): 146–169; vol. 24 (Dec. 1968): 273–298; vol. 29 (Mar. 1973): 51–71; and vol. 34 (Mar. 1978): 21–50.

6. Adele Goldberg and David Robson, *Smalltalk-80: The Language and its implementation* (Reading MA: Addison-Wesley, 1983); Adele Goldberg, *Smalltalk-80: The Interactive Programming Environment* (Reading, MA: Addison-Wesley, 1984).

7. Fremont Rider, *Rider's International Classification*, Prelim. ed. (Middletown, CT: the Author, 1961).

8. S.R. Ranganathan, *Colon Classification*, 6th ed. (New York Asia Publishing House, 1960).

9. Classification Research Group Reports (See Ref. 5).

10. Donald M. MacKay, "The Wider Scope of Information Theory," in Machlup, *Study of Information*, 485ff.

11. William Whewell, *Novum Organon Renovatus, Being the Second Part of the Philosophy of the Inductive Sciences*, 3d ed. (London: John W. Parker, 1858), 88,114.

12. Goldberg, *Smalltalk-80*. A brochure on *Methods* is available from Digitalk, 5200 West Century Blvd., Los Angeles, CA 90045.

13. Robert A. Fairthorne, "Content Analysis, Specification and Control," in *Annual Review of Information Science and Technology*, vol. 4 (Chicago: Encyclopedia Britannica, 1969), 73–109.

14. *Broad System of Ordering* (BSO), 3rd revision (London: FID/UNESCO, March 1978).

15. John R. Anderson, *Cognitive Science and Its Implications* (San Francisco: W.H. Freeman, 1980), 94–116, 127.

16. Phyllis A. Richmond, "Smalltalk-80 for Information Access," 13th ASIS Mid-Year Meeting, Indiana University, Bloomington, Indiana, May 20-23, 1984; "Smalltalk-80 as an Indexing Language," Symposium on Subject Analysis, North Carolina Central University, March, 1985. For Smalltalk-80 itself, see note 6.

17. Julia Pettee, *Subject Headings: The History and Theory of the Alphabetical Subject Approach to Books* (New York: H.W. Wilson, 1946), 22–25, 57–60, 79–80.

3

Classification: What Should We Be Training People to Do?

Nancy J. Williamson

It is now well established fact that the introduction of computer technology into the field of information retrieval has led to greatly increased emphasis on the development of systems that provide for improved subject access to information. Various mechanisms and methods of subject retrieval are being reexamined and redesigned. One aspect of this inquiry is the reconsideration of the role of classification, in particular its role in online systems. Numerous questions are being asked. Is there a new and more sophisticated role for classification in online systems, which was not feasible with manual catalogues and indexes? Is classification, instead, to remain the mere location device, which it has become in most North American libraries? Should it be completely superseded by Boolean operators? Whatever the answers to these and other related questions, this is an opportune time to take a serious look at what we *should* be doing to educate and train information professionals in the use of classification in the design of information systems and in the process of online searching.

This chapter begins with a survey of background information on the way in which, at present, library and information programs are preparing, or attempting to prepare, students in the essentials of classification. Then it examines the concerns, needs, and requirements of employers. Finally some questions are raised as the basis for further debate and discussion of problems and possible solutions.

THE STATUS QUO: A SURVEY

In the spring of 1985 a survey was conducted in which three kinds of data were collected in order to gather factual information on education and training in classification and on the professional requirements of libraries. Library and information science educators who teach classification and related subjects in the accredited library and information science programs were invited to complete a questionnaire on the nature and content of courses on classification and related subjects, on the teaching methodologies used, and on the relative importance of classification in library and information science education. Second, technical services directors in 40 randomly selected libraries of various types and sizes were surveyed to determine the nature and use of classification in libraries, the characteristics of persons who classify, and the kinds of provisions that are made for training and retraining of subject cataloging personnel. Technical services directors were also asked to identify what they considered to be the major deficiencies in new graduates' knowledge of classification and its application. Finally, employment opportunities were scanned in the 1984 and 1985 issues of *College and Research Libraries News* and *American Libraries* to see what kinds of references were made to qualifications in classification for library technical services positions.

With respect to the questionnaires, responses were received from 46, or 68.6 percent, of the 67 schools of library and information science contacted. These responses came from 62 instructors in the institutions responding. Three questionnaires were returned unanswered because the instructor was unavailable or no longer taught in the school to which the questionnaire was addressed. From the technical services directors contacted there was a 52.5 percent response. In both cases the returns were sufficient to provide substantial and useful evidence on aspects of the investigation.

DATA ANALYSIS—LIBRARY SCIENCE PROGRAMS

Required Courses

Of the 46 schools of library and information science from which responses were received, 43, or 93.4 percent, offer one or more required courses, which include some classification. In the case of three schools, there was no evidence of a required course that included classification, but this is not necessarily conclusive, since the instructor in the required course may not have responded to the survey. At the other end of the scale, one institution reported three required courses, while five other schools each indicated that they had two required courses that deal with aspects of classification.

The number of contact hours devoted to classification varied greatly depending on the nature of the course and ranged from a low of two hours to a high of 48 hours. Eleven of the required courses, which provided for two to six contact hours, tended to be very general in nature and had titles such as "bibliographic control," "bibliographic organization," and "introduction to information science." One of the 11 courses had a title as specific as "cataloguing and classification." In all but one case, the breadth of coverage appears to account for a small number of contact hours in classification. In three of these cases the school had another required course with many more contact hours in classification. Because of the special nature of these 11 courses they were excluded from the calculation of contact hours. Also excluded were three other courses where 100 percent of the contact hours in the course were designated as being used for classification, even though there was strong evidence that the courses included other elements. The remaining 32 institutions provided courses that have from ten to 42 contact hours on classification. The median number of contact hours was 26, and the average 17.8 hours. Percentage of course time spent on classification was also calculated, but the figures were less meaningful because of the wide variation in the total number of contact hours among particular courses and among library programs.

In general, the content of required courses, insofar as this could be determined from titles and brief calendar descriptions, suggested that these courses fall into three categories based on the breadth of topical coverage. The first category contained courses that appear to give a very broad overview and are described by such terms as "bibliographic control," "organization of knowledge," "storage and retrieval," and "introduction to information science." Twelve courses belong in the second category, which could be described as dealing specifically with cataloging and classification; while the third group consisted of three courses, which deal precisely with subject access, subject cataloging, and subject indexing. No respondent revealed a required course that dealt specifically and solely with classification. Of course, this kind of analysis is based on what can be observed. Library educators are well aware that calendar descriptions are frequently vague to allow for flexibility in course content from year to year, and/or to permit different faculty members to teach the same course at different times, and to fit the course to their perceptions, and to individualize the course to the needs of a particular group of students. Indeed the survey revealed that the same course taught by different instructors frequently has a difference in content and in the number of contact hours devoted to classification.

To provide for some consistency in the data gathered, respondents were asked to describe the kind of content and the percentage of time spent on each aspect in terms of seven categories of information. A provision was also made for adding categories not mentioned in the questionnaire. Aspects of classification covered in required courses are shown in Table 3-1.

Clearly, all of the educators feel that the principles of classification are essential and fundamental (100 percent). Theory gets slightly less attention (89.7 percent) but this may be attributed to the difficulty of defining "theory" and of separating "theory" from "principles." The percentage of courses covering historical background (89.7 percent) is high, given the scarcity of time that exists in most courses; but perhaps it is not unusual for required courses, which may also be basic, to include the historical aspects. The most surprising statistic is the 81.6 percent representing courses that cover "objectives." It would surely be difficult to impart an understanding of classification to students without discussing the reasons for having classification at all. Virtually every required course covered one or more specific classification systems with emphasis on the Dewey Decimal, and sometimes the Library of Congress, classification systems. The 97.9 percent result reflects the fact that included in the required courses reported was one course that appeared to be a general "foundations" type of course and included theory and principles only in its content. It is inevitable that facet analysis (40.8 percent) and automatic text analysis (14.2 percent) would be taught less often in a basic required course. However, the concept of facet analysis is becoming more and more important as a basic concept because it is the basis for thesaurus development, it is an underlying principle in Boolean searching, and indeed it is an essential principle in standard classification systems such as the Dewey Decimal Classification (DDC). Post-coordination was also mentioned by several respondents. It too is a fundamental concept, which seems almost essential to a required course.

TABLE 3-1 Categories Covered in Required Courses

Category	% of Courses Including
Principles	100
Theory	89.7
Historical background	89.7
Objectives	81.6
Specific classification systems	97.9
Facet analysis	40.8
Automatic text analysis	14.2
Other	2

When it came to analyzing the percentage of time devoted to each of the categories of course content in the required courses the calculations were difficult because respondents interpreted the question in two ways. However, it was possible to ascertain a reliable percentage for each of the major categories of coverage based on all but four of the responses. The results are shown in Table 3-2.

Notable is the fact that the least amount of time is spent on historical background, whereas the greatest amount of time is devoted to specific classification systems. Again, this is not a surprising result in a basic required course. In a time-pressured situation, history is probably the least essential of the components of a course that is intended to develop technical knowledge and skills.

TABLE 3-2 Percentage of Time Spent on Each Category in the Required Courses

Category	% of time
Principles	15
Theory	11.5
Historical background	7.2
Objectives	9.7
Specific classification systems	56.1

When the data on specific systems were analyzed further it was entirely predictable that the Dewey Decimal and Library of Congress systems would be the systems most often covered in required courses. However, the details merit closer examination. Forty of the 46 schools reported the inclusion of either DDC *or* DDC *and* LCC. Thirty-nine of the schools provide instruction in DDC, while only 32 schools also covered LCC in their required courses. Five of the eight schools that did not include LCC in a required course did so in elective courses, and one school had a full required course in LCC. Some years ago a major criticism was the lack of attention given to instruction in LCC. Is there still a problem? If so, why? Is it lack of available time? Do we think LCC is not essential to a required course? Where the emphasis is on principles, is DDC sufficient as one example? Or, perish the thought, is the problem that the instructors are reluctant to teach it? Surely, in the North American context, LCC is at least as important as DDC. These questions deserve further discussion.

A majority of instructors also endeavor to include some coverage of other (or nonstandard) classification systems in required courses. As one might expect responses often had an added note of caution. Several indicated that the coverage was "brief," or stated that other systems were "mentioned," or suggested that there was "some" coverage. Faceted classification was identified as a component of 13 of the 43 required courses, and the Universal Decimal Classification (UDC) was included in ten such courses. Bliss, Cutter, and the National Library of Medicine (NLM) systems were mentioned in conjunction with less than five of the required courses. PRECIS was identified as a component of six courses. One respondent covered several additional classification systems, but it should be noted that this was a course in which 42 contact hours in a 63 hour course were devoted to classification. Few classification instructors find themselves in such a fortunate position.

What is essential for all graduates to cover in required courses? Views on this are probably divided. With greater emphasis on technology and increased interest in subject access to information, is it time to consider a new kind of required course? Should there be required courses that would bring together various aspects of technology, indexing and subject access into one course? The results of the survey suggest that this may already be happening in some cases.

Elective Courses

Similar data were gathered on instruction in elective courses, but understandably the information received was less precise and more difficult to analyze for several reasons. Most important, there is a greater flexibility in the content of elective courses from year to year and from one instructor to another. Very precise data would have required a much longer and more complex questionnaire than the one used, but it was felt that the advantages to be gained by a long questionnaire might be negated by a reduced number of returns. Even so the information gathered is sufficiently reliable to identify some significant trends. The summary data for elective courses is shown in Table 3-3.

TABLE 3-3 Categories of Information Covered in Elective Courses

Category	% of Courses Including
Principles	83.3
Theory	77.7
History	66.6
Objectives	61.1
Specific systems	81.4
Facet analysis	55.5
Automatic text analysis	50

There were 95 elective courses on classification and related subjects reported from 46 schools and taught by 54 of the 62 respondents. When the percentage of time spent on each aspect of the subject was calculated it was discovered that the percentages were lower than for the same aspects in required courses. For example, principles were covered in 83.3 percent of elective courses, whereas it is 100 percent for required courses. Some of this discrepancy can be attributed to the fact that for some courses "specific systems" was the only topic identified by the respondent. However, it seems inconceivable that such things as theory and principles would not be covered in discussing UDC, Colon, and other systems. In conjunction with elective courses the most significant finding was the greater attention given to facet analysis, which was covered in 55.5 percent of the courses reported, and automatic text analysis, which was included 50 percent of the time.

A wide spectrum of classification systems was covered by the elective courses. Ten institutions had advanced courses in DDC and LCC, while eight schools had elective courses devoted to LCC alone. With respect to other systems taught, Colon and the Universal Decimal Classification lead the way. Each of these systems was cited as being included in 13 elective courses. They were followed closely by Bliss and PRECIS with the NLM classification being included less frequently. Mention was also made of Brown, Rider, the Classification Research Group Schemes, the Superintendent of Documents system, CODOC, and a number of local schemes.

A separate question was directed specifically at the inclusion of PRECIS and thesaurus instruction in courses of instruction. Thirty of the 46 schools provide instruction in some aspects of PRECIS. Only one institution had a full course on PRECIS, while others spent from one to 15 contact hours on it. The most frequent number of contact hours spent on PRECIS was from three to six hours. Slightly more attention was given to thesaurus construction than to PRECIS. Thirty-two schools have courses that included thesaurus construction. Three had full courses, and the number of contact hours in particular courses ranged from three to 15 hours. Most courses fall in the six to ten contact hour range. Several courses had substantial assignments requiring the construction of a thesaurus of several hundred terms. In general other findings of the survey suggest that there are a substantial number of courses available that permit students to gain a knowledge and understanding of systems of classification and subject access other than the standard systems. It would be interesting to know what percentage of students avail themselves of the opportunity to take such courses and the kinds of use made of this knowledge by graduates of library and information science programs.

Methods of Instruction and Evaluation

Two other aspects of instruction and training in classification, which were investigated, were the methods of instruction used in both required and elective courses and the kinds of testing used to evaluate students' performance.

Methods of instruction were reported in six categories—lectures, seminars, laboratory sessions, out-of-class exercises, practice, and computer-aided instruction. Fifty-eight instructors reported using the lecture method, and 29 used seminars. Seminars were overwhelmingly used in elective courses. Out-of-class exercises are more popular than laboratory sessions. Two instructors used only laboratory sessions; 16 used only out-of-class exercises and 42 instructors used both methods. Computer-aided instruction was reported in conjunction with about 50 percent of the courses but respondents appeared to have different interpretations of the term *computer-aided instruction*. It would be interesting to know more about the kinds of CAI that are being used to teach classification.

Methods for evaluating student performance were reported in six categories: closed-book, open-book, and take-home examinations; theoretical papers; practical projects; and combinations of two or more of these. Most instructors appear to prefer some combination of methods. Of the individual methods, practical projects were highly favored and used by 50 of the 62 instructors reporting. Almost equal use was made of open-book examinations (33 instructors), theoretical papers (32 instructors), and take-home examinations (31 instructors). Closed book examinations were the least popular method, and used by 27 instructors. When used, closed-book exams were usually applied to required courses. In only three cases was this method used for electives.

There was little that was surprising in the methods used either in providing instruction or in evaluating students. It would be useful to know more about the relative effectiveness of these methods.

THE IMPORTANCE OF CLASSIFICATION IN LIBRARY AND INFORMATION SCIENCE EDUCATION

Two final questions in the survey were directed at gathering information on the educator's perception of the place of classification in library education. Respondents were asked how they would rate the importance of classification in the curriculum: essential, very important, important, not important, or not necessary. The results were encouraging with very strong support for classification as an essential element of the curriculum. Thirty-five of the 62 respondents rated classification as essential; 14 thought it was very important. Only one person thought that classification was not important, and no one thought that classification was unnecessary.

When asked about the relative importance of classification, 37 respondents felt that classification would be more important and 21 felt that it would be of at least equal importance in the future. A number of respondents qualified their positions. Some felt DDC and LCC will be less important in the future, but that other aspects of classification will increase in importance. Does this augur a change in what is taught?

In general comments on education and training in classification many respondents expressed their conviction that it should be "different" in the future, and that the difference would be related to the use of classification in online systems. What do we mean by different? This is a question we might explore further. Others deplored the mark-and-park approach to classification taken by North American libraries, while one of the major problems cited was the lack of sufficient contact hours in which to provide adequate instruction for students. It was also noted that we are living in a period of transition and that it is impossible to know what direction the needs for education and training will take.

DATA ANALYSIS—LIBRARIES AND CLASSIFICATION

We must attempt to answer the question, What are we doing about formal education and training? But, before that, we must consider whether we need formal training at all. Part of the answer comes from knowing what libraries expect and need in the way of knowledge and training on the part of its new professionals. Therefore, technical services directors in 40 academic and public libraries were asked to provide information on their catalogs, their cataloging staff, and their observations on how well the new graduate performs as a classifier and to identify the major problems. Slightly more than one-half of the directors replied—52.5 percent or 21 libraries were represented. The responses were almost evenly divided, with replies from ten public and 11 academic institutions.

There was a relatively good cross section of institutions in the groups. Libraries ranged in size from a public library with 120,000 titles and 2,400 periodical titles to a large research library with between 5,000,000 and 7,000,000 volumes. A majority of the libraries uses either DDC or LCC. One library has its own classification scheme, and many of the libraries use nonstandard schemes for audiovisual material, music, and microforms. Ten of the libraries had online catalogs and nine of the remaining 11 were planning such catalogs. All of the existing catalogs had call number access and two-thirds provided for browsing by classification number. Responsibility for classification for copy cataloging was almost evenly divided between professional and nonprofessional staff with both groups being involved in five libraries. For classification for original cataloging all but one library always used professional staff, and in six libraries paraprofessionals were used sometimes. In only two libraries were subject specialists involved in any these operations.

What did the technical services directors expect of new graduates? Eight directors expected a general knowledge of classification, and in three instances this was the only requirement. Ten directors expected the ability to do copy classification and 16, or three-fourths, of the directors felt that new graduates should be able to do original classification. Most qualified this with statements such as "simple materials" or "under supervision." In nine cases new graduates would be expected to handle reclassification problems but only after some training. Only 13 of the 21 institutions provided for retraining and updating of staff when new schedules or new editions of schemes were published. All 13 provided for some in-house on-the-job training; six provided for special workshops. Only two indicated that updating would be through formal courses in library schools. Updating was used in only three continuing education programs. What do these figures indicate? Are there not suitable formal courses? Does continuing education fall down on the job? Or, do the directors think that the most effective approach is within their own institutions?

Perhaps the most interesting and rewarding data from the technical services directors were their comments on the deficiencies in the knowledge of new graduates who were classifiers. Strange as it may seem to educators, the instruction given in classification was not cited as the foremost complaint. The most serious problem appears to be the lack of general knowledge and, in some cases, specialized subject knowledge. This points to deficiencies in undergraduate education and the practical need for classifiers to have a second master's degree in a subject field. The second most prevalent deficiency referred to was lack of ability to handle schedules, particularly tables, and this seemed to be a more serious problem with LCC than with DDC. There was also concern for lack of understanding of how classification was used, or should be used, and the problem of keeping current.

WHAT DO LIBRARIES ASK FOR
WHEN THEY ADVERTISE POSITIONS?

Scanning job openings in major library periodicals did not prove very fruitful. The information given in the advertisements is too brief to be useful. However, two observations are pertinent. The need for knowledge of one of the major schemes was usually indicated, although classification was referred to less often than LC subject headings, AACR2, and OCLC. Sometimes ads asked for "LC practice." In one case the ad asked for either experience or evidence of excellent grades in formal courses taken in library schools.

CONCLUSION

With this background information there appear to be several main issues for future discussion. Among the most important questions are:

1. The content of required courses at present.
2. How to meet the challenge of the online world with respect to training people in classification. There is a feeling that things need to be "different." What do we mean by "different"?
3. Are new kinds of courses needed? Classification is more than book classification. This will be an important factor in the future. How do we bring together the bits and pieces that are presently separated by the barriers of formal courses based on established distinctions?
4. Are there new methodologies that we ought to be incorporating into our teaching? Do some of these already exist and could they be shared with others?

At the University of Toronto we have developed a computer-aided instruction program, which we call DDT, meaning Dewey Decimal Tutor. We have set up the exercises so that the students can assign classification numbers, put in their numbers at the computer terminal, find out whether they are right, and get some feedback on where they might go next.

The correct answers to the exercise on the student work sheet are shown in Figure 3-1, and the machine responses to student input in Figure 3-2. In preparing the example, I deliberately played with the answers for purposes of illustrating the system. For example, with the topic "Journal of Canadian Music," I have typed the number one incorrectly using an illegal character. A further comment on the possible answers to this particular topic is that 780.971 is technically the correct DDC number (based on the table of precedence for DDC Standard Subdivisions). However, we suggest to the student, that, for some libraries, 780.5 may be a more practical DDC number, since it will collocate all journals on the subject music. Thus, if 780.971 is correctly typed, the computer will respond with a note of explanation on the applicability of the number.

FIGURE 3-1   Student Work Sheet

University of Toronto Faculty of Library and Information Science

DDT Program
This exercise is provided to give introductory practice in the use of the Dewey Decimal Classification schedules. Your classification numbers for the topics can be checked and evaluated by computer.

Assign classification numbers to the topics in the Exercise, using the *Dewey Decimal Classification, 11th abridged ed.* When you are ready to have some or all of your answers evaluated, take them to one of the terminals in the CAI Lab and follow the instructions on the accompanying sheet.

Exercise A
1. Ethical aspects of the abuse and improper use of drugs by athletes   174 or 175
2. Journal of Canadian music   780.5 (780.971 technically correct)
3. Biographical accounts of twelve famous Canadian scientists and engineers   509.2
4. The cataloging and classification of books written in Braille   025.3 or 025.3028
5. A history of research on lung cancer among cigarette smokers   616.99

On topic 3, "Biographical Accounts of Twelve Famous Canadian Scientists and Engineers," the response on the incorrect number (DDC 620.9) is to indicate to the student that, unless there are other criteria evident, the two-topic book should be classified under the first topic rather than the second. That is, the number should be 509.2 not 620.9. To reinforce the learning process, the student is referred back to the Editor's Introduction in DDC in order to better understand the reason for the choice. As another example, topic 5 illustrates the fact that standard subdivisions should not be added where the DDC instructs "Do not use standard subdivisions." The exercises are designed with the learning process in mind as well as to provide a testing mechanism.

FIGURE 3-2 DDT Program: Responses to Input

---

the ddt student program begins>   15.47.25   jul 2, 1985
please standby>

please give exercise name> exercise a

please give your classification for question 1

174
did you type the number correctly: "yes or no" yes
Good. You have classed this topic correctly.

please give your classification for question 2

780.971
did you type the number correctly: "yes or no" yes

Your Dewey number contains an illegal character. Be sure you have not used a capital "O" (letter "O") instead of a zero, or a lower-case letter "l" instead of the numeral "1", or made some similar error. Check your typing and try again. If you cannot detect your error consult your instructor.

please give your classification for question 3

620.9
did you type the number correctly: "yes or no" yes

When you have a topic which deals with two subjects, you should examine the DC schedules for both subjects to see whether there are instructional notes. Recheck sections 6.1.2.2.1 and 6.5.2 of the Editors' Introduction. Examine the schedules again to locate relevant special instructions. If you do not understand your error consult your instructor. Try again.

please give your classification for question 4

025.3028

did you type the number correctly: "yes or no" yes

Good. Your classification of this topic is technically correct according to the 1st note at the -028 Standard Subdivision (Table 1). While this is an acceptable answer for a topic, where you cannot see the emphasis of a document, -028 s.s. should only be used where the "how-to-do-it" emphasis is predominant.

please give your classification for question 5

616.9909
did you type the number correctly: "yes or no" yes

In the Dewey schedules notations from the Standard Subdivisions (Table 1) may, in theory, be added to any number. However, in practice they are prohibited by specific instructions at some points in the schedules. Reconsider this number and instructions for it in the DC schedules, and consult section 6.4 of the Editors' Introduction. Try again.

Development time for such CAI programs is significant. The dean of the faculty, a graduate student in computer science, and a classification instructor worked over a period of time from one to two years on the project, supported by some Research and Development money. Beyond the initial design of the systems, the development of the classification topics for the exercises and the error messages is very complex. The instructor indicates that the first topics took approximately ten to 12 hours per topic. Above all, the instructor warns that this kind of system is "not at all something one embarks on lightly."

4

The Atlantic Divide: Classification Outside the United States

Russell Sweeney

The main themes to be considered in this chapter are:

1. The view of classification in countries other than the United States;
2. the different roles of classification outside the United States; and
3. the use made of the available general schemes of classification throughout the world.

It is fairly obvious that these themes are so interdependent that it would be difficult, if not impossible, to treat them separately. My observations will be concentrated primarily on the situation in Europe, and in particular in the United Kingdom. Information about the Third World is very sparse. What little there is shows that each country's views and practices emanate from a former colonial power or come from the country that predominates in the education of their librarians.

There is little doubt that there is a marked difference of views between North American and European librarians on the question of classification, and it is my purpose to try to shed some light on those differences. They can be explained by:

1. The different *types of subject catalogs* predominating in the two continents;
2. the *role of classification as a tool for information retrieval* in most European libraries; and
3. the greater acceptance of the *ideas of faceted classification* in Europe, reflected in the curricula of library schools.

European librarians have long favored the systematic arrangement of their subject catalogs, and to this day the great majority of European libraries possess a classed catalog.

THE CLASSED CATALOG

It is appropriate to give a brief explanation of the classed catalog. In a classed catalog the subject entries are arranged by the notation of whatever scheme is in use in the library, in what is known as the *classified file*. In Figure 4-1 there are two entries in the classified file for the item. In a classed catalog, the "main entry" is the primary subject entry in the classified file. Since the notation for a particular subject will not be known by the patron, the catalog must be equipped with an *alphabetical subject index* (Figure 4-2). It provides the entry vocabulary enabling the patron to translate the search terms into the notation used to arrange the entries.

FIGURE 4-1   Classified File Entries

Main subject entry:

711.4
   Urbanization and its problems: essays in honour of E.W. Gilbert/edited by R.P. Beckinsale and J.M. Houston.—Oxford: Blackwell, 1968.
   443 p., 19 p. of plates: ill.; 24cm.—
   16 essays dealing with both the social and planning aspects of the subject, in this country and abroad.—Bibliography: p. 420–432.—
   ISBN 0-631-11040-2 : £4.95.—

Added subject entry

307.76
   Urbanization and its problems: essays in honour of E.W. Gilbert/edited by R.P. Beckinsale and J.M. Houston.—1968.—
   Shelved at:- 711.4

FIGURE 4-2   Alphabetical Subject Index Entries

Cities: Planning	711.4
Cities: Sociology	307.76
Communities: Sociology	307
Planning: Town and country	711
Sociology	301–307
Town and country planning	711
Towns: Sociology	307.76
Urban areas: Planning	711.4
Urban communities: Sociology	307.76

The above two files deal solely with the question of subject searching. So, in addition, a third file is required, which enables the user to conduct a "known item" search. This file contains entries under authors, titles, editors, series, etc., and is frequently described, misleadingly, as an *"author" file* (Figure 4-3). The classed catalog, therefore consists of three files: classified file, alphabetical subject index, and "author" file.

FIGURE 4-3   Author File Entries

Beckinsale, R.P.
   Urbanization and its problems: essays in honour of E.W. Gilbert/edited by R.P. Beckinsale and J.M. Houston.—1968.—

                                                                              711.4

Gilbert, E.W.
   Urbanization and its problems: essays in honour of E.W. Gilbert/edited by R.P. Beckinsale and J.M. Houston.—1968.—

                                                                              711.4

Houston, J.M.
   Urbanization and its problems: essays in honour of E.W. Gilbert/edited by R.P. Beckinsale and J.M. Houston.—1968.—

                                                                              711.4

   Urbanization and its problems: essays in honour of E.W. Gilbert/edited by R.P. Beckinsale and J.M. Houston.—1968.—

                                                                              711.4

The dominance of the classed catalog in Europe, and indeed throughout the world, is reflected in a survey of classification systems in national bibliographies[1] which showed that the favoured method of arrangement in national bibliographies is:

	Number of Libraries	Percent
Alphabetically by author, title, etc.	56	25%
Alphabetically by subject	52	24%
Systematically		
—by Universal Decimal Classification	38	
—by Dewey Decimal Classification	44	49%
—by other classification schemes	26	
Other means	5	2%

You can see that the systematic arrangement accounts for 49 percent of the total. This contrasts very sharply with the methods usually employed in North American libraries. Despite the fact that the greatest library systematizer, Melvil Dewey, favoured the use of the classed catalog, American librarians overwhelmingly favour the *alphabetic* subject catalog as a means of organizing their material for retrieval. The classed catalog is virtually unknown in America, and one is able to count the libraries that use it on the fingers of one hand. It is this difference that has led to a different view of classification in the respective continents. But before looking at this difference of viewpoint a little closer, we should first of all consider similarities of view.

SIMILARITIES IN CLASSIFICATION
IN EUROPE AND THE UNITED STATES

Librarians in both continents require classification as a means of shelf arrangement of *books* and other documents. In other words, both sets of librarians require the facility to mark and park and to allow the user to browse. However, because American librarians and users are less dependent on the classification as a means of *retrieving information,* as opposed to browsing among similar material, they have tended to regard the shelf-location device and the browsing function as the only reasons for classing books.

In the circumstances it is easy to see why American librarians may be unable to appreciate the need for clear citation order, the ability to synthesize, and high specificity in a given classification scheme. They may ask, "Why is all this necessary when all that is required is the ability to browse among a number of shelves of books broadly on the same subject?" If a user wishes to retrieve material on a specific subject, then the alphabetical subject catalog would be used. In this type of catalog, although there is frequently a relationship between the subject heading and the class number assigned to a book, the subject heading is largely independent of the class number. This view is both reinforced and encouraged by the lack of systematic order and inconsistent citation order in one of the most widely applied classification schemes in America, the Library of Congress Classification, but it is also fostered in libraries classified by Dewey as well.

THE EUROPEAN APPROACH TO CLASSIFICATION

For the European librarian, however, this will not do. The librarian and the users are much more dependent on the classification as a means of retrieving information because it is the notation of the classification that determines the order in the subject catalog. Classification is no longer just a device for shelf-arrangement and the browsing function, but it is required to provide a coherent and helpful order of subjects for the purpose of information retrieval. Such a librarian will see the need for a coherent and helpful display of relationships, clear citation orders for classing of compounds, ability to synthesize those compounds, and higher specificity.

It is difficult to grasp these different requirements and roles of classification without an example. Therefore, let us take a fairly straightforward title, "Insect pests of wheat," and see what could happen in four different libraries, which I will label A-D. Library A uses 16th edition Dewey Decimal Classification and has a dictionary catalog; Library B also uses 16th edition Dewey and has a classed catalog; Library C uses 19th edition Dewey and has a dictionary catalog; Library D uses 19th edition Dewey and has a classed catalog.

In Library A and Library B, both using 16th edition, the book would be classed at 633.11, Wheat. There is no provision for synthesis, but a note at 632 indicates that the book should *not* be classed at 632.7, Insect pests. In Library A, with a dictionary catalog, the Library of Congress subject heading for this book would be WHEAT—DISEASES AND PESTS. As a matter of interest neither the class number nor the subject heading describes the subject content of the book precisely. Now for the mark-and-park librarian this would probably be considered satisfactory. The user browsing around 633 would come across the book eventually, whereas the user requiring this specific subject would be led to its location from the alphabetical subject heading, imprecise though this is.

Now let us consider the librarian who has a classed catalog, in Library B. In the first place there would be some consternation at the lack of synthesis for now it is not just the shelf location that matters but the position of the entry in the subject catalog. Placed at 633.11 the entry files among all the entries dealing with "wheat," *generally*. The classed catalog would not enable the user to differentiate between general books on "Wheat" and those that deal with "Insect pests of wheat," because there is not a piece of notation to specify "Insect pests." A comparison between the two types of catalog for information retrieval cannot be fairly made because the dependence on the classification with the defects mentioned greatly weakens the classed catalog as a retrieval device.

If we now consider Library D, we can see what an improvement there is in the classed catalog as a result of the provisions of 19th edition Dewey:

633.11   Wheat
633.1197   Insect Pests [From 632.7]

There is now a piece of notation to specify "Insect pests," and the classed catalog is now superior to the dictionary catalog because in the latter one still can only give the subject heading, WHEAT—DISEASES AND PESTS. But the librarian in Library C, with the dictionary catalog, may not be concerned with that ability to specify and synthesize because as far as he or she is concerned it may not be necessary.

This belief in the supremacy of the classed catalog has been at the root of the European librarian's attitude to classification. For many of them, classification is necessary for retrieval purposes and, that being the case, their demands have been for coherent, logical and helpful order; ability to synthesize; clear citation order; and high specificity. This serves to explain the major differences between the continents over the question of classification. It can be used to explain the criticisms of the Dewey Decimal Classification and the demands for its reform over the last 30 years or so; it provides one of the reasons for the development of Universal Decimal Classification; and it also explains why the Library of Congress Classification has never found a secure position in Europe or the United Kingdom.

There is another reason for differences in attitude over classification, which can be traced to the curricula differences in education for librarianship on the two continents. The syllabi of American schools of librarianship tend to concentrate on what I would call the *how* of classification.[2] That is, the greatest emphasis is placed on how to apply the schedules of DDC and LCC, and in some syllabi as much time seems to be spent on the construction of Cutter numbers as on any other factor. While the European, and particularly British, student would spend some time on applying the schedules, though not those of the Library of Congress Classification, they would concentrate as much time on the *why* of classification. That is, why certain orders are preferable to others, why synthesis and citation order are necessary, what governs the citation order, and so on.

In order to investigate the *why* of classification there is a greater emphasis on the theory of classification in Britain, and in particular the theories of faceted classification established by Ranganathan and developed by many British and European librarians. The ideas of faceted classification took hold in Great Britain far sooner than in America and formed the basis for the teaching of classification in every British library school since the 1950s. Those ideas are regarded as the most fruitful for the development of classification schemes, particularly those required for information retrieval and particularly for libraries that maintain a classed catalog.

The ideas of faceted classifications are often regarded with suspicion by American librarians because they do not require the facilities provided by such ideas. For example, in the proceedings of one American institute in 1968 there was a complaint that the add notes provided in 914–919 in DDC 17th edition were unnecessary. These enabled the *function* (or activity) facet to be added to the *place* facet:

914–919   Add "Areas" notation from Table 2 to base number
               91; then add further as follows:
               02 Physical geography) FUNCTION or ACTIVITY
               04 Travel   )   FACET
914.21   London   PLACE FACET

So 914.2102   London - physical geography
914.2104   London - travel

The writer maintained that when she checked with her local libraries, no one was using the add notes. Since all the libraries had dictionary catalogs, this is not at all surprising. However, for the librarian with a classed catalog and, particularly in this case, a library in London, the need for this provision is apparent.

There is no doubt that the acceptance of the ideas of faceted classification in Europe, and particularly in the United Kingdom, had an immediate effect on the European librarians' views of classification and is why considerable dissatisfaction over the slower acceptance of these ideas in the United States was expressed. Without a more widespread acceptance of these ideas in America the development of the existing general schemes of classification, particularly DDC, would be that much less satisfactory. There is no doubt also that these ideas were only slowly accepted in America. For example, the word "facet" was first used in the introduction to Dewey only in the 19th edition in 1979. Now, no one is seeking to lay any blame for this state of affairs. I am merely attempting to explain why there are different views on classification in our respective continents.

In summary, the difference in views can be traced primarily to the different types of subject catalogs that predominate in our respective countries; second, to the greater requirement of the European librarian for classification to act as an information retrieval tool, not just as a shelf location device; and third, to the greater acceptance of the ideas of faceted classification in Europe, reflected in the curricula of their library schools.

THE DISTRIBUTION OF CLASSIFICATION SCHEMES IN GREAT BRITAIN AND EUROPE

The distribution of classification schemes outside the United States are interpreted for our purposes as the application of the general schemes of classification. It is here that one can obtain evidence of the differing attitudes toward classification on both sides of the Atlantic. For American libraries there are only two general schemes: Dewey Decimal Classification and Library of Congress Classification. The latter is purely and simply a shelf location device, a mark-and-park scheme. For many American librarians Dewey is also a mark-and-park scheme though it has some potential to be a scheme for information retrieval.

In a survey conducted in 1975 it was shown that 85 percent of libraries in the United States and Canada used Dewey Decimal Classification and the remaining 15 percent used the Library of Congress Classification.[3] No other classification scheme was mentioned in that survey. The 15 percent of libraries using LCC included most of the large academic and some large public libraries in North America.

Great Britain

During the 1960s and 1970s many American libraries changed over from Dewey to Library of Congress Classification. Most British librarians viewed this activity with a great deal of skepticism, for it looked to be jumping from the frying pan into the fire. Re-classification from Dewey to Library of Congress Classification did not occur in Great Britain, and the reasons are not hard to find. In the first place, for British and European librarians there are four general schemes to choose from, not just two. These are Dewey, Library of Congress, Universal Decimal Classification (UDC), and Bliss's Bibliographic Classification.

Of these four schemes, two easily outstrip the other two in the number of libraries that apply them. These two are Dewey Decimal Classification and Universal Decimal Classification.

Bliss Bibliographic Classification, now in its second edition, is the most up-to-date general faceted classification available, but it suffers from the fact that (a) it only became available, even in its first edition, very much later than the other three; (b) it is incomplete in its second edition, and though it is likely to be completed, there must be a doubt over any future development; and (c) it is not used by any large library in Great Britain. One university library is using the scheme, and it is used in several small academic and special libraries, but its economic base is very narrow. It is probably only being used in 80 to 100 libraries, mostly in Great Britain. Its up-to-dateness has an appeal but the most telling factor for librarians seems to be whether or not USMARC or UKMARC records carry a class mark from a classification scheme. In the case of Bliss, the answer is no.

Library of Congress Classification is used in some British libraries and one or two in Europe, but its use is largely confined to university libraries. In the 1967 survey it was shown that LCC was used in 25 university libraries.[4] This is only about one-third of the libraries in this category; the remainder use either their own homemade schemes, Dewey, UDC, or some other scheme. A calculation made in 1973 showed that only 5 percent of all monograph materials in all libraries in Great Britain were classed by LCC. I do not know what the figures are for American libraries, but one imagines they are considerably higher than this. It can be seen from this that the Library of Congress Classification has very little influence in Europe, including Great Britain. It is widely regarded as a "local" American scheme, used in some libraries in Australia and Africa, but not elsewhere.

The two general schemes that dominate in Europe are, of course, Dewey and UDC. In the case of the United Kingdom, UDC is used in more libraries than Dewey. A survey conducted in 1979 and 1980 showed that the scheme was in use in 640 libraries out of a total of 2,895 libraries and information services in Great Britain.[5] These included some university libraries. The use of UDC, however, is largely confined to special libraries, some of which, like the libraries of the United Kingdom Atomic Energy Authority, Central Electricity Generating Board, and the British Steel Corporation, are very large organizations, but most are fairly small. The UDC system appeals to them because it is a highly specific, faceted scheme very suitable for information retrieval. Most, if not all, of the libraries who use it have a classed catalog.

As a scheme UDC confers a great deal of autonomy on the individual librarian in the crucial area of citation order. The following example is typical of its power in this respect. The system has a general relationship device, the colon, enabling parts of the classification to be joined together; square brackets may be substituted for this device to give a different arrangement.

(a) Using the colon (:)

620.1:		Materials Testing	
620.172:		Tensile Testing	[Type of Test]
620.172:	669.24	Nickel	
620.172:	669.26	Chromium	
620.176:		Shearing Tests	[Type of Test]
620.176:	669.24	Nickel	
620.176:	669.26	Chromium	

Citation order is TYPE OF TEST—MATERIALS

(b) Using square brackets ([]) instead of the colon (:)

620.1	Materials Testing	
620.1[669.24]	Nickel	[Material]
620.1[669.24]72	Tensile Tests	
620.1[669.24]76	Shearing Tests	
620.1[669.26]	Chromium	[Material]
620.1[669.26]72	Tensile Tests	
620.1[699.26]76	Shearing Tests	

Citation order is MATERIALS—TYPE OF TEST

Paradoxically this autonomy is also one of the weaknesses of UDC because there can be no standard UDC class number as there is in the case of Dewey or LCC. Therefore, despite its widespread use in the UK, UDC class numbers only appear on a UKMARC record if they are provided by the agency from which the document originates. So, a library committed to UDC must expect to be committed to totally original classification. Those users of UDC are unlikely to regard this as a serious weakness, however. Most will make their own interpretation of the schedules, decide their own citation orders, and so on. The use of UDC for monograph materials in most of these libraries is insignificant, in part because UDC is a bibliographic classification, not a shelf location device. It is used to classify documents in many different physical forms—unpublished reports, periodical articles, conference papers, patents, letters, etc. Physical location is a secondary consideration. The classification role is one of information storage and retrieval.

A survey on the use of Dewey in the United Kingdom in 1984 was conducted by the Library Association Dewey Decimal Classification Committee.[6] A questionnaire was sent to 1,000 libraries, most of which were known to be using Dewey. Dewey is used in all 173 public library systems, all 32 polytechnic libraries (the nearest equivalent to state universities in the United States), 21 university libraries, and about 85 percent of the 772 institutes and colleges of higher and further education. For the classification of monograph materials in British libraries no other general scheme of classification approaches Dewey in the extent of its application.

Europe

The situation regarding the use of the general schemes of classification in Europe closely follows that of Britain except that there is a decreasing use of Dewey the further east one goes and an increasing use of UDC. In the USSR and the countries of Eastern Europe UDC is widely used, but recently has been challenged by BBK (Bibliotechno-Bibliograficheskaya, Klassifikatsiya), also known as LBC (Library Bibliographical Classification).

In addition, many academic libraries in the Germanic countries do not have open stacks and have tended to develop in-house schemes rather than utilize existing published general schemes of classification. In a closed stack situation the use of classification for browsing by users does not arise; such "browsing" must be performed at the catalog. Can one imagine anything more dreary than that?

It is clear that the different distribution of classification schemes in the two continents emphasizes the very different view of the role of classification in a library's operations European libraries favor those schemes that have the greatest potential for information retrieval; American libraries favor those schemes whose main function is seen as a shelf-location device. This different view is brought about largely because of the predominance of different types of catalogs in our respective continents.

ONLINE CATALOGS AND CLASSIFICATION SYSTEMS

Considerable interest has been expressed in the potential use of classification as a search key in online catalogs; and there is a research project proceeding that is jointly funded by OCLC, the Council on Library Resources and Forest Press. Since the introduction of the British Library Automated Information Services (BLAISE) in 1978, British librarians, and I emphasize librarians, *not* patrons, have had the facility to search both UKMARC files and USMARC files online using the DDC class number as a search key. All the sophisticated paraphernalia of truncation, expansion of class numbers, and the use of Boolean operators are available. So, for British librarians, the use of classification search keys for searching a database is not new. Permitting patrons to conduct such searches on their own database, therefore, is going to be but a small step for them. Indeed, a number of libraries in Great Britain now have online public access catalogs, with the facility to interrogate the database with a DDC class number as a search key.

It is hardly surprising that the facility just described is available in British libraries. Many cynics would say those who are only just discovering the potential of classification for online subject searching are about to rediscover the classed catalog and what they are attempting to do online has been done in a manual environment for the last 80 years. However, the emergence of online public access to bibliographic records means that we can look forward to a synthesis of the two types of catalog. In the manual environment no library could afford to provide two types of catalog so that the user could search using alphabetical subject headings and/or class numbers. In the machine environment the ability to search the database by a variety of subject search keys must inevitably bring about the removal of terms such as *classed catalog* and *dictionary catalog* from the vocabulary, and therefore the minds, of librarians and patrons.

It is virtually certain that if classification is to be used as a search key by patrons, then our classification schemes will have to be equipped with all those devices that enable the schemes to be used as tools for information retrieval, and not used solely for shelf location purposes. That will then bring forward the question of whether libraries, which at present do not have the requirement of classification for information retrieval, will be prepared to face the additional costs that this will involve.

The European view of classification, in the past, has led to searching files using keywords, or other alphabetical designators, in addition to the norm of searching using the classification as a search key. The American view of classification, in the past, has led to searching files using the classification numbers, in addition to the norm of using alphabetical designators. Future developments in the area of online public access catalogs are likely to ensure that our respective views on the functions of classification will more closely coincide.

REFERENCES

1. E. R. Sukiasian, "Classification Systems in National Bibliography: Survey and Recommendations," IFLA, 1984 (Report prepared for the 50th General Conference of IFLA, Nairobi, 1984).
2. Mary Ellen Michael and John Comaromi, "A Survey of Classification Instruction in the United States and Canada." Prepared for Forest Press, January 1976.
3. John P. Comaromi, Mary Ellen Michael, and Janet Bloom, *A Survey of the Use of the Dewey Decimal Classification in the United States and Canada* (Albany, NY: Forest Press, 1975).
4. Joan Friedman and Alan Jeffreys, "Cataloguing and Classification in British University Libraries: A Survey of Practices and Procedures," *Journal of Documentation 23 (September 1967): 224–246.*
5. Richard Hindson, "UDC in the UK: A Report on the 1979/80 Survey," *Aslib Proceedings* 33, no. 3 (March 1981): 93–101.
6. Russell Sweeney, "Dewey in Great Britain: Survey on the Use of the Dewey Decimal Classification in Libraries in Great Britain and Northern Ireland," *Catalogue & Index* 76/77 (Spring/Summer 1985): 1, 3–7.

5

Dewey Decimal Classification: History and Continuing Development

John P. Comaromi

HISTORY

Every librarian is familiar with some parts of the history of the Dewey Decimal Classification as shown in Figure 5-1. This chapter will give you an idea of how we came to be where we are now, how Dewey is being developed and maintained today, and some of the things that you can expect to see in the near future.

Figure 5-1 Brief History of the Dewey Decimal Classification

1873	Conceived in 1873, published in 1876.
1900	By 1900 the DDC had spread to virtually all public libraries, school libraries, college libraries, and university libraries (but not to the Eastern research libraries).
1927	The editorial offices of the DDC moved from the Lake Placid Club to the Library of Congress.
1930	DDC numbers are recorded on LC cards.
1931	Melvil Dewey dies. The ALA moves to give the profession a voice in the development and application of the DDC. The DC Committee—the direct ancestor of the present Decimal Classification Editorial Policy Committee—was established.

1942	The 14th edition, one of the all-time favorites of librarians, is published. For reasons that time has concealed, the editor of the edition was fired, and his assistant not elevated to his place. Apostolic succession had been disrupted, and the ground was prepared for the disaster soon to visit the DDC family.
1951	The 15th edition appears, developed upon principles laid down by American librarians: exhaustive specification through brief numbers. In a hierarchical notation (which was also desired) the principles were in conflict. But American librarians then thought little and cared less about such ideas in opposition.
1953	LC assumes responsibility for editing the DDC. David Haykin was the first LC editor, until driven from his post by librarians inimical to his ideas of change. Replacing him was Benjamin Custer, who was responsible for the highly regarded 16th edition published in 1958.
1965	The 17th edition is published. Condemned by all but theorists.
1982	Expansion of 301–307, manual.
1985	004-006 Computer science, the first schedule published under the policy of continuous revision.
1985	By 1985 U.S. use declines from the high levels enjoyed earlier in the century: most public libraries, most school libraries, less than half the college libraries, and few university libraries use the DDC. Use outside the United States is widespread. Except for Eastern European countries, several Central European countries, and a few Eastern countries, the DDC has become or is becoming the world's bibliographic classification.
1988	Forest Press acquired by OCLC, Inc.
1989	The 20th edition is published, incorporating instructions for application.

Melvil Dewey conceived the idea of a classification system using Indo-Arabic numerals as the notation device in 1873 while he was at Amherst College. He published the first edition—a 44-page pamphlet—in 1876. Typically for Dewey, he had more copies printed than he needed, and he sold them on his own.

In 1885, the second edition appeared. The expansion over the first edition was colossal. It was probably the most important development of any classification system in the history of library classification codes. At the time the second edition was published, Dewey was librarian at Columbia College, which was an influential position in American librarianship, and his classification swept the field. It was adopted by small libraries in the East, public libraries in the Midwest and West, and by school libraries everywhere.

The large research libraries and largest public libraries in the East, however, did not adopt Dewey's classification. Most of the men in charge of those libraries did not like Dewey as a person, and they could not bring themselves to adopt his classification. But not everyone knew Dewey personally: by 1900, the DDC had spread to virtually all other American public, school, and college libraries, and to most university libraries.

In 1906 Dewey was forced to leave the job he held at that time, the directorship of the New York State Library, and was at the same time removed from any position of importance in ALA, because of the anti-semitic policies of the Lake Placid Club, a resort in which he had substantial interest. It was a blow from which American librarianship took a long time to recover.

In 1901, the Library of Congress began to sell catalog cards, which included the LCC (Library of Congress Classification) call number, but no Dewey numbers. The presence of the LCC number acted as a very powerful magnet for libraries, and immediately many of them, including some of the very largest university libraries, began to switch from DDC to LCC. Dewey recognized the potential impact of the cards, and almost from the beginning he tried to get DDC numbers included on them. At one point he wrote to Herbert Putnam, who was then Librarian of Congress, "Hundreds of librarians weep and wail because our numbers are not on the cards they buy."

In 1922, Dewey's longtime editor, May Seymour, died. By 1927, Dewey himself was getting very old, as was his next editor, Dorcas Fellows. Partly because of Dewey's advancing age, and partly to be near a very large library that could help in the development of the classification system, Dewey moved the DDC editorial offices from Lake Placid, NY to the Library of Congress. Soon afterward, in 1930, DDC numbers started to appear on Library of Congress printed cards. David Haykin was the first head of the Classification section. In their first year of operation they classified about 4,000 titles. The next year they did 25,000. In 1985 they did about 124,000.

While he lived, Melvil Dewey fought hard to retain control of the DDC and its development. The American Library Association thought that librarians using the system also should have a voice in how it was developed, and in 1930 ALA established a classification committee. At first the committee had little impact, but after Dewey's death in 1931, ALA moved more strongly to give the profession a voice in the development and application of DDC. In 1936 or 1937, the ancestor of the current Decimal Classification Editorial Policy Committee was formed. It was much more powerful then than now, in that the committee essentially determined the structure of the classification, what new topics would be included, and so forth. The committee also chose the editor, and could fire him or her if it wanted to.

In 1942, the 14th edition was published. This edition became one of the all-time favorites of librarians, and it is still used in many libraries. For reasons that time has concealed, the editor of the 14th edition was fired, and his assistant was not elevated to his place. The ALA committee seems to have gotten rid of the people who knew how the classification was put together, and the results for the classification system were horrible. The new Director of the Decimal Classification Office, Esther Potter (notice she was not called Editor), traveled around the country talking to librarians, asking what they wanted. Librarians told her they wanted exhaustive specification, they wanted every important topic to have its own number, they wanted short numbers, and they wanted the hierarchy maintained. And the Dewey people tried to give everything to them. The 15th edition was published in 1951, based on the results of Esther Potter's talks, and it was an unmitigated disaster. Almost the only nice things about it are that it was a pretty color and it was well printed. It was so universally disliked that it gave great impetus to libraries moving toward Library of Congress Classification.

Then Sputnik went up in 1957, and a lot of federal monies began to be directed into education. Libraries suddenly had more money than they knew what to do with, and a lot of them decided to re-classify their collections, which helped put Forest Press on shaky financial ground. In 1953, the Library of Congress obtained control of the editor's position and began to dominate the classification in most respects. Forest Press still had influence over the choice of editor, but they did not have total control as they had in the past.

David Haykin, who was the first head of the Classification Office, was named editor, and he set out to update the schedules in a hurry. However, he was in too much of a hurry and was fired after two years for making too many changes too fast for most librarians.

Managers and experts, such as Hugh Atkinson and Phyllis Richmond (see Chapters 1 and 2), say that classification schedules need to remain current, that the Dewey Phoenix schedules are important, that libraries simply have to adopt new numbers and reclassify their older titles to use them. That's theory. When I conduct workshops on Dewey classification, I almost never find anyone who is willing to reclassify books they have already cataloged. When changes are made in the schedules, I hear instead, "You must be kidding! We haven't got time. We haven't got money."

That is the kind of pressure that caused David Haykin to be fired. He was replaced by Benjamin Custer, who developed the classification as he was told. Custer kept some of the good features of the 15th edition, but mainly he modernized the 14th. As a result, the 16th edition was very successful.

Development of the Manual on the
Use of Dewey Decimal Classification

In 1965 Forest Press funded a survey to see what librarians needed most in the DDC. The press sent a long questionnaire to every tenth library listed in the North American directory. They asked about the problems of using Dewey for reference work and the problems of applying it in cataloging. They asked librarians if they liked biographies where they were, whether they liked the index, and so forth. It turned out that most librarians did not like the index. Melvil Dewey liked it, but almost no one else did.

The most important things that Forest Press learned were that classifiers were in great need of assistance, and that workshops and a manual of application were absolute necessities. We have now given more than 40 workshops. The manual took a little more time to develop than the workshops.

I was hired to work on the manual. My first step was to ask the staff in the Decimal Classification Division to send me all the notes they had about how they applied the schedules. I started with language, education, law, and literature. Using the notes that the Decimal Classification staff sent me, I wrote an introduction for each area of the schedule, explaining how Dewey had developed these classes and divisions, and why he had ordered them in a particular way. Then I set about trying to explain how to build numbers, and I included any tables, comparisons, or hints I could come up with. I was very proud of the result. I sent my notes to Custer at the Library of Congress, and asked, "Well, what do you think?" He wrote back, "We don't think very much of it at all. We don't use the system that way." So I said, "You're kidding! Those instructions come right off the notes you sent me." It turned out, of course, that every classifier had developed his or her own body of rules and was applying them independently of every other classifier. We started over.

Each classifier was assigned a portion of the schedule to prepare instructions for. All the sections were sent to the assistant editor, Margaret Warren, who read them and discovered they were all different. So she would go to the classifiers and say, "You can't mean this is what you're doing. Please tell me you aren't." And they would say, "Yes. Yes. This is really the way I do it." And she would say, "Not any more." So Margaret would negotiate a compromise and rewrite the section. Then she sent each section to me, and I'd say, "You can't mean this is what they're doing. Please tell me they aren't." And she would say, "Yes. Yes. This is really the way they do it." And I would say, "Not any more," and I would rewrite it. In the end, after all the sections were combined and compared, we had written a manual that was unified in concepts, and consistent throughout. It was published in 1982 and is called *Manual on the Use of the Dewey Decimal Classification: Edition 19.* Everyone classifying with Dewey should have used the manual, but most did not. A lot of people have never heard of it. I don't think it was ever even reviewed in this country. In the future it will be harder to ignore the manual, though, since the instructions are incorporated throughout the schedules in the 20th edition, and the manual will no longer be a separate publication.

Revision Policy

Another publication landmark was the expansion of 301-307 (Sociology) in 1982. Next, in 1985, came the Phoenix for computer science, data processing, and related areas. It was called a Phoenix, but it was really the first schedule to be published under the policy of continuous revision. Under this policy, whenever the Decimal Classification Division develops something new in the schedule, it will be printed, and librarians will not be able to tell from the printing what is new and what is not. If a large area is developed, something that can stand by itself, it will be published separately and sold. Then at the next cumulation, all of the changes will be combined into a single whole.

If you look carefully at the computer science Phoenix, you will be able to tell what major revisions will look like in the future. The Phoenix is 60 or 70 pages, with maybe 17 pages of schedules, an index, a baby manual of application just for these numbers, and a glossary. This is the first glossary to be done by DDC. So many unfamiliar words were used in the schedule that we decided that rather than define them wherever they occurred, we would create a glossary, and only define the terms once.

I am often asked if the Decimal Classification Division devises the schedules entirely with staff in the division, or whether we get help from outside experts in particular subject fields. In the past, the schedules were generally developed by experts and specialists within the division, without much recourse to outside expertise. Once we develop a schedule, however, we often ask an outside expert to look at it, especially if we are unsure of something. Experience has shown that we do not get very far by asking for outside opinions until we have a schedule fairly well developed. Our present pattern is to work through the Subject Analysis Committee (SAC) of the Cataloging and Classification Section of the Reference and Technical Services Division (RTSD). For every large schedule we produce, SAC sets up a subcommittee to study it and make recommendations. This arrangement seems to work very well.

We had a Subject Analysis Committee subcommittee for education, 370. We prepared a Phoenix for those numbers, but the subcommittee did not like it, so it was tabled. There will be a subcommittee to study public administration. The subcommittee that worked on 780, music, prepared a report that governed the final decision on what we did with those numbers.

By 1985 use of DDC in the United States had declined considerably from the position it held earlier in the century. Most school and public libraries still use DDC, but less than half the college libraries and only a few university libraries use DDC in their collections. Outside the United States use of Dewey is widespread. Except for Eastern European countries, some Central European countries, and a few Eastern countries, the DDC has become or is becoming the world's bibliographic classification. It has been translated into many foreign languages, including Arabic, with Greek and Turkish translations in the works.

CURRENT DEVELOPMENT AND
MAINTENANCE OF DEWEY DECIMAL CLASSIFICATION

Today the Decimal Classification Editorial Policy Committee, the Forest Press Committee, and LC's Decimal Classification Division each play a role in the maintenance and development of the classification system.

The Decimal Classification Editorial Policy Committee has three *ex officio* members: one from ALA, one from the Library of Congress, and one from Forest Press. In addition to these, there are three ALA appointees, and three people appointed by the Lake Placid Education Foundation. Committee members are selected to represent different types and sizes of libraries and are supposed to see that the librarians who use DDC are not undermined by something that the editors do.

This committee looks at everything the Decimal Classification Division produces. If they like what they see, they recommend acceptance to the Forest Press Committee. This group is "the money people." Their main concern is to see that the Dewey Classification and Forest Press survive. They are not particularly interested in the beauty of an expansion, or with whether the concepts are right, except that they know that the beauty of the expansion, or the rightness of a concept makes a difference in the success of the classification. The Forest Press Committee takes the recommendations of the Editorial Policy Committee and considers what the impact on Dewey is going to be. If they decide that the impact will be positive, then they tell the Decimal Classification Division at the Library of Congress, and we start to work on getting the revisions or expansions ready for publication.

Of course, the Dewey Decimal Classification Division does not just work on developing the DDC. We are the smallest division in the Processing Services Department of the Library of Congress. Books pour out of Descriptive and Shared Cataloging and are sent to Subject Cataloging, where the subject headings are added, the Library of Congress classification number is formulated, and the work is shelflisted. Then the books come to the Decimal Classification Division.

The Decimal Classification Division handles about 180,000 titles a year, but we do not classify them all. In 1985 we classified about 124,000, or approximately 70 percent, of all the titles that the Library of Congress handled. It is likely that the percentage of titles classed in Dewey will decrease in the near future, because in the interest of expediting the flow of cataloging copy through the Library, we will be instituting a policy of five-day turn-around. This means that any book arriving in the DC Division has to be out of there five work days later, whether it has a Dewey number on it or not. An outline of Divisional operations is given in Figure 5-2.

FIGURE 5-2 Operations in the Decimal Classification Division

I. Application (123,000 titles in 1984)

    A. Languages: English (including summaries in English), Chinese, Spanish, French, German, Portuguese, Italian, and other languages as time permits and words reveal.

    B. Staff responsibilities: by subject

        1. 301–307 (sociology)
        2. —68, —52 (South Africa, Japan)
        3. 004–006 (data processing, computer science)
        4. 780 (music)
        5. 560/590 (life sciences)
        6. 351/354 (public administration)
        7. Area tables
        8. Index

6

Library of Congress Classification

Mary Kay Pietris

This chapter covers five different topics relating to the Library of Congress Classification system: historical background, recurring problems, the tables, revision and updating, and future plans.

HISTORICAL BACKGROUND

Library of Congress classification began in 1897 with the decision to create a new classification to replace Thomas Jefferson's system. The first two schedules published, E-F and Z, are the only schedules that do not use double letters. The practice of expanding classification through double letters began with M.

The order in which the schedules were published is interesting and has had a permanent impact on the classification system. In Figure 6-1, you will notice that the ones published in 1910 include geography, social sciences, and political science. The year 1910 was, of course, before World War I. Eastern Europe was dominated by Germany, Austria-Hungary, and Russia; and Africa was ruled by colonial powers. The classification schedules developed before 1918 reflect this. To a large part, they still do now, which is one of the difficulties with LC classification.

FIGURE 6-1 Order of Publication of LC Classification Schedules

1901	E-F	History: America (Western Hemisphere)
1902	Z	Bibliography. Library science
1904	M	Music
1905	Q	Science
1910	B-BJ	Philosophy. Psychology
	G	Geography. Anthropology. Recreation

	H	Social sciences
	J	Political science
	N	Fine arts
	R	Medicine
	T	Technology
	U	Military science
	V	Naval science
1911	A	General works
	L	Education
	S	Agriculture
1915	C	Auxiliary sciences of history
	PN,PR,PS,PZ	General literature. English and American literature. Fiction in English. Juvenile literature
1916	D	History: General and old world (Eastern Hemisphere)
1927	BL-BX	Religion
1928	P-PA	General philology and linguistics. Classical languages and literature
1933	PB-PH	Modern European languages
1935	PJ-PM	Languages and literatures of Asia, Africa, Oceania. American Indian languages. Artificial languages
1936	P-PM supplement	Index to languages and dialects
	PQ (Part 1)	French literature
1937	PQ (Part 2)	Italian, Spanish, and Portuguese literatures
1938	PT (Part 1)	German literature
1942	PA supplement	Byzantine and modern Greek literature. Medieval and modern Latin literature
	PT (Part 2)	Dutch and Scandinavian literatures
1948	PG	Russian literature
1969	KF	Law of the United States
1973	KD	Law of the United Kingdom and Ireland
1976	KE	Law of Canada
1977	K	Law (General)
1982	KK-KKC	Law of Germany
1984	KDZ, KG-KH	Law of the Americas, Latin America and the West Indies
1985	KJV-KJW	Law of France
1989	KJ-KKZ	Law of Europe

In 1915 the only part of the literature schedule to come out before the 1930s appeared—General Literature, English and American Literature (PN, PR, PS, PZ). Class D (History) regrettably came out before World War I was over and still reflects the old organization of Europe. Only one schedule came out in the 1920s and that was the Religion (BL-BX) schedule.

The imprint dates do not reflect the dates the schedules were developed. In the past, the Library of Congress would use a schedule for quite a long period of time before publishing it. For example, BL-BX was published in 1927 after it had been applied at the library for ten years to over 105,000 volumes. The library no longer has the same time lag now in publishing the new Law (K) schedules. These have generally appeared within two to three years of application at LC.

Figure 6-1 shows that the rest of the literature schedules were published in the 1920s and 1930s, except for the last one, PG, in 1948. By 1948 the LC classification was complete except for Law. The Law Library of the Library of Congress used the traditional form arrangement of law libraries. In addition, law materials were accommodated in the other classes, such as in HF for legal materials relating to finance.

Work on Class K began in 1949 with the establishment of specialized committees. Working papers were published and revised, resulting in the preliminary edition of KF, Law of the United States, being published in 1969. A draft outline of Class K was published in 1970. Later study revealed that substantial changes would be desirable, and in 1979 that outline was abandoned. *Cataloging Service Bulletin,* no. 23 contains the announcement of that decision and a rough outline of the new Class K arrangement of countries.

We began applying Law of France, KJV-KJW, at the Library of Congress in May 1985. It is the last schedule to be created that is unique to one country. Law of Europe, KJ-KKZ, contains the first use of a generalized civil law table of topics.

Law of the Soviet Union, Africa, Asia, and Australia (KL-KZ) will probably be in two volumes, a volume of jurisdictional listings, similar to the one in KJ-KKZ, and a volume of tables, consisting of a civil law table, a common law table, and tables for provinces, cities, forms, and so on. The tentative jurisdictional allocations are as follows:

KL Soviet Union
KM-KPZ Asia (Near East, South and Southeast Asia, Far East)
KQ-KTZ Africa (North Africa, Sub-Saharan Africa)
KV-KW Australia, New Guinea, New Zealand, Melanesia, Micronesia, Polynesia, Antarctica

Schedules for theocratic legal systems (canon law, Islamic law, Jewish law, etc.) will be developed in Class KC after J-JX is revised. That revision is scheduled to begin when KL-KZ is completed. Theocratic legal systems as applied in a specific country will class with that country.

Figure 6-2 shows the schedules according to recency of publication. The schedules are arranged by date in which the most recent edition was published. Revision and updating of schedules will be discussed later in this chapter. This is simply a handy chart to show you how old some of the schedules are.

FIGURE 6-2   Dates of Latest Editions

1962	BL-BX
1965	E-F; PG; PJ-PM; PQ, Part 2; PT, Part 2
1966	D; J; PB-PH; PQ, Part 1; PT, Part 1
1968	P-PA; PA Supplement
1969	KF
1970	N
1971	T
1973	A; KD; Q
1974	U; V
1975	C
1976	G; KE
1977	K
1978	M; PN,PR,PS,PZ
1979	B-BJ
1980	HM-HX; R; Z
1981	H-HJ
1982	KK-KKC; P-PZ Tables; S
1983	P-PM Supplement (Index)
1984	BL,BM,BP,BQ; KDZ, KG-KH; L
1985	BX; KJV-KJW
1986	BR-BV
1987	DJK-DK; DS
1988	PJ-PK
1989	Q; KJ-KKZ

RECURRING PROBLEMS

Enumeration and Hierarchy

The first category of recurring problems is those that are inherent in LC classification. The first inherent problem is enumeration; that is, we specifically list most topics in the schedules. The system has very little notational synthesis. For instance, in the Dewey Decimal system -05 represents periodicals. So in Dewey you do not have to specify every time you have a periodical, you just add -05 to the number for the topic. With

LC classification it is necessary to create and print a unique number for periodicals, such as HC10 and HD4421. Library of Congress classification does use tables for geographical places. Otherwise we spell everything out. Of course, this means that LCC schedules take up more feet of shelf space than the Dewey Decimal schedules. The second inherent problem is that the system is not hierarchical. The hierarchy of subject matter is not expressed in any manner in the notation. You cannot just cut off the number and have any confidence that you are anywhere near the same topic. Also, A to Z arrangements are frequently used instead of logical arrangements. If you think that is a cop out, you are right. But that is how the system was designed.

Shelflisting

The second category of recurring problems is in the area of shelflisting. Any new call number that is developed must fit into the Library of Congress shelflist. Now that is not a problem for us—we have the LC shelflist. Other libraries do not have the shelflist, and I think this is a problem. A microfiche version of the shelflist was published in 1978, but quite a few books have been added since then. The problem with numbers having to fit into the shelflist is that no matter what one constructs theoretically, that theory is then readjusted upon seeing what already exists in the shelflist.

The second shelflisting problem is that the Library of Congress changed the author number table. It was called the book number table and was printed in *Cataloging Service Bulletin*, nos. 104 and 3. The basic change is that now two digits are used instead of one as in the past, even if it is not absolutely necessary. Let me give you an example. Before the change, if you had a book by a person whose name began with the letters "St", you Cuttered "S7." So authors whose names were Steele or Stone or Sturgis could get "S7" as a Cutter if this was the first author into the shelflist at that spot. Now, most of the time two digits are assigned. So Steele would get "S74"; Stone, "S76"; and Sturgis, "S78," even if there is nothing in the shelflist at S7. One more digit will provide those famous Cutter-Sanborn tables, which have been used for years with Dewey. The Library of Congress expanded the Cutters in order to keep them from getting too long if the shelflister injudiciously chose a Cutter that did not allow sufficient expansion.

That was not as much a problem as the change in the shelflisting of corporate bodies. This took place in 1974 and is described in *Cataloging Service Bulletin,* no. 110. The basic purpose was to simplify things. According to the *Cataloging Service Bulletin:* "All publications cataloged under a corporate heading and classified under the same number are assigned the same Cutter number. In formulating a Cutter number for a corporate heading all subheadings are disregarded." The American

Library Association with all the different divisions ending up intermixed on the shelves is given as an example in the *Bulletin*. If you then have two publications by the same corporate body or parts of it, to complete the call number and make it distinctive, the date of imprint is added: "Publications with identical dates of imprint are distinguished by adding successive work letters to the date in the call number." The library has been doing this since 1974. It has resulted in works not being arranged tidily on the shelves.

New rules for including dates in call numbers is the next shelflisting problem. This change was made in 1979 and was described in *Cataloging Service Bulletin*, no. 19. The old policy on the use of dates in call numbers for monographs was extremely confusing for shelflisters. They had a full sheet of paper with 12 rules defining when to add a date, and six rules for when not to add one. For example, if the edition was new, enlarged, revised, reprinted, improved, second, third, First American, or U.S., etc., then a date was added to show it was an edition. If, however, it said first, preliminary, limited, and so on, a date was not added. The rest of the rules were similarly complicated. The rules were difficult to apply, so in 1979 we went to the rule of always adding a date to call numbers for monographs.

Integrity of Numbers and New Developments

The third category of recurring problems is those shared by other classification systems. The old question of integrity of numbers versus keeping up with new developments is not quite as much of a problem as it is for other systems. The LCC system is hospitable to new topics. We seldom create phoenix editions. However, the introduction to the third edition of Class R (Medicine) in 1952 states that there is "more thorough-going revision" than in any other schedule done previously. If you are working from old cataloging copy with pre-1952 numbers in R, the numbers may bear no relation at all to the current ones. For instance, RC116 in the second edition meant transmission of diseases by mosquitoes and mosquito eradication, but according to the third edition it is used for an A to Z listing of specific bacterial diseases. In the second edition RC367 was for alcoholism, but in the third edition it is for vascular lesions as a disease of the central nervous system.

Currently, when making revisions the Library of Congress classification prefers to separate books on the same subject instead of putting books on several different subjects into the same number, as was done with the medical topics cited above. I believe that it is far worse to mix up subjects on the shelf than it is to separate them.

One example of this problem is trying to come up with a development for solar energy. It was difficult to figure out where to put it. Its companions had to be appropriate ones, but without mixing up the numbers too much or reusing old numbers. *LC Classification—Additions and Changes,* List 213, has the new development on renewable energy sources after TJ805, including solar energy and wind power. This enabled the use of the number that had previously meant solar engines, but many of the books previously classed in the single number TJ810 should be reclassed into the expanded and more specific numbers now available. (The problem of reclassification will be discussed later in this chapter.)

Another problem that LCC has in common with other systems is concern over the change of names and boundaries of countries. Keep in mind that much of the classification was developed before World War I, and so the problem has been particularly acute.

A letter from 1937 deals with the need to change classification to reflect boundary changes. A woman in Philadelphia wrote to the Chief of the Classification Division about Finland and Poland and the fact that they were classed in DK in what was the Soviet Union. The reply to her letter was, "We did not, after the European War, feel the necessity of reconstructing our classification of history with its quarter of a million books and corresponding cards. Inasmuch as such countries as Finland and Poland are complete units as they stand in the scheme, we see no advantage in changing the letters from DK to some other combination of letters which would seem to emphasize their independence." Well, about 40 years later we did change the numbers for Finland and Poland, but in 1937 we justified not doing it. Another letter written during World War II explained that there were too many cards on the European War to change the subject heading to anything else. The moral in this is to change as fast as possible, once you are reasonably sure the world is going to stay stable for a while.

Library of Congress classification is still working on the DT schedule to make it reflect the independent status of countries that were once under colonial rule. The library has completed major developments, except for Southern Africa where parts of the Republic of South Africa are scattered among independent countries.

The next problem shared with other classification systems is re-classification. When do we do it? We don't re-classify if we are just developing the schedules. When a new number is created, the older books are not reclassified. They just stay on the shelves in the old numbers. If an error was made in analysis or if there has been a typographical error, the book is re-classed. Errors are corrected if they are in the MARC database. If there is a new edition of a work, the classification is changed to a limited extent, as described in *Cataloging Service Bulletin,* no. 12.

As a result of developing numbers for new topics and when needed because of name and territorial changes, we may end up with a new classification schedule with a nice tidy organization. But you cannot take the new edition to the shelves and have it explain very much because the shelves are full of books classed by the old numbers. The new edition does not contain the old numbers at all. It just tells how to classify from now on. It does not explain what is already on your shelves. Therefore, it is important not to throw away old editions of the schedules.

One recent event that had an impact on classification and shelflisting was AACR2. Classification and shelflisting policies under AACR2 are fairly well explained in *Cataloging Service Bulletin,* nos. 8 and 11. According to the policies in the bulletin, when there were changes caused by AACR2 in the form of name of a person or corporate body printed in the classification schedules, a decision would be made on a case-by-case basis whether to alter the printed caption and make a reference from a new form or to create new numbers to match the revised form of heading. In most cases the caption was altered, but the material was not moved.

Names of jurisdictions not printed in the schedules posed a special problem. If the schedules provide for arrangement by place, A to Z, the classification started to use the latest form of name as the basis for arrangement. For instance, we would start using Zambia, a "Z" Cutter, instead of Rhodesia, Northern, an "R" Cutter. However, if the initial filing word was unchanged, as in Paris to Paris (France), we would trust that the shelflisters would recognize that these were the same place and would perpetuate Cuttering for the old name.

Other plans dealing with AACR2's impact involved trying to keep literary works by a single person together, regardless of the number of names by which a person might be found in the author catalog. This policy is fairly successfully. Cross-references are printed from the name now used to the name used before. An attempt is also made to continue existing numbers when Cuttering for a work about something. A work *by* an organization or a person whose name has changed is going to get separated on the shelves, even under one class number. But books *about* an organization or person are generally kept together.

The 1981 adoption of the new version of Library of Congress Filing Rules also affected shelflisting. A word is now filed by the way it looks, not the way it sounds. Numbers go before letters, abbreviations are arranged as written, and initial articles and prefixes are treated as separate words. Shelflisting is done according to these rules, which is separating materials on the shelves. *Cataloging Service Bulletin,* nos. 8 and 11 contain announcements of these policies.

Policy Confusion

Another recurring problem is that general policy is often overridden by instructions in the schedules and by the call numbers for works already classified and shelflisted. If we do not know what to do by looking at the schedules, we check the shelflist. Cutters derived theoretically are adjusted according to the realities of the shelflist.

Automation of Schedules

Another recurring problem is when and how the classification schedules will be "automated." Research on this topic is underway now. The major obstacle to automating is lack of a MARC format for classification. The only automation being used at this point is that some of the new schedules are in a word processor.

Disseminating Information on Classification Policies

The last recurring problem is how to inform others about the classification policies. The *Cataloging Service Bulletin* is the primary channel of communication.

Significant policy changes were the announcements of the alternative class numbers for fiction in English in *CSB* no. 84, (1968), the alternative class numbers for collected sets in *CSB* no. 104 (1972), and alternative class numbers for bibliography in *CSB* no. 113 (1975). In between, in 1974, is *CSB* no. 110 with the instructions on shelflisting materials cataloged under corporate bodies that were discussed earlier. In *CSB* no. 116 is the announcement that in Class P only the names of those authors who wrote before 1900 are generally listed individually.

Moving now into much more recent history, many of the announcements related to classification and shelflisting are immediately relevant. In *Cataloging Service Bulletin,* no. 124 the classing of society publications is described, and the announcement is made that all bellelettristic works are now classed in the literature schedules, not by topics. There are a few cases in which, for example, novels relating to music might have been classed in M. That practice was discontinued in 1978.

Cataloging Service Bulletin, no. 3 contains several important announcements. One explains how authors who write in more than one language or who have lived and written in more than one country are handled. In the same issue are the classifying of congresses and the new version of the book number table.

Cataloging Service Bulletin, no. 6 contains the announcement that the Library of Congress was discontinuing use of PZ1-4. *Cataloging Service Bulletin,* nos. 8–12 give the basic policies about the impact of closing the catalogs and AACR2. In *CSB,* no. 17 the publication of the language and literature tables was announced. This was an extremely important publication, as you will see shortly.

In *Cataloging Service Bulletin,* no. 19 the policy of adding dates to monographic call numbers to shelflist editions was announced. In *CSB,* no. 20 the circumstances under which names of individual literary authors are printed in class P is again discussed, this time relating to AACR2 changes.

Aside from answering individual letters or holding workshops, it is through *Cataloging Service Bulletin* that classification policies are announced.

TABLES

Tables are an important feature of LC Classification because they provide a method of avoiding repetition. In the center of Figure 6-3 is a table that lists topics that can be used under the names of countries specified at the bottom of the figure. You will notice that there are four different tables. The five-number table is the only one that has a number reserved for each of the topics listed on the right. In the three-number table you will notice that there is no number next to the "Local" caption. Why is there no need for a local number for three-number countries? If you will look at a three-number country, you will see why. America has three numbers, 1048, 1049, and 1050. A local number is not needed because the locals are all spelled out below. West Indies has three numbers. It does not need a local because the locals are spelled out. It is the same with the British West Indies.

In the two-number table, you will notice that with the first number, the .A1-6 Cutters, are reserved for documents followed by what will be the listing by author for history and general works. The second number is devoted to the locals with the colonies all crowded into .Z5 at the end. In the one-number table the emphasis is on general works, not on documents or locals; the documents and locals are put into A to Z Cutters.

We will do a very simple problem here. What number would you use for the abolition of slavery in Puerto Rico? Your first task obviously is to read the schedule to find Puerto Rico. You see that it is the span HT1086 to HT1090. How many numbers is that? Five. You use the five-number table for this five-number country. Which number are you going to use for abolition of slavery? The third number; the number for the abolition of slavery in Puerto Rico is HT1088.

How about slavery in Yucatan, Mexico? You use the second number of this two-number country: HT1054. Since you must arrange it by local area, A to Z, it will be Y something—probably .Y8. You cannot be sure until you check the shelflist because, no matter what the rules for creating Cutter numbers say, the result has to fit into the shelflist.

What about slavery in the American colonies? This is a trick question. It does not go here. It goes in E, because just under America it says "United States, *see* E."

FIGURE 6-3 Example from HT Schedule

| HT | | | COMMUNITIES. CLASSES. RACES | | HT |

```
HT                           COMMUNITIES.  CLASSES.  RACES                    HT

                    Classes
                      Slavery - Continued
                        Abolition of slavery.  Anti-slavery
                          Periodicals, see HT851
                          Societies, see HT853
                          Congresses, see HT855
                          Collected works (nonserial), see HT857
        1025              History
                          Biography of abolitionists
        1029.A3             Collective
            .A4-Z           Individual, A-Z
        1031              General works
        1033              Addresses, essays, lectures
                          Influence of economic conditions, see HT901
                          Influence of religion, see HT910+
        1037              Conditions under emancipation
                          By region or country, see HT1048
                        By region or country
                          Under each country:
```

5 nos.	3 nos.	2 nos.	1 no.	
(1).A1-6	(1)	(1).A1-6	.A1-6	Documents
.A7-Z		.A7-Z	.A7-Z8	History and general works
(2)	(2)			Slave trade and its suppression
(3)	(3)			Abolition of slavery and conditions under emancipation
(4)		(2).A-Z4	.Z9A-Z	Local, A-Z
(5)		.Z5A-Z		Colonies

```
1048-1050            America
                       Including "Asiento" contract
                       Use also for North America and Spanish America
                     United States, see E
1051-1052            Canada
    1052.5           Latin America
1053-1054            Mexico
1055-1056            Central America
1071-1073            West Indies
1076-1080              Cuba
                         Including works treating Cuba and Puerto
                           Rico together
1081-1085              Santo Domingo.  Dominican Republic
1086-1090              Puerto Rico
1091-1093              British West Indies
                         Cf. HT1165, British colonies
1096-1100                Jamaica
    1105                 Other, A-Z
1107-1108              French West Indies
1112-1113              Dutch West Indies
    1119               Other islands, A-Z
                     South America
    1121               General works
1122-1123              Argentina
1124-1125              Bolivia
1126-1130              Brazil
1131-1132              Chile
```

Now we are going to deal with the biography table. Let's look first at the part of the classification schedule to which you will apply the biography table. It is in Figure 6-3, HT1029, or "Slavery"—"Biography of abolitionists." HT1029.A3 is for collective biographies; HT1029.A4-Z is for individual biographies, A to Z. If you are classifying the biography of an individual abolitionist, you would apply the biography table.

Where do you find the biography table? Out in the real world it is in *Cataloging Service Bulletin,* no 19. Here it is reproduced in Figure 6-4. In *CSB,* no. 19 is an explanation of the use of this table.

FIGURE 6-4 Individual Biography Table (unless otherwise provided for)

(From *Cataloging Service Bulletin*, no. 19)

.x	Cutter for the individual
.xA2	Collected works. By date
.xA25	Selected works. Selections. By date
	Including quotations
.xA3-39	Autobiography, diaries, etc. By title
.xA4	Letters. By date
.xA5	Speeches, essays, and lectures. By date
.xA6-Z	Biography and criticism

Let us say that you are going to classify a biography of William Wilberforce, who was a British abolitionist. The country does not matter here because all of the biographies of abolitionists are together. Let us also assume that Wilberforce has a .W5 Cutter, which, in fact, he does because a work about him was shelflisted before we started using two-digit Cutter tables. In the table the "x" is the Cutter, in this case .W5. If the book you are classifying is a biography or criticism, you simply add a second Cutter based on the author's last name. So if you had a book by Carter, it would be .W5C35 or whatever, depending on the shelflist. If, however, you had Wilberforce's letters you would use .W5A4 and then the imprint date.

Now let's look at the H tables, a section of which is reproduced in Figure 6-5. The H schedule is one of the more complex ones. It uses ten different tables of geographic divisions frequently to avoid spelling out individual countries in the schedules. In the newer edition of H, the span of numbers allotted in each table is not indicated. Table I is a 100-number table, II is 200, III is 300, IV is 400, V is 130, VI is 200, VII is 830, VIII is 840, IX is 420, and X is 1000 numbers. Charles Martel and his associates who developed Class H were unnecessarily elaborate. Some of these tables are very popular and frequently used. Others are hardly used at all. Tables IV, V, IX, and X are popular tables.

As you look at this table, notice the decimals. Decimals in LC Classification usually tell you that the numbers are a relatively recent

FIGURE 6-5 Section Of Class H Tables

TABLES OF GEOGRAPHICAL DIVISIONS

I	II	III	IV	V		VI	VII	VIII	IX	X
					Europe - Continued					
55	107-108	160-162	213-216	74-77	Russia	105-109	411-420	421-430	211-215	551-560
55.3	108.3	162.3	217	77.3	Finland	110	421-425	431-435	215.5	561-565
55.7	108.7	162.7	218	77.7	Poland	111	426-429.5	436-439.5	215.7	566-567.5
56	109-110	163-165	219-220	78	Scandinavia	113-114	430	440	216-220	570
57	111-112	166-168	221-224	79	Denmark	115-119	431-440	441-450	221-225	571-580
58	113-114	169-171	225-228	79.5	Iceland	120-124	441-450	451-460	226-230	581-590
59	115-116	172-174	229-232	80	Norway	125-129	451-460	461-470	231-235	591-600
60	117-118	175-177	233-236	81-84	Sweden	130-134	461-470	471-480	236-240	601-610
61	119-120	178-180	237-240	85-88	Spain	135-139	471-480	481-490	241-245	611-620
61.3	120.3	180.3	240.3	88.3	Andorra	139.3	480.3	490.3	245.3	620.3
61.5	120.5	180.5	240.5	88.5	Gibraltar	139.5	480.5	490.5	245.5	620.5
62	121-122	181-183	241-244	89	Portugal	140-144	481-490	491-500	246-250	621-630
63	123-124	184-186	245-248	90	Switzerland	145-149	491-500	501-510	251-255	631-640
64	125-126	187-189	249-252	91	Balkan States	150-154	501-510	511-520	256-260	641-650
64.5	126.5	189.5	252.5	91.4	Albania	154.4	510.5	520.5	260.5	650.5
65	127-128	190-191	253-254	91.5	Bulgaria	154.5	511-520	521-530	261-265	651-660
65.5	128.5	192-193	255-256	91.6	Yugoslavia	154.6	521-525	531-535	265.5	661-665
67	131-132	196-198	261-264	91.8	Romania	154.8	531-540	541-550	271-275	671-690
67.5	132.5	198.5	264.5	91.83	Greece	154.83	540.5	550.5	275.5	680.5
68	133	199	265	91.85	Asia	154.85	541-545	551-555	276	681
68.2	133.3	200	265.5	91.9	Middle East. Near East	154.9	546	556	276.5	682
68.25	133.4	200.5	265.7	91.93	Turkey	154.93	546.5	556.5	276.7	682.5
68.3	133.5	200.6	266	91.95	Cyprus	154.95	547	557	277	683
68.35	133.7	200.9	266.5	92	Syria	155	548	558	277.5	684
68.4	133.9	201	267	92.15	Lebanon	155.15	549	559	278	685
68.45	134	201.3	267.5	92.2	Israel. Palestine	155.2	550	560	278.5	686
68.5	134.3	201.6	268	92.25	Jordan	155.25	551	561	279	687
68.55	134.5	201.9	268.5	92.3	Arabian Peninsula. Arabia	155.3	552	562	279.5	688
68.6	134.7	202	269	92.35	Saudi Arabia	155.35	553	563	280	689
68.65	134.9	202.3	269.5	92.4	Yemen (Yemen Arab Republic)	155.4	554	564	280.5	690

development. In the H tables almost every country with a decimal in its number reflects a change that was made during the big H table revision in 1977. Old numbers were reused with new meaning when tables are revised, just as in the Dewey system. Some of the countries that have not changed are Russia, Sweden, Spain, Portugal, and Switzerland. How can you tell? They do not have decimals. That is a pretty good tip-off. Looking at either Table V or VI, you can assume that the listing of the Balkan States and Asia has been reorganized.

FIGURE 6-6 Tables for HV1001-1420.5

HV	SOCIAL PATHOLOGY. SOCIAL AND PUBLIC WELFARE. CRIMINOLOGY			HV

```
                    Protection, assistance and relief
                    Special classes.  By age
                      Children
                        Orphanages.  Orphans - Continued
   1001-1420.5                Other regions or countries.  Table IX 1/

      10 nos.      5 nos.      2 nos.      1 no.
       (1)          (1)                    .A1-5      Collected works
                                                        (nonserial)
       (4)          (2)         (1)        .A6-Z7     General works
                                                        Including history
       (5)                                               Early through 1800
       (6)                                               1801-
       (8)          (3)                               Other
                                (2)                   Local, A-Z
       (9)          (4)                    .Z8        By region or state, A-Z
      (10)          (5)                               By city, A-Z
                                                        Under each state or city:
                                                        .x   General works
                                                        .x2  Particular
                                                               institutions,
                                                               A-Z
```

For Table IX, *see* pp. 135-44. Add country number of table to 1000.

You are now going to use the table in Figure 6-5 in combination with the section of the HV class for orphans reproduced in Figure 6-6 to classify a book on the problems of orphans in eighteenth-century Portugal. Note that in HV1001-1420.5 you are instructed to use Table IX and to add the country number to 1000.

Your first problem is to find Portugal, which is a little above the middle in Figure 6-5. Looking to the right at the column of numbers for Table IX you find that five numbers, 246-250, are assigned to Portugal. Back in Figure 6-6 the column under "5 nos." shows how the five numbers are allotted to various subjects. Remember this is a book about eighteenth-century Portugal. Can you bring out eighteenth century? No. The time period can be brought out only if you have a country to which a span of ten numbers has been assigned. According to the instructions for five-number spans the second number, 247 in this case, should be used. You add that to the base of 1000 and get 1247. HV1247 is the number for orphans in eighteenth-century Portugal.

A visitor to the division thought that he had worked out the tables: he had been adding the number as a decimal to the base number. He would have come up with HV1000.247 for orphans in eighteenth-century Portugal. Do not add to base numbers as a decimal—add as a whole number.

Now let us classify a work on orphans in Finland. Finland is a one-number country in Table IX. From the one-number table instructions in Figure 6-6 you see that you must decide what kind of work you have, a non-serial collected work, a general work, or a work by locality. In this case you have a general work, so the classification number would be HV1000 plus 215.5 from the table resulting in HV1215.5 plus a Cutter by author.

FIGURE 6-7 Tables for HV6801-7220.5

HV	SOCIAL PATHOLOGY. SOCIAL AND PUBLIC WELFARE. CRIMINOLOGY				HV
6801-7220.5	Criminology Crimes and criminal classes By region or country - Continued Other regions or countries. Table IX 1/ Under each country:				

10 nos.	5 nos.	2 nos.	1 no.		
	(1)		.A1-5	Collections	
(1)				Documents	
(2)				Other	
		(1)		General works	
(3)	(2)			History	
	.A01-26			General	
	.A3-5			By period	
				Subarranged, A-Z	
(4)	.A6-Z5			Recent	
(5)	.Z6A-Z			Biography (Collective)	
				For individual, see HV6248	
(6)	(3)			Statistics	
(7)			.A6-Z7	General works	
		(2)		Local, A-Z	
(9)	(4)		.Z8	By state, province, etc., A-Z	
(10)	(5)			By place, A-Z	

For Table IX, see pp. 135-44. Add country number in table to 6800.

If you look at Figure 6-7 we will now deal with the criminal classes. You are instructed to use Table IX and this time to add the base number HV6800. Assume that you have a title on criminal statistics in Sweden. You find in Figure 6-5 that Sweden is assigned a five-number span, 236-240. From the five-number instructions in Figure 6-7 you see that the third number is used for statistics. Therefore, your final number is HV7038; i.e., 6800 plus 238. Then you Cutter by author.

Let's try another one. How about crime on the Rock of Gibraltar? You see Gibraltar is listed in the tables in Figure 6-5, assigned one number, 245.5, which is added to 6800 to get 7045.5. Now you must settle the question of whether the Rock of Gibraltar is a local under Gibraltar. You start by running out to the shelflist to see what you already have classed here. If you are lucky there is going to be another book on crime on the Rock of Gibraltar and you will see if it is treated as a local of Gibraltar or not, and then you will do the same with this book. If you have absolutely nothing, then you go to the geographical dictionary to find out how big the rock is, whether it seems possible to divide by locals at all. And then, if you do not have anything else in your shelflist about Gibraltar at all, it is not going to matter what number you pick. You have to be a little loose about these things. At LC we have nothing in the shelflist yet for Gibraltar.

This brief practice should give you an idea of how the tables work. The tables are a method of mathematical interpolation in order to avoid specifying the same information over and over throughout the schedules.

A summary of the revised language and literature tables appears in Figure 6-8. *Cataloging Service Bulletin*, no. 17 contains an explanation of them. Previously there were tables in each of the separate schedules for literature and languages. Similar tables had different table numbers. The tables may have started out the same, but over time deviations and peculiarities for each appeared. To reduce the confusion and to become more consistent the tables were removed from each individual schedule, small adjustments were made, and they were published separately. In the process some tables were cancelled while others were renumbered. The Library of Congress tried for a minimum of disruption to previously classified materials. In *LC Classification—Additions and Changes*, List 206 (1982) the numbers of the new tables were printed. It is necessary to use this booklet of tables in classifying materials for your libraries. If not, you are probably skewing the materials a little bit compared to what the Library of Congress is doing.

FIGURE 6-8 Language and Literature Tables

I	Language: 900 numbers
II	Language: 500 numbers
III	Language: 200 numbers
IV	Language: 100 numbers
V	Language: 50 numbers
VI	Language: 29 numbers
VIII	Language: 9 numbers

VIIIa	Language: 9 numbers
IX	Language: 5 numbers
XI	Language: 4 numbers
XII	Language: 8 numbers
XIV	Language: 4 numbers
XV	Language: 1 number
XVa	Language: 1 number
XVI	Language: Cutter number
XX	Literature: 200 numbers
XXI	Literature: 20 numbers
XXII	Literature: 48 numbers
XXIII	Literature: 19 numbers
XXIV	Literature: 9 numbers
XXV	Literature: 1 number
XXVI	Literature: Cutter number
XXVIII	Anonymous works in fiction, poetry, drama, etc.
XXIX	Author number determined by second letter of the name
XXX	Translations into foreign languages
XXXI	Authors with 49 numbers
XXXII	Authors with 19 numbers
XXXIIII	Authors with 9 numbers
XXXIV	Single works with 5 numbers
XXXV	Authors with 4 or 5 numbers
XXXVI	Authors with 2 numbers
XXXVII	Authors with 1 number
XXXVIII	Authors with Cutter number
XXXIX	Authors with 1 number
XL	Authors with Cutter number
XLI	Separate works with 1 number
XLII	Authors or works with 3 successive Cutter numbers
XLIII	Separate works with successive Cutter numbers
XLIV	Authors with 2 successive Cutter numbers

You will notice in the P tables (see Figure 6-8) that there are two different ones for authors with one number (Tables XXXVII and XXXIX) and for authors with Cutter numbers (Tables XXXVIII and XL). The difference is whether biography and critical works are emphasized more than the original works. The logic is that dead authors do not write very much. There are more books written about them than by them, and so more expansion room is needed for biography and criticism. Live authors are still writing and may not have much written about them.

REVISION AND UPDATING OF SCHEDULES

We are now going to turn to the fourth topic—revision and updating.

In the last 15 years there have been significant changes in the LC schedules. First of all, the development of BQ, Buddhism, in 1972 was extremely important. Buddhism had previously been classed in a range of 95 numbers in BL; now in BQ it takes up almost 100 pages in our new edition of BL-BQ.

In Class D, one of our pre-World War I schedules, we have often made significant changes that, more or less, disrupt things. Changes were made in Subclass DS for Bangladesh and Burma (1973) and for Cambodia, Laos, and Vietnam (1974). We moved Poland (1975) and developed an extremely short schedule for Eastern Europe, DJK (1976). Since then changes were made in Hungary (1976), Czechoslovakia (1977), and Yugoslavia (1982). In 1977 work began on Africa, with Egypt, Sudan, and Somalia in 1978. In almost every issue from 1977 to 1982 there were some changes in Africa. In 1984 numbers were added for the recent administration in Iran.

Class P also has undergone significant revisions. Subclass P was reprinted in 1979 in an attempt to reflect additions and changes to that point. PZ1-4 was cancelled in 1980. In 1982 *LC Classification—Additions & Changes,* List 206 contained numerous revisions to reflect the new language and literature tables.

I might now point out the impact of these changes. Works cataloged and classified before the changes have the old numbers on the LC cataloging copy. It means, for example, that numbers assigned for Yugoslavia before 1982 are obsolete. If you have LC copy from 1978 about Yugoslavian history, it is classed in DR. If you want to be up-to-date, you should check what the class number really means.

These changes are ones that usually are made as needed in cataloging. The big developments, particularly the relocation of Poland and the change in Yugoslavia, required releasing catalogers from other cataloging responsibilities for a substantial period of time to work on them. We do not have the luxury now of being able to do that. For the most part a new Cutter number is made up here and there, following fairly standard patterns. Trying to actually revise a schedule can take years. It took about eight years to do a revision of H-HJ.

How does LC cope with change internally as far as updating the cataloger's copies of the schedules is concerned? Until the early 1970s, an annotator, who would come around each week, was employed—because new class numbers are approved every week—and take the copy of our schedules from our desks and handwrite in the new numbers. This was great. Catalogers lost their schedules for a few hours, but the schedules would come back with the new numbers all written in. We did this for years. Of course, when you got your copies of *LC Classification—*

Additions and Changes you wrote all the numbers into all your schedules too. If you wished to keep up-to-date more quickly you could cut out a development from *LC Classification—Additions and Changes* and paste it onto a page instead of handwriting it. It looked a little nicer than handwriting.

In the early seventies we changed our system. Because the number of catalogers had increased to 60 and because each of the catalogers had two or three classification schedules, the annotator could not keep up. So we took the master copy of the classification schedules and photocopied them, giving the copied pages to our catalogers. When a new number was approved, it was annotated on the master copy. The master was then photocopied, and replacement pages were given to the catalogers. This made it a lot easier for catalogers, but of course they had the workload of filing to do. Currently we do have a word processor and if a page is old and heavily annotated, we will retype and Xerox it for our own catalogers. Our complete set of loose-leaf schedules takes up about ten feet of space: a full book truck with some left over.

Other libraries can subscribe to *LC Classification—Additions and Changes* and the Gale supplements, which makes updating easier than it used to be in the old days. For example, in 1937 someone in Canada wrote to the Chief of the Classification Division inquiring about Class B, Philosophy. The first edition had come out in 1910. The second edition would not come out until 1950. She wrote, "Is there any likelihood of scheme B being reprinted in the near future? If not, would it be possible for the University of Western Ontario to borrow for a short time the manuscript editions [that's the handwritten annotated copy] covering the European philosophers of the late nineteenth and twentieth centuries? We noticed from the cards we have received for the books in this class that some numbers have been assigned; and we would find it useful to have the complete scheme."

The chief answered, "In reply to your letter I regret to say we do not have copies of our scheme available for loan." We used to lend the manuscript version and people would copy them by typewriter, we presume, and send them back. The chief went on to say, "Many of the additions to the printed scheme have been incorporated in the list of additions issued by the Card Division. This list can be had by subscribing libraries for a small charge. I venture, however, to suggest a better plan, one that has been satisfactorily adopted by other libraries. That is, to employ one of our assistants to secure a copy of the scheme and make in manuscript all additions found in our official copy. [And then there is a name here of a person from the Shelflisting Section] has done similar work for other libraries. Her charge is 75 cents an hour and she will, if you desire, give you an estimate of the cost of the work."

I can just see this person who is moonlighting—it had better be moonlighting—who goes to the Card Division, buys a copy of the schedule, and sits at home handwriting in all the numbers. I do not know what we would charge if we were doing that today, but it wouldn't be 75 cents an hour. Now you get *LC Classification—Additions and Changes* from us regularly instead.

Related to the updating of schedules is the publication of new editions. Three different kinds of new editions are now being done. First are the new editions of schedules that never existed before. Second are revised editions in which our catalogers work over the numbers and make changes. It takes quite a lot of time to revise a schedule. Not only our catalogers work on the revisions, but the staff of the Principal Cataloger's Office must take time out from their regular duties as well. Some schedules badly need revision and updating. However, at this point, we do not have the staff to ever again do a revised edition. The third kind of edition is a cumulative edition. PN, PR, PS, PZ was the first cumulative edition, done in 1978. When we do a cumulative edition the classification editorial staff integrates all of the additions and changes into the main volume. The catalogers are not involved. The editors do a little tidying and then they re-index the entire volume. All editions of schedules since 1978, except for H-HJ, were done like that.

FUTURE PLANS

The Law classification is expected to be completed soon. Otherwise, classification developments will consist of more of the same. Big revisions are not anticipated. New numbers will be created as needed. We expect to continue publishing *LC Classification—Additions and Changes*.

One question that occasionally surfaces is whether to stop using classification at LC as a shelf location? We have closed stacks and storage problems. It could be a lot easier to go to accession numbers since the patrons have to request the books through call slips anyway. On the other hand, most patrons rely on our assigning full LC class numbers; and so even if we went to accession numbers for internal purposes, we would still have to give you a full call number. It might be possible to use a class number without the full Cuttering for subject retrieval purposes; but you have been relying on a full call number, and I expect that we would be unable to stop supplying that.

Several years ago there was talk about closing the catalog at LC. We discussed what would happen if we closed the shelflist and tried to shelflist only against the MARC database. One result would be duplicate call numbers. Some of you may remember that we had floated a trial scheme to just shelflist against the MARC database and to identify with an asterisk those numbers as being new ones that might conflict. This was described in a document distributed at the January 1978 ALA meetings entitled "Freezing the Library of Congress Catalog." Shelflisting only against the MARC database has not been discussed since then. When online cataloging is implemented at the Library of Congress, we will begin to plan whether online shelflisting is possible.

BIBLIOGRAPHY

Birket-Smith, Kjeld. *Local Applicability of the Library of Congress Classification: a Survey with Special Reference to Non-Anglo-American Libraries.* International Federation for Documentation, Committee on Classification Research, FID/CR Report Series no. 10. Copenhagen: Danish Centre for Documentation, 1970.

Chan, Lois Mai. *Immroth's Guide to the Library of Congress Classification.* 3d ed. Littleton, CO: Libraries Unlimited, 1980.

Comaromi, John P. *Book Numbers: a Historical Study and Practical Guide to Their Use.* Littleton, CO: Libraries Unlimited, 1981.

Comaromi, John P. *The Eighteen Editions of the Dewey Decimal Classification.* Albany, NY: Forest Press, 1976.

Comaromi, John P. and Margaret J. Warren. *Manual on the Use of the Dewey Decimal Classification, Edition 19.* Albany, NY: Forest Press, 1982.

Eaton, Thelma and Donald E. Strout, eds. *The Role of Classification in the Modern American Library: Papers Presented at the Institute Conducted by the University of Illinois Graduate School of Library Science, November 1-4, 1959.* Champaign, IL: distributed by Illini Union Bookstore, 1959.

Foskett, A. C. *The Subject Approach to Information.* 4th ed. Hamden, CT: Linnett Books, 1982.

Henderson, Katherine Luther, ed. *Major Classification Systems: the Dewey Centennial.* Allerton Park Institute, no. 21, Urbana-Champaign, IL: Graduate School of Library Science, 1976.

LaMontagne, Leo E. *American Library Classification, with Special Reference to the Library of Congress.* Hamden, CT: Shoe String Press, 1961, reprinted 1973.

Lehnus, Donald J. *Book numbers: History, Principles, and Application.* Chicago: American Library Association, 1980.

Matthis, Raimund E. and Desmond Taylor. *Adopting the Library of Congress Classification System: a Manual of Methods and Techniques for Application or Conversion.* New York: R. R. Bowker, 1971.

Mills, Jack. *A Modern Outline of Library Classification.* London: Chapman & Hall, 1960.

Sayers, William C. B. *A Manual of Classification for Librarians.* 5th ed., rev. by Arthur Maltby. London: Deutsch, 1975.

Schimmelpfeng, Richard H. and C. Donald Cook, eds. *The Use of Library of Congress Classification: Proceedings.* Chicago: American Library Association, 1968.

7

Classification and Copy Cataloging

Arlene G. Taylor

How copy cataloging is affected in the realm of classification depends to some extent on whether the library uses Dewey Decimal Classification (DDC) or Library of Congress Classification (LCC). Revision occurs regularly with both schemes, but Dewey has more reused numbers. Library of Congress tends to add numbers to its classification scheme whenever new materials appear needing new classification. These numbers can be inserted wherever needed. There are many unused letters and numbers; but if a new concept needs to be inserted where no unused numbers fall, decimals may be used. A decimal number is not required to be a conceptual subdivision of the subject represented by the number without the decimal. Library of Congress also occasionally revises a number or section of numbers, but this is done only when the need is very great, since it necessitates the reclassification of LC's collections. An example of revision of a section occurred in 1973 when PR9080-9899 (for English Literature outside of Great Britain) was reworked, and new numbers were developed for most countries of the world. More often when a section of numbers is inadequate, completely new schedules are constructed using letters and/or numbers not previously used, as occurred when BQ was developed for Buddhism, and the numbers in BL for Buddhism were abandoned.

Dewey schedules also are revised on an irregular basis. Changes in Dewey are often reworkings of sections of numbers that were previously used with other meanings. This is necessary because of Dewey's hierarchical structure. New concepts cannot just be inserted in their logical place between numbers, as in LC, unless there happens to be an unused number at that spot, or unless numbers that once stood for other concepts are reused. When this is done immediately from one edition to the next without allowing the numbers to go unused for an edition or two, the new section of the schedule is called a Phoenix schedule.

There is, of course, merit in the periodic updating of classification schemes. If they were not updated, local libraries would have to invent many more numbers for new topics than they now do. However, these variations have definite implications for the library that uses outside cataloging, especially if the intention is to mix new and retrospective copy. The class numbers suggested at any point in time will not necessarily have the same meaning in the latest edition of the classification schedules being used, nor will they necessarily be the most current class numbers available for the subject being covered.

A difference faced by users of LC copy is that most suggested LC numbers are complete call numbers, while suggested Dewey numbers are classification numbers only. Also, the percentage of copy lacking a suggested Dewey number is much higher than the percentage lacking an assigned LC number. These differences suggest a higher efficiency in classifying with LC since less time must be spent completing call numbers and assigning original classification. In the library where I once supervised copy catalogers, LC classification was used without pre-checking the shelflist. Alternatives were sometimes used, and there were some local exceptions to the LC classification scheme. An attempt was made to keep editions and translations together. Even with these changes, an informal survey showed that 85 percent of the exact copy had LC call numbers that were being used without change. Since many of the 15 percent changes were made in the Cutter numbers, an even higher percentage of the classification part of the numbers was acceptable. In a large Dewey library such a percentage is not possible because it is highly unlikely that a Dewey number will be suggested for 85 percent of the copy. However, if one is using cards from a commercial service such as Catalog Card Corporation of America, the service will, of course, provide Dewey classification for everything.

Dewey classification from LC is also affected by the fact that the numbers are not assigned against a shelflist, as LC classification is. We will discuss this in greater detail later in this chapter.

DECISIONS NECESSARY REGARDLESS OF SCHEME USED

Is the Call Number Strictly a Location Device?

A very basic decision concerns the importance of browsing in the library and whether the classification should reflect this importance. Each library should have a policy about whether the call number assigned to an item is strictly a location device or whether there is to be an attempt to put related materials together in such a way that a browser can find needed material by knowing certain classification numbers.

The latter is virtually impossible to achieve completely. Interdisciplinary subjects have proliferated recently, and supporting materials must be placed in one discipline or the other, in either Dewey or LC unless separate copies of an item are classified separately. Items that are parts of a serial or set that is classified in a general number may be related to very specific materials on a topic, but cannot be classified with them. There are also topics that fit equally well in two or more places in the schedules, depending on which aspect of the subject is emphasized. It is possible, therefore, for two copies of the same book to be classified in different places by different catalogers or by the same cataloger at different times. Classification schemes are revised, but the suggested numbers on the copy reflect the edition of the scheme in use at the time of cataloging. Thus, the cataloger deals with old copy reflecting some abandoned classification numbers, new copy with some new numbers, and the local shelflist, which contains all classification used during the library's existence. These and other problems caused a number of libraries to consider the call number a location device only and to rely on subject headings to serve the browsing function. They leave older materials in old classifications while putting new materials in the current classification number. Other libraries decided not to use new editions of the schemes or revised numbers as they appear. Instead, they continue to use the earlier classification for new materials; this means that many suggested numbers on new copy cannot be used. Still other libraries made a decision to reclassify materials from an out-of-date classification into the new revised classification, so that new copy can be used and all materials on the subject will appear together in the new classification. The latter practice requires that sufficient personnel be available to do the reclassification each time changes appear. This is a particular financial burden for large collections when Phoenix revisions of Dewey occur. Since Phoenix schedules reassign all values for a particular area of the scheme, every item already in a collection in that area must be reclassified if a decision is made to reclassify completely into a new edition.

A slightly different but related decision concerns whether later editions of a work should be shelved next to earlier editions and whether translations should appear beside originals. This can be a problem with any classification scheme. One cause of variation is the occasion when the classification scheme is changed between editions or translations of a work. In such a case, the suggested classification numbers reflect the edition of the schedule in use at the time each edition of the work was cataloged. In the case of LCC, cataloging for an earlier edition published less than three years earlier is revised if the classification changes, but that does not change the record that has already been entered into a local library's catalog. In some cases the classification may differ because the classifier did not know of the existence of the other edition at the time of cataloging. In another situation, one edition may have been classified locally before appearance of outside cataloging, and thus the number may differ from the number assigned to another edition by the outside source. Still another situation involves a serial that has changed its title and its subject matter coverage in some way. Both Dewey and LC classification numbers can differ on cataloging for the new title, meaning that the volumes of the old and new parts of the serial are shelved in different places if the library arranges them by classification number. Monographs also can change in content between editions, with the same resulting differences in classification numbers. This, too, usually accompanies a change in title. Similar problems occur in a library that changes classification schemes (e.g., from Dewey to LC), but has not reclassified materials that were classified under the old scheme.

In a library with closed stacks, the separation of editions or translations will probably not affect their being found. The patrons in such a library learn that they must find what they want through the catalog and then make a request by call number (essentially a location device). Patrons also learn to find wanted items through the catalog in libraries that have changed from one classification scheme to another but have not reclassified.

In a library with open stacks, however, where patrons enjoy browsing and expect to find subject materials together, there may be some expectation that editions and translations will be shelved together. In some universities, for example, researchers may expect new editions, about which they have received prepublication notices, to appear beside older ones. They may not even check the catalog to determine whether classification has changed.

If the library decides that editions and translations should be shelved together, there must be some mechanism for advising catalogers of the call numbers of other editions or of originals owned by the library. If catalogers do their own searching, they will have find this information themselves. However, if searching is done by others, there must be some method for giving the cataloger this information. There must also be a decision on how to go about getting the editions and translations together. There are basically two options—reclassify the old with an adjusted form of the new number, or use an adjusted form of the old number on the new. Most libraries will probably use a combination of methods. If the items already in the library are always reclassified, this does not satisfy the needs of the patron who is looking for the new edition to appear beside the old. On the other hand, if the old classification number is an outdated, inadequate one, placing a new edition in that classification does a disservice to other patrons. The library must also consider the cost of reclassification, especially if multiple copies, sometimes from many locations in the library system, and/or several editions are involved.

The question of whether call numbers will serve a browsing function or a location function has definite implications for use of outside copy. Suggested classification numbers can be used as they appear on the copy, without change, only if the call number is to be a location device and if editions and translations do not have to be together. Most libraries seem to take a stand somewhere between the extremes. An attempt is made to get similar subjects near each other where possible, but it is understood that only one classification number can be affixed to any one piece of material; thus, there will necessarily be a certain amount of scattering of materials on a given subject.

Do All Items Require Classification?

A second basic decision concerns whether all kinds of materials require classification numbers, or whether they simply require some code as a shelving device. Each library has its own list of types of material that it will not classify. Recordings, for example, may simply be numbered in order of receipt; periodicals may be shelved in alphabetical order by title; maps may be marked with the drawer number of the case in which they are housed. It is possible, too, that some libraries will choose not to classify even the monographs, but this discussion is predicated on the assumption that at least some items in the library require classification/call numbers.

The alphabetical vs. classified arrangement of serials debate is still going strong. Classified arrangement places serials in proximity with other kinds of material on the subject. But it is argued that most people who want a serial have a citation to a title that they would just as soon find alphabetically rather than having to look up a call number. But this only works if serials with title changes are split up—i.e., if a person has a citation to *Journal of Library Automation* and looks in the "Js" only to find that the *Journal* is now shelved with its new title, *Information Technology and Libraries* in the "Is," a second look-up is still required and one might as well have looked up a call number. The value of the classified approach is questioned in a specialized library where most serials are on the same general subject in any case. But an alphabetical arrangement can be difficult to administer in large collections because of the massive shifting necessary when, for instance, more space is needed in the "As." So the answer to this problem lies, in part, in the type and size of library involved.

Another situation that calls classification into question and that has become more common in recent years is compact storage. Storage of little-used items is much more efficient if it can be by size of materials rather than by classification.

In any case, whatever items are not to be classified must be identified so that copy catalogers will know when to substitute some other location device.

Do Some Items Require a Different Kind of Classification?

Related to the question of whether or not certain types of material will be classified is the question of whether there are certain groups of materials that will be handled with a different type of classification or call number device than that used for the majority of the collection. For example, biographies may be pulled out to be classified or shelved together rather than with the subject area with which the biographee is associated. Juvenile collections for children and/or young people are often given separate treatment. Superintendent of Documents numbers are used to organize government documents in some libraries. There are also situations where the classification schemes suggest inclusion of a kind of subject matter in one area of the scheme, but the local library prefers to use another area or areas of the scheme. An example is bibliographies, which Dewey and LC both prefer to bring together in one part of the scheme, but which many libraries prefer to classify with the subject area covered by each bibliography. All of these special handlings mean that the person cataloging with outside copy must be fully aware of local classification policy so that the suggested classification numbers can be adapted when necessary. Libraries that receive preprinted cards must select a company that will cater to these special handlings. Then the library should be willing to accept the judgment of the company, in most instances, if optimum use of the outside copy is to be made.

Is it Necessary for Each Item to Have a Unique Call Number?

Regardless of whether the classification used is for browsing or location, a library must decide whether each item must have a call number that is not duplicated by any other call number in the system. Use of cataloging from an outside source is directly affected by the answer to this question. Most of the commercial firms that sell cards with preprinted call numbers cannot attempt to provide unique call numbers for each item because each local shelflist is not available to them for checking to see if they are duplicating call numbers already used for other items. Only with the use of LC call numbers printed on the cards can unique call numbers be approached by an outside source. Even those cannot be assured of being different from some number assigned locally, and because companies must sometimes supply the call numbers for items that for some reason do not have LC numbers, the company-supplied number may later conflict with an LC-assigned number. Some libraries affix a letter "x" to the Cutter of locally assigned LC call numbers to help avoid conflict with numbers assigned by LC. With Dewey numbers it is virtually impossible for an outside source to supply unique call numbers. This must be done at the local level.

Libraries need to consider whether their circulation system, for example, requires unique call numbers for satisfactory operation. Perhaps an accession number or other device would more economically serve this purpose. The cost of local assignment of numbers should be considered, especially in situations where checking the shelflist is required before any number can be assigned. Another factor to be considered is whether there is so much material in a classification that it cannot be kept shelved in a meaningful order without unique call numbers.

The questions raised in the preceding sections represent decisions that must be made regardless of the classification scheme used. The direction these decisions take, however, may be affected by the particular scheme in use. There are also specific decisions to be made which are related *only* to the scheme being used. So let us discuss each of the major schemes now, in order to point out decisions required when using a particular one.

LIBRARY OF CONGRESS CLASSIFICATION

The library that uses LCC should try to accept, unaltered, as many LC-assigned call numbers as possible if greatest efficiency is to be achieved. But there are situations where accepting the LC call number may not be desirable. Some of these situations include: cases where items on the same subject, or editions or translations, will be separated; items that are classified by LC only as analyzed parts of serials while the local library wishes to classify them as separate titles; copy that has no LC-assigned call number at all; and other copy with only a suggested *classification* number, not a complete call number.

Acceptance of LC's Choice of Classification Number

A primary early decision concerns whether to accept the classification part of an LC call number. This decision is related to the library's philosophy about whether the call number is to serve a browsing function or to act purely as a location device. If it is to be mainly a location device, a library may decide to accept LC's number without checking it in the classification schedules. It may be decided that the small percentage of error inevitable in printing, as well as errors made by the classifier, can be tolerated since the item should be retrievable as long as the number in the catalog matches that on the item.

In a recent study of LC cataloging, Charles Simpson and I compared the books from a sample of English language items with the LC copy to determine rate of error in cataloging. Library of Congress Classification numbers were checked against the outline of LC class numbers produced by the CDS Alert Service. Granted, this method would not have found some inversion typos (e.g., PN2278 instead of PN2287). But it was designed to identify class numbers that were completely out of place. We found that 1.2 percent of the LC class numbers fell into this category.

It may be decided that differences of opinion about which classification number is best suited to the item are just that—differences of opinion—and time spent searching for a better number will result only in another difference of opinion. Libraries that accept LC's classification also find merit in the idea that acceptance of the number will have value in networks and union catalogs. If many libraries wish to share an online catalog, the system would be much less complicated if all the libraries were to have the same call number for any one item.

Other libraries, however, have the philosophy that the call number serves to draw together materials on a subject, and these materials should be drawn together in the best way to serve a local user. Such a library may believe that an item that is assigned to "ZA" number when it should have had an "AZ" number is "lost" to certain types of users. It may be decided that there are certain areas in which it is better to classify materials reflecting the needs of the local clientele. For example, a book of religious poems would serve some users best if classified with religion, while others would be better served by finding it with other poetry in the literature section.

Along with the user-service consideration, a library needs to consider the length of time it takes to verify correctness of every suggested class number and to change those deemed unsuitable. The value of such change to the local user should be balanced against the extra time required to make materials available to the public.

Whichever philosophy is followed, there are certain cases where there is no class number to accept or where it is necessary to choose among alternatives offered by LC. The number of items with no LC class number have diminished. The largest group lacking class numbers were items in the field of law. As law schedules appeared beginning in 1969, LC began classifying new materials with the new schedules. Libraries will find much retrospective copy, however, that lacks the classification, and for these items it must be supplied locally. Another group that lacks classification is recordings, which are not classified by LC; since 1972, however, a classification number only has been offered for these items. It appears in brackets on cards. Titles that LC does not wish to retain also have bracketed numbers, some of which are classification numbers only. These are identified by first indicator 1 in the 050 field in a MARC record. If any of these suggested classification numbers are accepted, a library is obliged to determine whether the call number is complete and to add its own Cutter if not. There also are items that receive a call number that is based not on LC classification but on a unique LC arrangement for that type of item. An example is incunabula (i.e., books printed before 1501). Library of Congress arranges these under the abbreviation "Incun." followed by the year of printing. They began in the mid-1970s to supply a suggested classification number in brackets (or in a second subfield a). Another example is microfilm call numbers that include the word "Microfilm" followed by a sequencing number.

Alternative Suggested Classification Numbers

In addition to copy with only a suggested classification number, there is copy that offers numbers as alternatives to the classification given in the complete call number used by LC. The first situation for which LC gave alternative numbers was for fiction beginning in 1968. They were still classifying fiction in PZ3 and PZ4. Beginning in November 1968, LC provided a bracketed classification number from the literature schedules for the benefit of libraries that wanted to place adult fiction with other literature. On July 1, 1980, use of PZ3 and PZ4 was abandoned, meaning that those libraries that used PZ3 and PZ4 were faced with either changing policy or creating their own call numbers. The advantage of using literature numbers, particularly in a research library, is that an author's fiction is not separated from that author's other literary works and biographical material. In addition, English translations of fiction in other languages are not separated from the originals. For other libraries, however, there is merit in placing all English-language fiction together in order to provide in one place a "leisure reading" section. Whichever policy is followed, copy cataloging is affected. For those libraries that follow LC's current policy, retrospective copy prior to July 1980 requires choosing the alternative number and making it a complete call number. For libraries wishing to use PZ3 and PZ4, copy for fiction after June 1980 must be identified and a local call number must be supplied.

In 1970 LC began supplying in brackets the secondary numbers that it uses in its classed catalog of music score holdings. (These appear in subsequent "a" subfields of the 050 field of a MARC record.) These numbers represent aspects of the works not covered by the call numbers assigned. A library that catalogs these materials could choose to use any of these classification numbers as the basis for its call number, since it might be better for local patrons if the score is placed with one of the alternative numbers instead of with the one used by LC.

Alternative numbers for monographic titles of items that LC classifies as collected sets began to appear on LC copy in 1972. However, they usually are supplied only when the number covering the content of the individual title would be different from the number for the collected set. These are useful in a library that prefers to shelve each title in the specific classification with other works that have the same content. The collected set number is usually a much more general one. Classifying all volumes of a series together is helpful to the patron who expects every volume of that series to be of value and who, therefore, appreciates finding the parts of that series together. Usually, an individual decision is made for each series or set, instead of having an overall policy that all items in a series will be classified together or all will be classified separately. If each case is decided on its own merit, the copy cataloger, or perhaps someone else before copy is sent to the cataloger, must be able to recognize an "analytic" call number (i.e., call number for the collected set plus an individual volume or identification number) so that a decision can be made on how to handle any series new to the library. If collected set numbers are not accepted, local classification must be supplied for items cataloged by LC before 1972. Most of the commercial producers of catalog card sets routinely classify parts of monographic series separately. They supply a complete call number on older copy or add a notation to the suggested call number on newer copy. This must be taken into consideration when choosing to purchase cards with preprinted call numbers.

Two other situations for which alternatives began appearing in the 1970s are "bound withs" and bibliographies. For the second and following titles that are bound with another title, the classification number that would be assigned that title is enclosed in brackets beneath the call number (or given as a second subfield a) for the first title (which is necessarily the one used for the physical volume when two or more works are bound together). This allows the library that receives the second or later title bound alone to assign a proper classification to it.

Requests from libraries for alternative classification numbers for bibliographies, which LC puts in Class Z, finally brought results in late 1974. Library of Congress now suggests a number to be used by libraries that prefer to classify bibliographies of a subject with other items on that subject, instead of all together as a group of bibliographies.

Whenever a library chooses to use the alternative classification numbers provided by LC, it must be remembered that Cutters have to be added to them to make complete call numbers, and that retrospective copy before a certain period of time does not provide the alternatives. Yet many libraries believe that these choices serve their patrons better than the classification used at LC.

A final choice, which LC sometimes "offers," although inadvertently, is provided when they revise copy to correct a classification number that was in error the first time. A library that used the initial version may wish to change it. Unfortunately, there is no way to know when classification for an item already in one's catalog has been revised by LC. It is discovered by accident or because of the acquisition of another edition.

Local Alternatives to LC Classification

In addition to the choices that are offered by LC on copy, there may be other situations where a local library may choose to assign classifications different from those given by LC. Local classification schemes may have been developed for use with certain kinds of materials, e.g., juvenile materials or local theses. These schemes may or may not be compatible with LC classification on an individual number basis. Certain LC classification numbers may be rejected in favor of a different number or a locally expanded run of numbers for that topic. For example, an expansion of the schedule for the local history of a state or community may have been devised. Also, there may be local approval for choice of a different number when the local cataloger disagrees with the number assigned by LC or other outside source. There may be series for which each title has been classified separately by LC but which the local library wishes to classify together as a group.

In any of these cases, the copy cataloger must be able to recognize situations where the LC classification will not be used locally or where a given alternative will be used instead. This may be done by annotating the classification schedules, if all classification numbers are checked before use. The decision on whether to use analytic or separate call numbers cannot be recorded in the schedule, however, since this decision can be called for with virtually any possible number. If all classification numbers are not checked before use, the library should limit the exceptions as much as possible and should teach the copy catalogers to recognize those exceptions.

DEWEY DECIMAL CLASSIFICATION

Some of the decisions that confront the library that uses Dewey Decimal Classification differ from those faced by Library of Congress Classification users. The source of the Dewey number has a definite impact on the decision to be made. If a library has contracted with an outside source to provide pre-cataloged books with preprinted cards and spine labels, undoubtedly it has decided to accept the numbers assigned. If a library purchases preprinted cards from a company that offers choices on such things as classification of fiction or biography, this library, too, probably has decided to accept the numbers with only a minimum amount of change. Libraries that choose to purchase card sets without classification numbers in the margin and libraries that use Library of Congress cataloging (either card format or MARC format) as the basis for their cataloging record must decide whether to accept or reject Dewey classification numbers suggested on the copy.

Accepting the Dewey Number Given on Outside Copy

For most libraries using Dewey when LC copy is used, the only decision is whether to accept or reject suggested numbers. There are no decisions involving acceptance of suggested Cutter numbers because none are given. Some commercial firms do offer to print one or more letters of the author's (or biographee's) name below the call number in the margin. A library may choose to have this done, if it has decided to accept that form as a complete call number or to use the letter as the basis for adding a Cutter to complete the call number. When member input copy is used from a network, there may be no Dewey number at all, or there may be a complete Dewey call number. In the latter case, there must be a policy about acceptance of Cutter numbers, as well as classification numbers.

The classification numbers supplied by commercial firms may be assigned wholly by the firms or may be based on the number suggested by LC, or a combination thereof. In all cases however, the numbers are devised from the edition of Dewey or Abridged Dewey in effect at the time of cataloging and they are not reclassed to reflect changes in a later edition. Whether or not the numbers can be used just as they appear depends on the library's philosophy regarding whether call numbers should serve a location or browsing function. For example, a copy cataloger may have two books in the area of mathematics, one on trigonometry and one on topology. The number 514 could be suggested as a classification number for both of these, the former according to the 17th edition of Dewey and the latter according to the 18th edition of Dewey. In a library with open stacks, a mathematician might be disturbed, to say the least, to find books on topology and trigonometry together in 514 while also finding some books on trigonometry in 516.24 (18th edition) and some books on topology in 513.83 (17th edition).

Many libraries, of course, already have on their shelves numbers representing many more than two editions of Dewey. Through the 14th edition new numbers were almost always expansions or reductions of numbers with the same meaning as before, but later editions have contained many relocations. Even a relatively new library with numbers on the shelf from only one or two editions must cope with suggested Dewey numbers from several editions on retrospective copy if it intends to use outside copy for any older material it acquires.

Besides the changes that occur when a new edition appears, there may be changes between editions; these are first instituted by the Library of Congress and are usually followed in time by other commercial producers of cards. An example of this is the change made in

January 1975, when LC began to use area notation -41 instead of -42 for British Isles, United Kingdom, Great Britain, while the area notation for Scotland was changed to -411. The notation -42 is now assigned only to England and Wales. This was a logical and long overdue change, since the former arrangement implied that Great Britain was part of Scotland. It affects libraries of all sizes, however, because in the 900s, the basic three-digit history number for Great Britain appears on new cataloging as 941 and on old copy as 942. Scotland's history number is 941.1 instead of 941; so a library that uses the new numbers without reclassifying the old has quite a mixture at the 941 spot. For larger libraries, which subdivide many subject areas by country, the area notation change can affect virtually every classification number in Dewey. However, with fewer materials at each spot, it is hoped that in most cases items stand so close together that the change is hardly noticed.

These changes were incorporated along with others into the 19th edition of Dewey, which was not implemented until 1980. More recent "between edition" changes were the implementation of the expanded revision of 301–307 Sociology in January 1982 and of the 004–006 schedule for computer science in May 1985. Such implementations are to be the norm from now on, with new editions of Dewey farther apart.

Accepting Dewey Numbers Assigned by LC

Because LC copy from MARC tapes, CDS Alert Service, or NUC is the basis for cataloging by many commercial sources and by individual libraries, the idiosyncrasies of Dewey numbers suggested by LC are discussed in this section.

As with LC class numbers, Dewey numbers assigned by LC are occasionally in error. In the study mentioned earlier Charles Simpson and I found that 1.9 percent of the records had an error in the Dewey number. We checked the Dewey numbers against the third summary in the Dewey schedules that gives the meanings of numbers to the decimal point. When one recalls that we looked at 1,808 records and found 35 errors, one has to consider the relative value to the patron of holding up 1,773 items with good numbers in order to find 35 bad ones.

An understanding of how the Decimal Classification Division at LC operates is a useful asset for anyone who uses LC's suggested numbers. One of the pertinent points is that Dewey numbers were assigned to only about 70 percent of all titles cataloged in 1985. In the mid-1970s Dewey numbers were assigned to only about 40 percent of the titles. The percentage has gradually increased since, but possible budget cuts and procedure changes will likely cause it to decrease again. Another useful piece of information is that Dewey numbers on CIP entries, as well as on the finished cataloging available on cards, MARC, or in NUC, are those assigned from proofs, galleys, or front matter. The finished book is not checked upon its arrival at LC unless requested.

The fact that not all LC cataloging receives Dewey numbers affects libraries more or less according to their size. Library of Congress assigns Dewey numbers to all CIP items, all English language items, and many items in the other major languages. Others are done as time permits. For many medium-sized and small libraries, the CIP and English items represent a high percentage of their acquisitions. Larger libraries and special libraries acquire and catalog foreign language materials, technical reports, retrospective materials, and non-print items, for which a substantial percentage of the LC copy does not include a suggested Dewey number. Since most of this copy does have an LC call number or suggested LC class number, libraries may derive some benefit from locating that number in the LC classification schedules and then attempting to locate the comparable classification in Dewey. This at least saves "starting from scratch" in supplying Dewey numbers.

When the Dewey number is present, the length of the suggested number presents a situation that requires a policy decision in each library. If allowances for number-building provided by Dewey are followed, the length of the number can render it practically unusable. Since 1967 LC has provided guides to meaningful shortening of such numbers in the form of prime marks ('). These appear as slashes in MARC records. With the adoption of the 11th abridged edition, the practices of segmentation were changed so that most of the time the first segment is the same as the number provided in the abridged edition. Most of the commercial firms that provide card sets based on LC copy allow libraries the option of cutting numbers at one of the primes. There is usually a limit, however, on the length of number they will print (one company cuts back to the closest prime if the number goes more than nine digits past the decimal point). Some libraries themselves set a limit that a cataloger may assign, or choose one of the primes at which they will usually cut a number. There may also be a variation within a library on use of standard subdivisions to lengthen a number. In subject areas where the collection is very small, for example, material may not have further breakdown by form or place. In other areas, however, size of the collection may demand as much subdivision as possible. In some cases, the local automation system may dictate the length of the number.

There are fewer suggested alternatives to Dewey numbers on LC copy than there are for the LC classification numbers, but several past policies and practices necessitate decisions before older numbers are used. Between 1952 and 1958 numbers were given for both the 14th and 15th editions when they differed other than in length. The 15th edition was starred. This is the only time numbers from more than one edition were given. Between 1961 and 1969 the *only* number given on many of the nonfiction materials for young people was assigned from the abridged Dewey and designated "3." Now numbers are assigned from the latest full edition. During the time that the abridged edition was not a literal abridgement (editions 9 and 10) if the abridged Dewey number was not the same as the digits to the left of the first prime, the abridged one was given in brackets following the regular one. In 1968 LC began providing Dewey numbers for adult fiction for the benefit of those libraries that do not place all fiction in one section. At about the same time, they began to identify fiction for children with "[Fic]" and books for very young children with "[E]" (meaning easy).

As with LC classification, there are some cases where alternative classifications are provided. Since 1965 LC has supplied "[B]" following a subject classification number for biographical material. This began because the 17th edition recommended that biographies be classified with the subject area associated with the biographee, rather than all together in the 920s. Biographies cataloged before 1965 bear 920 numbers. Another application of alternative designations is with monographic series, which LC classifies as a set. At the time they started supplying alternative individual title numbers for LC classification (1972), they also began supplying the equivalent Dewey numbers in brackets below the number for the series as a whole, which is identified by the letter "a" following it. The "a" has been added only since 1969. Before 1959, such numbers were enclosed in parentheses, and between 1959 and 1969 they were not identified. This alternative number may also be followed by "[B]," thus providing two alternative designations to the series number. As with LC classification, most commercial sources of preprinted cards supply the number for the individual title, rather than the number for the series.

In December 1980 LC's Decimal Classification Division began assigning two numbers to works classed in 340, Law. The first number is built by first indicating the branch of law, then the area notation for the jurisdiction, and last the notation for subdivision of the branch of law. The second number is built according to Option B in Dewey and indicates first the jurisdiction, followed by the branch of law and the subdivision for the branch. If a library believes its users are best served by having works about a branch of law together, the first number should be chosen. If it would be more useful to have works about a particular country or other jurisdiction together, the second number should be chosen. When LC classes a legal series together, there will be four Dewey numbers given: the collected set number and the specific analytic number for the first option, and the collected set number and the specific analytic number for Option B.

Local Alternatives to Dewey Numbers

Most of the situations in which local libraries deviate from use of Dewey classification have been mentioned already. The more common ones include placing fiction together in a section given a label "F" or other such designation, and keeping biographies together in either the 920s or labeled "B." Juvenile materials may be marked in a special way above the classification or may not be classified at all.

Some libraries may wish to classify bibliographies with their subject areas instead of all in 016. This is quite easy to do with the suggested bibliography number, since one can simply move the decimal point three places to the right, remove 016 from the front of the number and put it on the end. Also, some libraries may wish to classify all literature of an author together instead of having it separated by form. Such a case requires massive local rewriting of the 800s, but it can be done. Most of the possibilities already mentioned in the section on "Local Alternatives to LC Classification" can also apply in a Dewey library—local history may need expanding, certain numbers may be preferred locally to the one usually used for a subject by the outside cataloging source, and certain series may be locally classified together instead of as separate titles. These types of local differences should be rewritten as policy if the library expects consistency in its cataloging practice.

HANDLING COPY IN UNUSUAL
CLASSIFICATION NUMBER SITUATIONS

Established procedures must exist to handle the following situations: the assignment of class numbers locally, the lack of a class number on copy, presence of an alternative classification number only, the decision to use a suggested alternative, or use of a local alternative.

When there is no call number at all, someone must assign one locally, if the item is to be retrievable by call number.

When there is *only* a suggested LC number, the copy cataloger must first determine whether it is a complete call number or a classification number only. If the latter, it must be completed.

When LC-suggested alternatives are given *in addition* to LC's complete call number, the alternatives are classification numbers only and must be completed locally, if chosen for local use. Occasionally LC acquires a "Copy 2" to which it assigns a different call number, and that may be used as is by the local library. It does not appear in brackets. It appears in a MARC record in a 051 field.

Use of local alternatives to LC call numbers requires that copy catalogers be able to recognize all LC numbers that cannot be used as they appear. Then there should be written instructions recording local decisions made and explaining in what way the numbers will be changed. If such policies and instructions are not written and accessible (i.e., indexed in some fashion), there can be no hope for consistency in handling such call numbers.

If a library does not assign its LC numbers locally but purchases card sets with numbers already assigned, it should have made known its requirements to the commercial firm that supplies cards. If the firm cannot supply cards with numbers desired locally, then the local library must either accept what can be supplied or arrange to receive certain types of cards with no call number supplied. In the latter case the library must be equipped with sufficient staff to supply its own call numbers. There is also the option of changing call numbers supplied by the outside source, but this is costly since supplied numbers would have to be erased on every card of the set before the locally assigned number could be typed.

Because of the nature of LC copy available to Dewey libraries—specifically, the lack of any number at all on much of the copy, the lack of a means of drawing together materials on the same subject, and use of long numbers divided by prime marks—the use of Dewey classification can be quite expensive in terms of time and personnel required to maintain it. Even in a library that uses the call number strictly as a location device, the suggested number often is too long and must be cut, and a number must be supplied when the copy provides no suggested number. As a result, Dewey copy catalogers must be more sophisticated in classification than LC copy catalogers. A Dewey library may need to have a person or group of people responsible for classification of materials with copy; this group of people might be separate from the people who handle the description and entry (and possibly subject headings, although subject headings and classification often go together). Since this separate group of people is often professionally trained, and therefore more highly paid, large libraries that believe themselves to be committed to Dewey and commercial firms that supply Dewey numbers would benefit greatly if the Library of Congress increased its Dewey Decimal Classification Division staff and thereby increased the percentage of copy being assigned Dewey numbers.

SUMMARY OF ACCEPTANCE OF
NUMBERS FROM OUTSIDE COPY

In the area of classification/call numbers, not only is it sometimes undesirable to use copy exactly as it appears, it is also sometimes impossible, since no classification may be given. The LC call number sometimes is not complete, and the Dewey number is a complete call number only on commercial preprinted card sets (and then only if unique call numbers for each item are not necessary), or on member input copy in a network (and then only if input by a Dewey library). Therefore, many decisions must be made in this area when outside copy is used. The following questions should be considered:

1. Which classification scheme will be used?
2. Is the call number strictly a location device, or does it contribute to browsing by keeping related subject materials together?
   a. If the call number serves as more than a location device, will the classification number be checked in the classification schedules or local shelflist, or both?
3. Is it necessary for each item to have a unique call number?
4. When new sections and/or revisions of the classification scheme appear, will materials already in the library be reclassified?
5. Is it necessary for editions to stand together on the shelf, or for translations to stand next to the original work?
6. Do all items require classification?
7. Do some items require a kind of classification different from the scheme chosen for the majority of the materials?
8. Where alternative classifications are suggested, which classification will be used?
9. Are there situations where local alternatives to the suggested classification are desirable?
10. What type of Cuttering, if any, will be used to make a complete call number?
11. Who may assign classification numbers and/or Cutters when they are missing or unacceptable?
12. If the library uses LC classification, have the following questions been considered:
    a. If LC's complete call number is accepted, are there certain situations where the Cutter assigned by LC will not be used?
    b. Are there times when a date on an LC call number should be changed locally or when a date should be added to the call number?
    c. Is LC's method of designating analyzed parts of a work in the call number acceptable?
13. If the library uses Dewey classification, have the following questions been considered:
    a. Which edition(s) of Dewey will be accepted locally?
    b. Are there certain revisions of Dewey, such as Phoenix schedules, which will not be accepted?
    c. Will Dewey numbers suggested by LC automatically be cut at one of the prime marks?*

---

* Questions adapted from: Arlene Taylor Dowell, *Cataloging with Copy: a Decision-Maker's Handbook* (Littleton, CO: Libraries Unlimited, 1976).

8

Keyword Searching in an Online Catalog Enhanced with a Library Classification

Karen Markey

In the Dewey Decimal Classification (DDC) Online Project, subject-rich terms from the DDC Schedules and Relative Index were incorporated into the subject searching capabilities of an experimental online catalog. The effectiveness of this DDC in an online catalog was tested in online retrieval experiments at four participating libraries. These experiments provided data for analyses of subject searchers' use of a library classification in the information retrieval environment of an online catalog. Recommendations were provided for the enhancement of bibliographic records, online catalogs, and online cataloging systems with a library classification.

In this chapter, subject searchers' use of the keyword (or direct) searching capability of the experimental online catalog is described. Failure analyses of direct searches demonstrated the ability of the direct search to retrieve items relevant to users' topics of interest. Users' post-search interview comments highlight their direct search experiences and their satisfaction with the results of this type of search. Based on the failure analysis and user's interview comments, recommendations are provided for the improvement of keyword searching in online catalogs.

BACKGROUND AND PROJECT OBJECTIVES

Mechanization of classification schedules for information retrieval purposes was first carried out by Freeman and Atherton (1968) in their study of the Universal Decimal Classification (UDC) as an entry vocabulary in an online bibliographic system. At the time of their study, there were few (if any) operational online retrieval systems available to library patrons. Interest in classification as a subject searcher's tool in online bibliographic systems was rekindled in late 1981 after a 13-year hiatus when the preliminary findings of the Council on Library Resources-sponsored Online Catalog Project demonstrated library patrons' (1) ability to use online catalogs to find library materials of interest, (2) their acceptance of this new form of the library catalog, and (3) their need for improved subject access in online catalogs (Besant 1982).

The realization that the printed 19th edition of the DDC (1979) was produced by computerized photocomposition prompted the OCLC Office of Research to ask Forest Press about the availability, for research purposes, of the print tapes used to produce this 19th edition. With the eventual support of Forest Press, the Council on Library Resources, and OCLC, the DDC Online Project team in the OCLC Office of Research obtained selected portions of a machine-readable DDC from Inforonics, Inc. which was converted from the print tapes that originally served to produce the 19th edition of the printed DDC using computerized photocomposition.

The objectives of this project were to:

1. Use the consensus of DDC experts to determine strategies for searching and displaying the DDC in an experimental online catalog.
2. Demonstrate the DDC as a searcher's tool for subject access, browsing, and display in the experimental online catalog.
3. Test the effectiveness of the DDC as a searcher's tool in this catalog.
4. Evaluate the demonstration and test results of the DDC as a searcher's tool and disseminate the results of the research project.

The experimental online catalog was actually composed of two online catalogs: (1) the Dewey Online Catalog (DOC), in which the Dewey Decimal Classification was incorporated as a searcher's tool for subject access, browsing, and display, and (2) the Subject Online Catalog (SOC), in which the DDC was not incorporated. Both DOC and SOC featured direct searching and other subject searching capabilities, but the direct search index of DOC was enhanced with terms from the DDC Schedules and Relative Index.

DEVELOPING THE EXPERIMENTAL ONLINE CATALOG

The databases of the experimental online catalog were created from three data sources: (1) machine-readable cataloging (MARC) records from the four participating libraries in selected subject areas of the DDC, (2) the 19th edition of the DDC Schedules, and (3) the Relative Index. Each participating library contributed between 8,000 and 15,000

MARC records in a subject area(s) selected by the library. Between 8,000 and 12,000 records per library were processed into the experimental online catalog:

1. Library of Congress (LC): Economics (330-339), commerce (380-382), and management (658); database size = 11,865 records.
2. New York State Library (NYSL): New York State geography (917.47-917.4799), United States colonial history (973.1-973.2), and New York State history (974.7-974.799); database size = 8,144 records.
3. Public Library of Columbus and Franklin County (PLCFC): Sports, recreation, and performing arts (790-799); database size = 9,719 records.
4. University of Illinois at Urbana-Champaign (UI): Mathematics (510-519); database size = 7,613 records.

The DDC Online Project team selected fields from libraries' MARC records and the machine-readable DDC Schedules and Relative Index for indexing and display in SOC and DOC. Class number captions and including, general, class here, and example notes from the Schedules and Relative Index entries were selected for indexing and display in DOC only. Classifier's notes and footnotes were not processed into DOC because these notes would not have been helpful to library patrons and staff performing subject searches. Special handling was given to DDC Schedules and Relative Index data to make this information more presentable, accessible, and understandable to DOC searchers. Dummy DDC class numbers with trailing zeros and captions had to be created in DOC to enable subject searchers to browse Schedule numbers with embedded zeros and their associated captions and notes.

A Schedules DDC class number field was specially created and added to bibliographic records in DOC. The Schedules DDC class number of a bibliographic record was defined as a DDC class number that exists in the Schedules *and* is the best match of the record's DDC class number. The Schedules DDC class number enabled DOC to automatically match class numbers in libraries' bibliographic records with class numbers in the DDC Schedules and Relative Index and, subsequently, to add class number captions and including, general, class here, and example notes from the Schedules and Relative Index entries to DOC bibliographic records. Subject Online Catalog and DOC bibliographic records contained the same information, but the *DOC records were enhanced with subject-rich captions and notes from the DDC Schedules and Relative Index entries.* Although DOC records were enhanced with the DDC, only schedule captions (of the DDC information added to records) were displayed in bibliographic records.

There were four Subject Online Catalogs and four Dewey Online Catalogs, i.e., one for each of the four participating libraries. We wanted first-time users of SOC and DOC to be able to search these catalogs with ease and find items relevant to their topics of interest, since most searchers in the library patron and staff retrieval tests would be using the experimental online catalogs for the first time. Therefore, the experimental online catalog was a menu-based system, which we felt was an appropriate interface for first-time users.

DIRECT SEARCHING IN SOC

Subject Online Catalog had the traditional subject searching capabilities of online catalogs, namely subject heading, subject heading and title keyword, and class number searching. When users selected the direct search in SOC, the words in their entered term were matched in a keyword, implicit Boolean AND search with words from title, subject heading, series, and notes fields in bibliographic records. The result of the search was the number of items retrieved matching the user-entered term and the option to display retrieved items. An overview of SOC subject searching is provided in Table 8-1. Figure 8-1 shows a direct search in SOC for the user-entered term "personal loans."

TABLE 8-1   SOC Subject Searching Capabilities

SOC Option Code	Functional Description	Source of Subject Terms for Indexing	End Result of the Search
SA	Search for subject and browse an alphabetical list of subjects near your subject	Assigned *subject headings* from the library's bibliographic records	Display of bibliographic records
SD	Search directly for subject and retrieve number of items on your subject	Keyword, implicit Boolean AND search of *title, subject heading, series,* and *notes* words in bibliographic records	Display of bibliographic records
SC	Search directly for call number and retrieve number of items with your call number	Class number search with implicit truncation of *class numbers* created from class number subfield of the library's bibliographic records	Display of bibliographic records

FIGURE 8-1   Number of Retrieved Items and Options in a SOC Direct Search
for "Personal Loans"

```
What would you like to do? > sd
>>>>> YOUR REQUEST...sd:personal loans
    139 ITEMS FOR "personal"
    111 ITEMS FOR "loans"
      3 ITEMS IN SET 1 (personal loans)

THE FOLLOWING IS A SUMMARY OF YOUR SEARCHES:
SET      ITEMS     REQUEST
1        3         sd:personal loans

OPTION       DESCRIPTION
DI           Display items
SO           Start over
```

Although the result of a direct search was a set of records whose indexed fields contained all the words in the user-entered term, SOC did not perform the search by checking for the presence of *all* given words in *each* record. Instead, it looked for a set of records containing the first word, a set containing the second word, a set containing the last word, and finally found the records common to these three intermediate sets. In this process , shown in Figure 8-1, the intermediate results were displayed, e.g., "139 ITEMS FOR 'personal' " and "111 ITEMS FOR 'loans,' " "3 ITEMS IN SET 1 (personal loans)." With this searching method, the order of terms in the entered term was not important. The only options provided to the user after the direct search were (1) the capability to display retrieved items (using the DI, display items, option) if items were retrieved or (2) the option to start over (SO).

Not all words in the user-entered term were selected by SOC to check in its index for the direct search. Conversely, not all words in the fields of bibliographic records were indexed in SOC's index for the direct search. In both, a selected list of words (called stopwords) and one-letter words were not selected by SOC for searching or indexing. Stopwords are usually prepositions, articles, and conjunctions, e.g., from, to, of, a, and the. Because stopwords were neither searched nor indexed, a direct search for "stocks or bonds," "stocks bonds," "bonds stocks," or "bonds and stocks" yielded the same results. For readers familiar with DIALOG or BRS searching, SOC treated any one of these four examples as DIALOG would treat the search statement "SS STOCKS AND BONDS" or as BRS would treat the search statement (in search mode) "STOCKS AND BONDS."

DIRECT SEARCHING IN DOC

Dewey Online Catalog had both the traditional subject searching capabilities of SOC and enhanced subject searching capabilities because the DDC Schedules and Relative Index had been incorporated in DOC. When users selected the direct search in DOC, the words in their entered term were matched in a keyword, implicit Boolean AND search with words from the title, subject heading, series, (bibliographic record) notes, DDC Relative Index entries, and DDC Schedules and notes fields in bibliographic records. The result of the search was the number of items retrieved matching the user-entered term and the option to display retrieved items. An overview of DOC subject searching is provided in Table 8-2. Figure 8-2 shows a direct search in DOC for the user-entered term "personal loans."

TABLE 8-2 DOC Subject Searching Capabilities

DOC Option Code	Functional Description	Source of Subject terms for Indexing	End Result of Search
SA	Search for subject and browse an alphabetical list of subjects near your subject	*DDC Relative Index entries* matching class numbers in the library's bibliographic records	Display of bibliographic records and/or display of the appropriate shelf location for a selected Relative Index entry or Schedule caption
SS	Search for subject and browse an outline of subjects related to your subject	Keyword, implicit Boolean AND search of *DDC Relative Index entries, DDC Schedules and notes,* and the *first subject heading* listed in the library's bibliographic records	Display of bibliographic records and/or display of the appropriate shelf location(s) for selected Schedule caption(s)
SD	Search directly for subject and retrieve number of items on your subject	Keyword, implicit Boolean AND search of *title, subject heading, series, note, DDC Schedule and note,* and *Relative Index entry* words in bibliographic records	Display of bibliographic records

DOC Option Code	Functional Description	Source of Subject terms for Indexing	End Result of Search
SC	Search for call number and browse an outline of meanings of call numbers	Class number search with implicit truncation of *class numbers* created from the class number field of DDC Schedule records	Display of bibliographic records and/or display of appropriate shelf location(s) for selected Schedule caption(s)

Although the result of a direct search was a set of records whose index fields contained all the words in the user-entered term, DOC did not perform the search by checking for the presence of all given words in each record. Like SOC, it looked for a set of records containing the first word, a set containing the second word, then a set for each subsequent word, and finally found the records common to these three intermediate sets. DOC displayed intermediate results to the user and employed the same stopword list as SOC to eliminate selected prepositions, articles, and conjunctions in searching and indexing operations.

FIGURE 8-2   Number of Retrieved Items and Options in a DOC Direct Search for "Personal Loans"

What would you like to do? > sd
Enter subject to search > personal loans

>>>>> YOUR REQUEST...sd:personal loans
    397 ITEMS FOR "personal"
    159 ITEMS FOR "loans"
     12 ITEMS IN SET 1 (personal loans)

THE FOLLOWING IS A SUMMARY OF YOUR SEARCHES:
SET   ITEMS   REQUEST
1   12   sd:personal loans

OPTION   DESCRIPTION
   DI   Display items
   SO   Start over

METHODS USED TO CONDUCT
THE ONLINE RETRIEVAL TESTS

Two online retrieval tests were conducted with the four participating libraries' patrons and staff: (1) partially controlled but authentic Comparison Search Experiment, in which library patrons conducted online searches on a topic of their own choosing—sequentially—on SOC and DOC, and (2) a controlled field experiment, the Sample Search Experiment, in which library staff performed equivalent but different subject searches in SOC and DOC for topics assigned to them by the DDC Online Project team. The design of the retrieval experiments was based on the design of comparable experiments by Siegel, et al. (1983) in their evaluation of two prototype online catalogs. Two retrieval experiments were employed to test the experimental online catalog to ensure a high degree of confidence and strength in the results of the experiments that were obtained under different experimental conditions with different user populations.

In both retrieval experiments, the time spent searching, estimated recall, and precision were dependent and quantitative measures collected in each SOC and DOC search and were submitted to quantitative data analyses. Patrons and staff in the online retrieval tests were asked which system was satisfactory for the search and their system preference. They also responded to open-ended questions about ease of system use, system differences, and the reasons for their system preference and search satisfaction. Qualitative data analyses were performed on patron and staff responses to such open-ended questions.

A total of 160 different library patrons searched the experimental online catalog at the four participating libraries and performed a total of 160 searches in SOC and 160 searches in DOC for a topic of their own choosing. A total of 60 different library staff searched the experimental online catalog at the four participating libraries and performed a total of 180 searches in SOC and 180 searches in DOC for different topics assigned by the DDC Online Project team. The online retrieval tests provided a wealth of data for a variety of analyses.

SELECTING THE DIRECT SEARCH

Comparisons of the number of times experimental online catalog users selected a particular subject search option in SOC and DOC cannot be made fairly because SOC featured three subject search options and DOC featured four subject search options. However, it is interesting that the listing of SOC and DOC options in the order in which they were presented to online searchers in options menus was not the same as a rank-ordered listing of SOC and DOC options in the order of their selection by SOC and DOC searchers. The SOC options menu listed subject search options in the following order. The number in parentheses is the rank order of the number of times each option was chosen by SOC searchers.

- SA   Search alphabetically for subject (2)
- SD   Search directly for subject (1)
- SC   Search for call number (3)

The DOC options menu listed subject search options in the following order. The number in parentheses indicates the rank order of the number of times each option was chosen by DOC searchers.

- SA   Search alphabetically for subject (2)
- SS   Search subject outline for subject (3)

- SD   Search directly for subject (1)
- SC   Search for call number (4)

Both patrons and staff chose the direct search (SD) in SOC and DOC more times than any other subject search in the experimental online catalog. Patrons and staff might have best understood the two-line description of the direct search of the three or four descriptions of SOC and DOC subject searches that resulted in their selecting this option most frequently. Also, the direct search was the most successful subject search of the three SOC subject searches and four DOC subject searches for retrieving items relevant to users' topics of interest (Markey, 1986, 176-79).

RETRIEVING RELEVANT ITEMS IN DIRECT SEARCHES

Table 8-3 shows how often SOC and DOC users were successful retrieving and displaying relevant items. The percentage of times that the direct search option led searchers to relevant items was greater in DOC than in SOC in retrieval tests with patrons and staff at most participating items. Furthermore, the percentage of times that no items were retrieved in direct searches was greater in SOC than in DOC. Direct searches in DOC were enhanced with the DDC, whereas direct searches in SOC were not enhanced with such subject-rich information. Thus, the results about retrieving relevant items and zero items in direct searches are evidence that the enhancement of bibliographic records with DDC benefited users in their subject searches by directing them to relevant items with greater frequency in DOC than SOC and retrieving zero items with lesser frequency in DOC than SOC.

TABLE 8-3 Direct Searches Directing Users to Relevant Items

	LC SOC	LC DOC	NYSL SOC	NYSL DOC	PLCFC SOC	PLCFC DOC	UI SOC	UI DOC	Total (Four Libraries) SOC	Total DOC
1. Patrons' selection of the SD (direct search) option										
a. Selected	116	90	97	75	80	57	78	50	371	272
b. Relevant items	36	34	40	28	26	27	28	23	130	112
c. Percentage of times SD option led directly to relevant items	31%	38%	41%	37%	33%	43%	36%	46%	35%	41%
d. Percentage of times zero items retrieved	35%	27%	41%	40%	33%	23%	23%	34%	34%	31%
2. Staff selection of the SD (direct search) option										
a. Selected	56	57	77	75	77	49	74	54	284	235
b. Relevant items	37	39	28	28	36	34	38	39	139	140
c. Percentage of times SD option led directly to relevant items	66%	68%	36%	37%	47%	69%	51%	72%	49%	60%
d. Percentage of times zero items retrieved	11%	5%	34%	23%	22%	16%	14%	6%	21%	13%

TABLE 8-4 Estimated Recall and Precision Scores of Users' Direct Searches

	LC SOC	LC DOC	NYSL SOC	NYSL DOC	PLCFC SOC	PLCFC DOC	UI SOC	UI DOC	Total (Four Libraries) SOC	DOC
1. Estimated recall in patron searches										
a. Recall	70%	78%	80%	61%	56%	66%	69%	63%	70%	66%
b. Combined total number of relevant items retrieved and displayed	64		117		96		64		341	
c. Number of relevant items retrieved and displayed	45	50	94	71	54	63	44	40	237	224
2. Estimated recall in staff searches										
a. Recall	59%	68%	64%	60%	65%	74%	56%	84%	61%	72%
b. Combined total number of relevant items retrieved and displayed	126		123		159		146		554	
c. Number of relevant items retrieved and displayed	74	86	79	74	103	117	82	123	338	400
3. Precision in patron searches										
a. Patron searches	27%	21%	51%	36%	51%	44%	46%	35%	43%	32%
b. Number of items retrieved and displayed	166	239	186	197	106	144	95	113	553	693
4. Precision in staff searches										
a. Precision scores	49%	75%	56%	54%	75%	75%	63%	59%	60%	65%
b. Number of items retrieved and displayed	151	114	142	138	137	157	131	207	561	616
5. Percentage of matched relevant items retrieved and displayed in SOC and DOC direct searches										
a. Patron searches	47%	42%	52%	69%	44%	38%	43%	48%	48%	50%
b. Staff searches	58%	50%	57%	61%	67%	59%	85%	57%	67%	57%

RECALL AND PRECISION OF DIRECT SEARCHES

The success of the direct search in DOC was also apparent in the estimated recall scores of subject searches in which the searcher(s) who performed a search for the same topic used the direct search in both SOC and DOC searches. (Estimated recall and precision are defined and expressed in a formula in Markey 1986, 144-45, 161-62.) Average estimated recall scores are listed in Table 8-4 for only those searches in which the searcher(s) who performed a search for the same topic used the direct search in both SOC and DOC searches. Estimated recall of patron and staff searches in DOC exceeded estimated recall of patron and staff searches in SOC at LC and PLCFC, and estimated recall of staff searches in DOC exceeded estimated recall of staff searches in SOC at UI. The precision of patrons' searches was greater in direct searches in SOC than in DOC, and the precision of staff searches was equal or almost equal in direct searches in SOC and DOC (except at LC, where precision of direct searches in DOC exceeded the precision of direct searches in SOC).

The percentages of matched relevant items that were retrieved and displayed in direct searches in SOC and DOC show that just about half of these relevant items were retrieved in one system and not in the other. That is, one of every two items retrieved and displayed in a DOC direct search by a patron was also retrieved in a direct search for the same topic in SOC. Four of every seven items retrieved and displayed in a DOC direct search by staff members were also retrieved in a direct search for the same topic in SOC.

SUCCESSFUL DIRECT SEARCHES

The major reason for searchers' success in direct searches in SOC and DOC was because the user-entered term contained words from a relevant subject heading describing the topic. In one direct search in DOC, the user first consulted the printed *LCSH* (Subject Cataloging Division, 1980) for the correct subject heading and then expressed his topic in a direct search using this subject heading. In most direct searches, users entered their terms without first consulting the printed *LCSH*, and, in some searches, their terms matched subject headings. Here are some examples:

Expressed Topic	Direct Search Access Point	Correct Subject Heading
Industry surveys	market surveys united states	Market surveys— United States

Uses of microcomput-ers in business	industrial management data processing	Industrial management—Data processing
History of the New York State capitol building	new york state capital and capitol	New York (State)—Capital and capitol
Integral geometry	integral geometry	Geometry, Integral
Role of New York (State) in the American Revolution	new york state history revolution	New York (State)—History—Revolution, 1775-1783
Traveling on the St. Lawrence River	lawrence river travel	St. Lawrence River—Description and travel
Boys' gymnastics	gymnastics	Gymnastics
Hyperbolic equations	hyperbolic equations	Different equations, Hyperbolic

Access points in direct searches composed of words from relevant subject headings that described the user's topic of interest were an effective way of retrieving relevant items. However, users did not always know the subject heading that best described their topic, nor did they bother to check the printed *LCSH* to find an appropriate heading. Instead, searchers expressed their topics of interest in a user-entered term in SOC and DOC direct searches that they felt best described their topic of interest. The best result of such direct searches was the retrieval of relevant items whose subject-rich fields of the item, e.g. title, subject heading, Relative Index entry (DOC only) fields. Some direct searches in DOC and SOC succeeded because the user-entered term matched words in various subject-rich fields of bibliographic records. Here are some examples:

Expressed Topic	Direct Search Access Point
Silver Trade	silver
Revolutionary War in New York State	new york state in revolutionary war
Television commercials	television commercials
Textbooks in advanced calculus	advanced calculus
Food problems in third world countries, especially in Africa	food problems

SYSTEM FEEDBACK IN DIRECT SEARCHES

When such direct searches resulted in the retrieval of relevant items, there was often one or more subject headings in retrieved, relevant items that, if entered into the system in another search, could have led to the retrieval of additional relevant items. For example, a patron whose

TABLE 8-5 Relevant Subject Headings and Titles Retrieved in Direct Searches

Expressed Topic	Direct Search Access Point	Number of Items Retrieved	Relevant Subject Heading	Number of Additional Items Retrieved
1. Incompleteness theorem	incompleteness theorem	1	Incompleteness theorems	1

Additional title retrieved: Formal number theory and computability

| 2. Stage movement | stage movement | 4 | Movement (Acting) | 7 |

Examples of additional titles retrieved: A movement approach to acting; Theatre movement: the actor and his space; and Movement for the performing artist

| 3. Aerobics | aerobics | 1 | Aerobic exercises | 6 |

Examples of additional titles retrieved: Aerobic dance and fitness; Aerobic weight training; Aerobic tennis; Aerobic dancing; and Dance aerobics

| 4. New Netherlands | new netherlands | 15 | New York (State)-- History--Colonial period, ca. 1600-1775 | over 100 |

Examples of additional titles retrieved: Henry Hudson and the Dutch in New York; History of New Netherland, or New York under the Dutch; The patroon's domain; Portrait of New Netherland; New York historical manuscripts: Dutch; and A sweet and alien land: the story of Dutch New York

| 5. Analytical geometry | analytical geometry | 30 | Geometry, Analytic | 344 |

Examples of additional titles retrieved: Freshman mathematics, a course in the essentials of algebra, trigonometry and analytic geometry; New analytic geometry; Analytic geometry and calculus; and A first course in analytic geometry

expressed topic was "French government: national trade and monetary policy" entered the phrase "french economy" into DOC, which retrieved one relevant item entitled *The French economy* that bore two subject headings: "France—Economic conditions—1945-" and "France—Economic Policy—1945-." If the searcher had entered the latter into DOC using the direct search, he would have retrieved an additional 11 items bearing titles such as *Public assistance to industries and trade policy in France, The politics of economic policy, France 1974-1982*, and *Economic policies in France, 1974-1982*, which might have been relevant to the user's topic of interest. Other examples are provided in Table 8-5.

Unfortunately, most online catalog searchers do not know that it is useful to check the subject heading field of retrieved, relevant records to find subject headings relevant to their topic of interest in order to enter the headings into the online catalog to find additional relevant items. When users display bibliographic records in online catalog subject searches, the catalog should occasionally remind the user to check the subject headings in retrieved records to enter later in the search.

UNSUCCESSFUL DIRECT SEARCHES

Many users' direct searches failed to retrieve relevant (or any) items because the user-entered term was not made up of relevant subject heading words describing the users' topic of interest. Often, users would display a half-dozen or so retrieved items and stop displaying them because no relevant items had yet been displayed. Here are some examples:

Expressed Topic	Direct Search Access Point (number of items retrieved)
Conducting successful business meetings	personnel meetings (0)
Descriptive statistics	descriptive (185)
How to invest in the stock market	how to invest in the stock market (0)
Photographs or sketches of the Hudson River (from 1850-1910)	hudson river photography (0) hudson river sketches (37) hudson river description and travel (99)
Bohemian life in Greenwich Village	bohemian york (0)
Game hunting without guns	primitive hunting (0) hunting implement (7)
Improving your golf swing	golf instruction (0) improving your golf swing (0)

General Montcalm (of New France)	general montcalm (2)
19th century experiences traveling on New York State's canal	canals (11) new york canals description and travel 19th century (0)
Current guide-books on what to do or see in New York (City)	contemporary new york city travel (1)
Black history of Albany, N.Y.	african-american history in new york state (0)

Such direct searches must have been frustrating to searchers, particularly those searches in which no items were retrieved. A number of searchers continued their searches by entering an access point that was a broader term than one previously entered. Here are some examples:

Expressed Topic	Direct Search Access Point
Black History of Albany, N.Y.	afro-american (5)
General Montcalm (of New France)	new france (41)
Bohemian life in Greenwich Village	york city (1640) york customs (151)
Current guide-books on what to do or see in New York (City)	new york state travel (825) new york city (900)
Descriptive statistics	statistics (234)
How to invest in the stock market	investment (272)
Improving your golf swing	golf (223)

These broader terms entered by users were either complete subject headings, i.e., new york city, statistics, and golf, or parts of subject headings, i.e., afro-americans, york city, investment, new york state travel, york customs, and see references to valid subject headings, i.e., new france. Most of the time, the user was overwhelmed by the number of items retrieved and did not display retrieved items. Had users consulted the printed *LCSH* under two of the complete subject headings, they would have been directed to the appropriate subject heading "Swing (Golf)," which is a see also reference under "Golf," and to the appropriate subject heading "New York (City)—Description—Guidebooks," which is a suggested subdivision under New York (City). The searchers in these two searches did not consult the printed *LCSH*, and subject searches for these two topics failed to retrieve relevant items in both SOC and DOC.

The major reason patron and staff direct searches failed to retrieve relevant (or any) items is because their user-entered terms in direct searches were not composed of words from relevant subject headings describing their topics of interest. Another reason for the failure of direct searches was the tendency of this subject search option to misguide users by directing them to a classification (or bookshelf) area where a number of books on a particular topic were located based on the retrieval and display of a half-dozen or so relevant items when in fact the area was not good for bookshelf browsing. For example, a direct search on "Combinatorial analysis" in DOC results in the retrieval of 35 items. The first six items bear the class number 510 because they are collections or conference proceedings on this topic, e.g., *Theory and practice of combinatorics: a collection of articles honoring Anton Kotzig...*, *Bonn Workshop on combinatorial optimization*, and *Studies in pure mathematics; papers in combinatorial theory*. A user who displays these first six items would probably be tempted to browse the shelves at the class number 510; however, 27 of the 35 items are classed in 511.6, and this class number area is probably the more fruitful area for shelf browsing. Another example is a direct search for "Leadership." The first six of 22 items displayed in a direct search in DOC are scattered into five different class areas and are about leadership of trade unions and leadership in a specific industry, trade, or profession. The last seven of 22 items are classed in 658.409 and more specific class numbers and are about leadership in business management. Thus, a searcher interested in the latter topic would find items on this topic if he persevered and displayed more than the first 10 items or used DOC's subject outline search for this topic.

The solution to this problem in direct searches is to alter the display of retrieved items so that items in the highest posted class area are displayed first. Reversing the display of retrieved items is not an adequate solution because high posted class areas for the user-entered term may be at the beginning of the classification. Another solution is DOC's subject outline (SS) search, which is intended to direct users to the most fruitful class area(s) for shelf browsing (see Table 8-2 for a brief description of this search). Had the user entered "Combinatorial analysis" into DOC using the subject outline search, DOC would have directed the user to the class number 511.6 and the 22 items bearing that class number.

In DOC, bibliographic records were enhanced with subject-rich information from the DDC Schedules and Relative Index. Sometimes this enhancement led to the retrieval of relevant items on a topic, and sometimes it resulted in the retrieval of many items. One example of the former result is the direct search for "third world economics." In SOC, a direct search for "third world economics" retrieves two relevant items entitled *Economics of the third world* and *Monetarism, economic crisis, and the third world*. These two items were retrieved because their title, subject heading, sponsor, and selected note fields contained the user-entered term. In DOC, a direct search for "third world economics" retrieves these same two relevant items and 22 additional items with titles and class numbers such as *The EEC (European Economic Community) and the third world* (337.4), *The international economy and industrial development: the impact of trade and investment on the third world* (337.7). The major reason these additional titles were retrieved is the enhancement of these items with the term "economics" from DOC Schedule captions or Relative Index entries. For example, the item entitled *The EEC and the third world* was enhanced with the Schedule captions "International economics" and "Foreign economic policies and relations of specific jurisdictions and groups of jurisdictions" and the Relative Index entry "Foreign—economic problems—international economics." Because this item did not bear the term "economics" in SOC, it was not retrieved in a direct search for "third world economics." After this item was enhanced with the DDC, it contained the term "economics" and was retrieved in a direct search in DOC. Searches for the two topics "Descriptive statistics" and "Probabilistic processes" succeeded in DOC and failed in SOC; the reason for their success in DOC was the enhancement of bibliographic records with subject-rich information from the DDC.

Such enhancement of bibliographic records did not always provide beneficial results. In a SOC search for "Linear algebra," 46 items were retrieved, the majority of which were classed in 512.5 and assigned the LC subject heading "Algebras, Linear." A DOC search for "linear algebra" retrieved 616 items. Of these 616 items, the 45 items bearing the class number 512.5 were probably relevant to the topic "Linear algebra," since this class number category bears the schedule caption "Linear, multilinear, multidimensional algebras" and Relative Index entry "Linear—algebras." However, many more items were retrieved in the direct search than these 45 items because of the enhancement of bibliographic records with the DDC. The class number, number of items, and reason for retrieving 616 records are provided for this direct search on "Linear algebra":

Class Number	Number of Items	Reason for Retrieval
516.35	443	"Linear algebra" contained in a general schedule note
512.55	60	"Linear algebra" contained in a class here note from the schedule
515.14	5	"Linear algebra" contained in the Schedule caption
512.57	5	"Linear algebra" contained in class here note from the Schedule

These reasons for retrieval account for 513 of 616 items in a direct search for "Linear algebra" in DOC. The remaining items were probably retrieved by matching words in the subject-rich fields of the record, i.e., title, subject heading, sponsor, and selected note fields, and words in the subject-rich fields added to the record, i.e., Relative Index, Schedule caption, and Schedule note fields.

A direct search in DOC for the topic "Linear algebra" yields many items (616) in comparison to a SOC search (46). In the online retrieval tests, a total of two DOC searches in the Comparison Search and Sample Search Experiments required the user to enter the term "linear algebra." The staff searcher entered this topic using the direct search; however, this searcher did not pursue this direct search but chose instead to reenter the topic using the call number (SC) search under 512.5, a class number to which he was directed earlier in the session using the subject outline (SS) search and the term "linear algebra." Displaying items under the class number 512.5, the searcher judged them relevant. The patron searcher did not use the direct search for the topic "linear algebra." Like the staff searcher, the patron found relevant items using the subject outline (SS) search for the topic "linear algebra." Other examples of search topics and direct search access points that were adversely affected by the enhancement of subject information from the DDC are :

Expressed Topic	Direct Search Access Point	Number of Items Retrieved in SOC	Number of Items Retrieved in DOC
Proof theory	proof theory	11	79
Vector analysis	vector analysis	26	54
Computer games	computer games	7	257
Derivatives	derivatives	2	409
Photographs or sketches of the Hudson River (from 1850-1910)	hudson river	112	1086

Subject searches in DOC were successful for four of the five searches above. Only the search for "Photograph and sketches of the Hudson River (from 1850-1910)" failed. Subject searches for the four other topics yielded relevant items through subject searches other than the direct search, particularly the alphabetical (SA) or subject outline (SS) search. These subject search options directed searchers to a class area in which they scanned retrieved items for relevant ones. The "Hudson River" search failed because alphabetical and subject outline searches in DOC did not direct searchers to a relevant class area for reasons that are unique to these two subject search capabilities. In SOC, the searcher was directed to relevant items on the "Hudson river sketches" topic because he had the advantage of browsing an alphabetically arranged list of subject headings and subdivisions beginning with the main heading "Hudson River."

SEARCHERS' EXPERIENCES USING DIRECT SEARCHES

In the post-search interview, the majority of library patrons and staff singled out direct search as the online catalog capability that was most helpful for directing them to relevant items on a topic. Their comments about direct searching are:

- I like the direct search because it is quick and pinpoints relevant items. (six staff, PLCFC; two staff, UI; one staff, LC)
- The direct search pinpoints relevant items and you can enter more than one term into the catalog. (two staff, PLCFC)
- I like retrieving items right away with a minimum of time and effort using the direct search. (two staff, NYSL; one patron, UI)
- In SOC and DOC, the direct search obtains the best results. Why should I need the other subject search options? (one staff, NYSL)
- I liked the direct search because it saved me from having to know all the subject headings describing my topic. (four staff, UI)
- List the direct search first because it is more likely (than other options) to lead you to relevant items. (one staff, PLCFC; two staff, UI)

A number of patrons and staff noted the direct search's report of successive postings, which helped them to identify words that were contained in few or no items, and later omitted these words from the user-entered term in subsequent searches. For example, a patron entered the term "implicit differentiation" into SOC, and the system reported that one item was retrieved for "implicit," three items were retrieved for "differentiation," and zero items were retrieved for "implicit differentiation." Then, the searcher entered the term "implicit" in a direct search and retrieved one relevant item entitled *Constrained equations in a study of implicit differential equations and their discontinuous solutions*.

Not all searchers' remarks about direct searches were favorable. Their unfavorable remarks note their dissatisfaction with the direct search's inability to alter the results of a direct search:

- I want to limit the results of a direct search without having to start over. (one patron, NYSL)
- With the direct search, it was difficult to limit the search. Sometimes thumbing through books is the only way to find relevant items. (one patron, LC)
- If you hit your topic using the direct search, you don't get a chance to see how your topic is organized or what you didn't retrieve using other search options. (one staff, LC)
- Using the direct search, your subject is either *in* the catalog or *not in* the catalog. When it's in the catalog, this option performs well. (one staff, LC)
- Using the direct search in SOC and DOC, you have to know the right words to find relevant items. When you find the right words, the direct search works well. (one staff, NYSL)
- The direct search gives no assistance for finding related terms. (one staff, UI)

IMPROVEMENTS TO DIRECT SEARCHING

Modification of Results

Users' experiences in direct searches helped us to reformulate the process of direct searching to include feedback and search modification. Direct searches are a linear procedure as shown in Figure 8-3. The user-entered term is matched with the subject-rich fields of the bibliographic record including fields enhanced by the DDC. The intermediate results of the number of items retrieved by the individual words in the user-entered term precede the report of the final result, which is the logical combination of the words in the user-entered term through the Boolean AND operation. When the final result is presented, the searcher has the option to display retrieved items or modify the result.

FIGURE 8-3 Direct Searching in a Redesigned Experimental Online Catalog

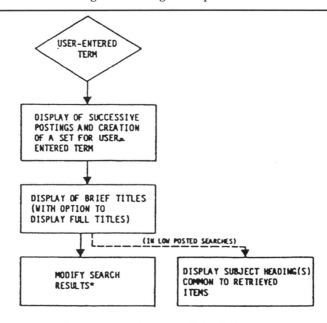

*By one or a combination of the following:
1. Another subject search
2. Restrict/limit search results
3. Boolean operators
4. Relational operators
5. Truncation

In a search for "Computers as an aid to mathematical statistics," the searcher first enters the term "mathematical statistics" and retrieves 170 items. After displaying items with titles, such as *Studies in statis-*

tics, Identification and informative sample size, and *Stanford studies in mathematics and statistics,* the searcher decides to limit the results (see Figure 8-4).

FIGURE 8-4   Direct Search for "Computers as an Aid to Mathematical Statistics" in a Redesigned Experimental Online Catalog

---

What would you like to do? > sd
Enter subject to search > mathematical statistics

>>>>> YOUR REQUEST...sd:mathematical statistics
     1221 ITEMS FOR "mathematical"
      274 ITEMS FOR "statistics"
      170 ITEMS IN SET 1 (mathematical statistics)

     THE FOLLOWING IS A SUMMARY OF YOUR SEARCHES:
     SET ITEMS   REQUEST
       1   170   SD:MATHEMATICAL STATISTICS

OPTION   DESCRIPTION
     DI   DISPLAY items
     SO   Start over

The searcher modifies the results of the previous direct search in Figure 8-4 by entering another search for the term "data processing" and combining it in a Boolean AND operation. In the search modification shown in Figure 8-5, the user performs another direct search for "data processing," displays a few titles, and then enters the option to modify the results of previous searches. The user selects the option to "Find items common to 2 or more sets" (FI) and combines the results of sets 1 and 2 in a Boolean AND operation. Three of the ten items in set 3 bear the titles *COMPSTAT: proceedings in computational statistics, Computational statistics and data analysis,* and *Basic statistical computing* and are probably relevant to the user's expressed topic.

FIGURE 8-5   Modifying the Results of a Direct Search for "Mathematical Statistics" by a Direct Search for "Data Processing"

What would you like to do? > mr

>>>>> YOUR REQUEST...mr

OPTION   DESCRIPTION
     MY   Modify results by year of publication
     ML   Modify results by language
     MS   Modify results by another subject
     MP   Modify results by previous search(es)

What would you like to do? > mp

>>>>> YOUR REQUEST...mp

THE FOLLOWING IS A SUMMARY OF YOUR SEARCHES:

SET	ITEMS	REQUEST
1	170	sd:mathematical statistics
2	47	sd:data processing

OPTION	DESCRIPTION
FI	Find items common to 2 or more sets
II	Include items from 2 or more sets
EI	Exclude items from 2 or more sets
SO	Start over

What would you like to do? > fi
Enter sets (separated by commas) > 1,2

>>>>> YOUR REQUEST...fi 1 and 2
10 ITEMS IN SET 3 (1 AND 2)

When direct searches or the modification of direct searches result in zero items, subject searchers usually have to conjure up additional search terms to enter into the online catalog in subsequent search statements. Okapi, an experimental online catalog of the Central Polytechnic of London, employs a hyper-OR search when a direct search for a search statement exceeding two words results in no retrievals. In the hyper-OR search, Okapi searches for items containing some but not all of the words in the user-entered term and retrieves items based on the postings for individual words in the user-entered term. Okapi also displays items retrieved in a hyper-OR search in an order that corresponds to the items' relevance to the searcher's topic of interest (Mitev, Venner, and Walker, 1985). The hyper-OR search of Okapi is an online catalog search strategy for direct searches when a keyword, implicit Boolean search using the AND operator fails to retrieve items for the user-entered term. The designers of Okapi have also considered automatic correction of misspellings and truncation of words in the user-entered term in both direct searches and hyper-OR searches to reduce such searches with no retrievals.

SYSTEM FEEDBACK

Direct searches that retrieve few items could be enhanced to automatically analyze the subject headings in retrieved items, find the headings common to the majority of the retrieved items, and suggest these to the searcher for entry in subsequent searches. Table 8-5 listed five direct searches that retrieved 30 or fewer items. Had the searcher entered the subject heading common to the majority of retrieved items, additional relevant items would have been retrieved. For example, the searcher looking for items on "new netherlands" obtains an option when completing the display of items that suggests an alphabetical search for the subject heading "New York (State)—History—Colonial period, ca. 1600-1775," which is common to a number of the 15 items retrieved in a direct search for "new netherlands" (see Figure 8-6).

FIGURE 8-6 System Feedback About Subject Headings Found in Retrieved Items

Would you like to see the next item? > n

*The subject heading "New York (State)--History--Colonial period, ca. 1600-1775" is listed in some of the items. Choose the SA option to browse an alphabetical list with this subject and others like it.

THE FOLLOWING IS A SUMMARY OF YOUR SEARCHES:

SET	ITEMS	REQUEST
1	15	sd:new netherlands

OPTION		DESCRIPTION
*	SA	Search alphabetically for "New York (State)—History—Colonial...
	DI	Display items
	SO	Start over

Direct searches provide much less feedback than alphabetical and subject outline searches about the controlled vocabulary assigned to bibliographic records. The system's analysis of subject headings common to retrieved items is one way in which the online catalog can assist searchers, whose direct searches retrieve few items, to find additional library material.

System designers are now implementing an online searching capability comparable to the feedback capability discussed. In the online catalog marketed by Innovative Interfaces, Inc. (III), users can search subject headings listed in a retrieved item by selecting option "I" (find other items with the same subject) from the list of options following the display of an item. Users of the Dynix online catalog can enter the "Related works" option following the display of a bibliographic record to find additional records bearing a subject heading or author name selected in a relevant item from a previous search. LUIS, the online catalog of Northwestern University, reminds searchers that they can enter a subject heading displayed in a record in a subsequent subject search by this message, which precedes the subject headings field of a bibliographic record: (Library of Congress; use s=) (Northwestern University 1982). The feedback capability of the III, Dynix, and LUIS online catalogs that directs users to additional items is based on users' selection of a relevant subject heading or another criterion in *one* retrieved record. The feedback capability discussed earlier in this section and shown in Figure 8-6 was based on the system's selection of a subject heading common to a number of items in a retrieved set.

SUMMARY

The direct search in SOC and DOC was a keyword and implicit Boolean search using the AND operator. In a direct search in SOC, a user-entered term retrieved items whose title, subject heading, sponsor, series, and note fields contain all of the words in the user-entered term. In a direct search in DOC, a user-entered term retrieved items whose title, subject heading, sponsor, series, bibliographic record note, Dewey subject, Dewey Schedule note, and Dewey Index (i.e., Relative Index entry) fields contained the words in the user-entered term.

The percentage of times that DOC's direct search retrieved relevant items for a user's topic of interest was greater than the percentage of times that SOC's direct search retrieved relevant items. The percentage of times that no items were retrieved in direct searches in SOC was greater than the percentage of times that no items were retrieved in direct searches in DOC. These results about relevant items and no retrievals are evidence that the enhancement of bibliographic records with the DDC improved subject access in DOC's direct searches.

The direct search was particularly effective in retrieving relevant items on a topic when the user-entered term matched words in a relevant subject heading. When the user-entered term was not composed of words from relevant subject headings, it sometimes retrieved relevant items. Access points in direct searches that were not composed of words from subject headings and led users to no retrievals or the retrieval of nonrelevant items provided them with little feedback about indexed terms in the online catalog except through the report of successive postings that told the number of items retrieved per word of the user-entered term.

A few users noted relevant subject headings in retrieved, relevant items in direct searches and entered these headings into the catalog using a direct or other subject search. Examples of retrieved, relevant items for certain topics were shown in which the subject heading(s) found in one relevant item could be used to find additional relevant items. The experimental online catalog did not feature such a capability. So, users whose direct searches resulted in no retrievals sometimes continued their search by entering an access point that was broader than their expressed topic and resulted in many retrievals, i.e., over 200. In a redesigned direct search for DOC, a feedback capability was recommended. This feedback capability would inform subject searchers of subject heading(s) common to items retrieved in low-posted direct searches. Some online catalogs are now equipped with a comparable feedback capability for searchers to select a subject heading (or some other criterion) in a retrieved item to find additional items bearing the selected heading.

Subject searchers of SOC and DOC criticized the systems for their inability to modify results of a direct search by another term or a limiting criterion, such as language or year of publication. In a redesigned direct search, the online catalog should offer users the capability to modify searches without losing the results of the ongoing subject search should the modification of the search result in no retrievals.

In general, there was no difference between direct searches in SOC and DOC with regard to estimated recall and precision. However, there was a marginally significant effect in the estimated recall of staff searches, and the recall scores of staff searches in DOC at the four participating libraries exceeded the recall of staff searches in SOC. The performance of direct searches in the two systems are comparable, but about half of the relevant items retrieved and displayed in direct searches in DOC were unique with respect to the relevant items retrieved and displayed in SOC direct searches.

The percentage of access points in direct searches that resulted in no retrievals was greater in SOC than in DOC. Bibliographic records in the latter were enhanced with subject information from the DDC. There were times when this enhancement helped users find relevant items on a topic by providing them with additional subject-rich words in items with which to match their terms. Sometimes this enhancement did not help users find relevant items and only contributed to producing searches with a large number of postings and false drops. Most searchers were able to circumvent such results by using a different search option in DOC, but one searcher needed the alphabetical list of subject headings in SOC to focus on the topic and was unable to find relevant items in the DOC search.

Another reason for failure in direct searches in SOC or DOC was the tendency of this search to misguide users by directing them to a classification or bookshelf area where a number of books on a particular topic were located based on the retrieval or display of a half-dozen or so relevant items. In DOC, subject searchers were able to use the subject outline (SS) search, which directed users to the most fruitful class area for shelf browsing for a topic.

The direct search was not always the most fruitful subject search for retrieving items relevant to the user's topic of interest. In unsuccessful direct searches, SOC and DOC searchers employed the other subject searches available in these systems. This chapter contained the results of direct searches in the experimental online catalog enhanced with the DDC and suggestions for improving the design of direct searches in the experimental online catalog and in online catalogs in general.

BIBLIOGRAPHY

Besant, Larry. 1982. Early survey findings: Users of public online catalogs want sophisticated subject access. *American Libraries* 13(3):160.

Dewey Decimal Classification and Relative Index. 1979. Devised by Melvil Dewey. 19th ed., ed. Benjamin A. Custer. Vol. 1. Albany, NY: Forest Press.

Freeman, Robert R. and Pauline Atherton. 1968 "File Organization and Search Strategy Using the Universal Decimal Classification in Mechanical Retrieval Systems." In *Mechanized Information Storage, Retrieval and Dissemination*, Edited by Kjell Samuelson. Proceedings of the FID/IFIP Joint Conference, 1967. Amsterdam: North-Holland Publishing Co.

Markey, Karen, and Anh N. Demeyer. 1986. *Dewey Decimal Classification Online Project: Evaluation of a Library Schedule and Index Integrated Into the Subject Searching Capabilities of an Online Catalog.* Dublin, OH: OCLC. OCLC Research Report OCLC/OPR/RR-86/1.

Mitev, Nathalie Nadia, Gillian M. Venner, and Stephen Walker. 1985. *Designing an Online Public Access Catalogue.* London: British Library. Library and Information Research Report 39.

NOTIS Public Access Catalog Display Screens. 1982. Evanston, IL: Northwestern University Library.

Siegel, Elliott R., Karen Kameen, Sally K. Sinn, and Freida O. Weise. 1983. Research strategy and methods used to conduct a comparative evaluation of two prototype online catalog systems. In *National Online Meeting Proceedings—1983.* Comp. Martha E. Williams and Thomas H. Hogan. Medford, NJ: Learned Information.

Subject Cataloging Division, Processing Services. 1980. *Library of Congress Subject Headings.* Washington, D.C.: Library of Congress.

9

Setting Classification Policy

Mary W. Ghikas

A public catalog design project was undertaken at the Los Angeles County Public Library System in 1975-76 in response to perceived problems in public access to library collections. The overall study was aimed at (1) reducing catalog production costs, (2) reducing the lag between acquisition, cataloging, and (book) catalog production, (3) economical distribution of holdings data within the 96-library system, (4) simplification of technical services procedures, (5) redesign of the public catalog to provide improved collection access *and* development of improved public information on catalog use, and (6) incorporation in the catalog (system) of previously-excluded classes of material, such as non-print material.

As part of the study, my staff and I observed people using the catalog in branches on Sunday afternoons. We discovered that more than 60 percent of the people who came in used the subject catalogs. Most people did not turn pages or scan multiple entries, nor did they make note of authors and titles. Most found the subject in which they were interested, wrote down the call number of the first entry under their subject heading or the call number that appeared most frequently, if they were really sophisticated. Then they went to the shelf and browsed. They had no interest in the author or title. They just wanted a way to get into the hierarchy of the classification schedule.

With this pattern of use in mind we began looking at ways to reorder bibliographic products. We put together an access tool that consisted simply of a list of subject headings that appeared in the library's catalog along with classification numbers that appeared in conjunction with those subject headings. We asked our software people to extract subject headings out of appropriately marked fields, pull the class number that appeared on the same record and make those a pair.

On the first pass we found that almost inevitably more than one class number had been associated with any given subject heading. Using the subject heading did not always get you to the same place in the classification hierarchy. It might get you to several places. We then asked for a count for each pair of subject heading and classification. For how many titles did the cataloger use both that subject heading and that class number? That number was placed in brackets next to the class number in the access tool, and the entries were sequenced in numerically descending order.

In looking up a subject heading, the first class number you saw was the one that appeared in conjunction with that subject heading most frequently. The assumption was that most of the time the user would be better served if directed to that place in the classification hierarchy where there were the most titles with that class number and that subject heading. We tried to use that as a way of increasing success and satisfaction.

The tool was created in book form. A hole was drilled in the upper left hand corner, and the book was simply hung up at the end of each stack row just as telephone books used to be hung up in phone booths.

It turned out to be a remarkably successful tool. People want to use the classification. It is basically a very efficient way of moving about a collection. The more effective a library has been in applying the classification, the better it works.

The tool has been replicated in a number of medium-sized public libraries and a handful of big ones. It probably works more successfully in the medium-sized ones than in the large ones. People would walk into the library of Baltimore County, Los Angeles, or Columbus and Franklin County, open the book, find the subjects they wanted, go to the appropriate section of the shelves and utilize the classification.

The Chicago Public Library used the same tool. On balance, it worked less effectively there. For one thing, the collection was larger, with 500,000 instead of 250,000 titles. That is a significant difference. The mechanics of handling a much larger printed volume were different in such a larger collection. Size, weight, and print type are important differences to people. The Chicago Public Library also has changed its classification system from Dewey to LC. So, in fact, it was much more complex to use the results of that kind of search. Users often became very frustrated where portions of the collection were handled much differently in those two classification systems.

But it is, I think, an example of the way that we can think about what potential tools we have in our classification systems and can begin to redefine what we are doing. We must begin to think more seriously about what the classification system can and ought to be used for and about how things are used. We must go back to the perception that classification really involves two different things: analysis of the text, in the sense of what is it about, and analysis of how it is likely to be used.

The awareness of this is being forced on administrators in many cases. While it is much easier to view classification as a neat way of getting the book on the shelf and forgetting about it, technology has given us options that we are obligated to examine. For library managers that means coming to terms with what the catalog is about, with what classification is about, and with how those have to be interfaced with library users and what they are about.

One thing that is likely to happen as library managers become more aware of potential tools is more experimentation with organizational structure. Hugh Atkinson commented that he does not have one big library anymore; he has 40 little libraries. Look at the kind of organizational changes that he tried at the University of Illinois in Urbana and nudged other folks into trying. Look at his kind of horizontal organization of the professional staff. The theory behind such changes begins by pointing out that you do not have to organize the staff in traditional ways because you no longer have a card catalog. Look at how much of the structure of the library has been imposed by the existence of massive files that were not transportable or replicable. Now you are free of that constraint. Additionally, if you accept the theory that the process of structuring the access tool has to do not only with the inherent qualities of the works themselves but also with some perception of how people are likely to use them, then it begins not to make sense to segregate catalogers off in the back room. They should be in contact with users to understand their needs.

Furthermore, it has long been apparent that, in many cases, the reference staff does not understand the catalog. In doing the first round of catalog conversion, I made a serious mistake in the sort sequence in one notable area, which put some entries into radically different locations. They were not arranged by the library's sort rules. So I did the appropriate thing and explained to the reference staff what had happened, how to cope with it, and promised a correction in six weeks. About three-quarters of them had not figured out that there was anything wrong. I found that more disturbing than the fact that I had made the mistake in the first place.

Increasingly, the perception of the people who are making the money decisions about collections and about access is that people doing the cataloging do not know anything about how the materials are used, and people doing reference do not know a thing about the catalog. So the kind of reorganization that Atkinson tried starts to make some sense. He said, "Why not take your mathematics library and the librarians therein and let them be bibliographer, classifier, and information specialist?" You can keep doing your support functions in a normal vertical fashion. Support staff can continue doing copy cataloging for all subjects. There are a lot of practical reasons not to do this, but also there are a lot of practical reasons why it makes sense. If not that kind of reorganization, we certainly will see over our careers some rather different ways of structuring organizations. And those different ways will have a great deal to do with the different ways we perceive the catalog, the way we organize the catalogs, the way we make catalogs, and catalog-based tools available for people to use.

One of the more economically viable options with online and computer-based catalogs rather than with card catalogs is the assignment of multiple classification numbers to works that are not adequately described by one classification number. The option for assigning multiple class numbers to a work was always there. Online catalogs make it affordable.

New kinds of catalogs and new kinds of reference tools, such as online indexing and abstracting services, provide access to our serial collection that is by and large far superior to access to the monograph collection. As a manager in charge of doling out dollars on collection development, my preference is pretty consistently for putting the money into the serials collection, when there is not quite enough money to go around. Dollar-for-dollar I got more out of the serials collection because of the better access provided by indexing and abstracting.

While there are many areas of our collections where traditional cataloging and classification provide quite reasonable access to the collection there are other areas where this is not the case. Think of conference proceedings, which from a user's point of view are very hard to find. Many users will not find them unless they are coming after them from bibliographies, citations, from other kinds of materials that provide a hook to get in. Classification is certainly not the only way to approach the problem, but it is one way. There are places in the collection where it makes eminently good sense to make the investment in assigning multiple classification numbers. We have an enormous capital investment in our collections, but we do not use those collections very well in most cases. Using the collections is more difficult than it ought to be. We get cheap at the wrong end of the operation. Multiple classification numbers would help to make it better.

From the point of view of a user, the hierarchical structure of classification, particularly the Dewey classification, gives you a way of getting into a discipline for which subject headings and thesauri do not substitute, even where the thesauri are more comprehensive and used more liberally than is done in cataloging. The user assumes when finding only one class number that a work fits into one of these hierarchical structures when in fact it may fit conceptually into several. While works cannot physically be shelved in several places, users would be better served by assigning multiple class numbers so that the same work could be found in several places in the hierarchy. Neither the hierarchical structure that classification imposes nor a straight vocabulary structure by itself is sufficient. Together they provide more powerful access to collections.

During a presentation to librarians, the following question-and-answer session occurred:

Karen Muller: I have been struck by similarities between classification theory and principles and authority and thesaurus structure. I am reminded of the art and architecture thesaurus that is now being developed at the Getty Museum in California. It is hierarchical. You can come in by an alphabetical index term or you can move up or down. This is the capability we have with our classification system. If you have ever had a public shelflist such as the Chicago Art Institute has, you know that people use it. They grub around in it and find what they are looking for a whole lot more efficiently.

Ms. Ghikas: An article by Karen Markey and Pauline Atherton in the June 1985 issue of *Information Technology and Libraries* is very good if you are interested in classification and the way you might begin to build on it in the future. Part of what they are investigating is the combination of the classification schedule and its A to Z index to create tools that will give you the ability to move up and down the hierarchy of the classification schedule without physically going to the shelves. If I were trying to design an ideal public access catalog, I would want some immediate access to classification as a point of entry and some way of going from that to search up and down the hierarchy. I would want some conceptual recombination of the dictionary catalog and the public shelflist. I find the shelflist to be still a first rate tool for getting people into the collection.

Alice Allen: I agree with everything you have said about addressing the needs of users, exploring different ways of organizing the way your cataloging gets done and all of that. But, in realistic, everyday terms in most libraries that belong to a utility, 75% or 80% of the cataloging is copied. At this point most libraries seem to feel that to be efficient about that, you have to have a group of people more or less accepting this information that has come from other places and that the options for any kind of local treatment of copy is very limited. Is that implicit in what you are saying?

Ms. Ghikas: As a professional community, we have to start looking at the access tools and the way to structure those tools. This does not mean that every library should do its own cataloging and classification, which I think is not particularly feasible.

If you look at the experience of libraries that have opted to do very nonstandard things in classification, and there are still some doing exceedingly nonstandard things in classification, it is apparent that it becomes not only very uneconomic but also very dysfunctional as far as the use of that collection is concerned. So, I am not advocating an increase in local, or nonstandard, cataloging.

Many new access tools are being designed with a tremendous amount of input from all over the place. If you do one you will discover that many people are interested in what you are doing and will have ideas and suggestions to contribute. They feel a proprietary interest in what you are doing and that is a positive thing. In talking about making these changes, I do not mean that we should do something nonstandard so that you can no longer use a bibliographic utility or any other products that are out there.

How are libraries represented here handling things like reclassification? Are all of you LC libraries?

Peter Lisbon: We started in 1977 at Harvard University and tried to keep reclassification to a minimum. We reclassify mostly when gross errors are discovered or when literary authors have been split because we classed in one place and LC eventually put the author in a different place. Then we try to bring the author's works together. Apart from that we have not done much. In copy cataloging there are sometimes questions about using the LC numbers which are now obsolete on old LC copy. We have decided we would not change old LC copy, even that which has become obsolete. I think some libraries attempt to catch those obsolete numbers in the shelflist. So we do minimal reclassification.

Ms. Ghikas: Do you see that as a user problem?

Peter Lisbon: I am not aware of any complaints. That doesn't mean they don't exist. For example, when Finland was abruptly split from DK to DL . . .

Ms. Ghikas: Is it a visible split in the catalog? Is there any explanatory information in the catalog?

Peter Lisbon: Not directly. Users must assume that by seeing under the subject heading that the recent material is in DL and the older books are in DK.

Unidentified speaker: Does anyone know of any studies of users' awareness of classification schemes?

Karen Muller: I don't know of any studies. But last year in a business school program I was surprised by how many of my classmates understood what classification was about, what it was, and that major libraries in the Chicago area used different classification schemes. Also, patrons at the Chicago Art Institute would come in and ask why didn't we use LC like the University of Chicago. We replied because we used Dewey like Northwestern University. People are aware of what is going on and they do ask such questions as "Why is this book in this place when another on the subject is there?" It means that people are more aware than we might think.

Kathleen Jackson: Duke is a large library using Dewey classification. I have been interested to find during freshman orientation tours that many of our freshmen understand Dewey from their experience in public libraries or their school libraries. They are glad to find we have Dewey and they really do know how to use it. Now, I'm sure that their level of understanding varies. But some of them know, for instance, that the geographic number can be found in different places in the classification number. We are not changing to LC.

Janet Hill: I'm from Northwestern, and neither are we. We find that people actually understand the numbers a whole lot better than we thought. One way we can judge that is by the number of people who use our online catalog comment forms for such questions as: "Why don't you have this classified in the same place the Springfield Public Library does?" or, "Why is that not located with this other literature?" A lot of people seem to be very aware of it for their own subject areas.

Linda Smith: That's what we found. I'm from a relatively new university with a new collection without a lot of old, historical volumes. One of the things we discovered right off was that often different editions of the same title were not going to have the same classification number on the cataloging copy. So we very early adopted a policy of using the newer class number for old editions. There was a trade-off in cost, of course. Now we find there is an underlying assumption on the part of our users that if one edition of a title is here and another there, then something is wrong and should be corrected. They bring it to our attention.

Audrey Yuen: I work at a very tiny public library compared with most of your systems. However, we do find, for example, that our younger students who are faced with finding state materials for their reports in two different locations in the 900's because the old ones have not been changed over are really very sophisticated about asking why we have some materials in the 917's and some in the 970's. There is a measure of dissatisfaction on their part when they have to go to two different places to look for the same material.

Ms. Ghikas: When the Chicago Public Library started using OCLC and changed from Dewey to LC in 1975 it was decided not to reclassify the Dewey collection. There was significant vocal opposition from the public to the change. People didn't like the change. They were used to Dewey. They knew where to go on the shelf. They knew what section was theirs. People got used to LC and accepted it; but, even so, there were specific things in the classification that they did not like. They were able to give reasoned evaluations from their point of view of the pros and cons of the two classification schemes for those particular subject areas or material types. They asked to have specific parts of the collection in Dewey even though everything else was in LC. For example, many people did not like, and they still don't like, the way that LC treated biographies. The fact there was a remaining Dewey biography collection, and substantial one, served to keep that issue very much alive.

Karen Muller: I once heard someone from the University of Michigan say that they had maintained Dewey classification for the literature and language part of their collection when the rest of the collection was reclassified to LC because the faculty demanded it. Does anyone have any experience with that kind of thing?

Ms. Ghikas: Can anyone answer that? I think that in many cases particularly committed user groups, like faculties, are likely to be sufficiently aware of the impact of classification on the way they can get at the collection to insist on, or at least try to insist on, certain kinds of action.

Alice Allen: I was formerly at the University of Michigan and that is, in fact, what happened to literature at the time the library reclassified. It is still true. They have a massive collection of literature and language materials in Dewey. It is not recognizable Dewey by any edition of Dewey but is a very modified local use of Dewey. They are still using that system specifically because the faculty like to browse and feel that they can do it better with the Dewey numbers than they could with LC. Because of its size at this time I can't imagine realistically reclassifying it.

Peter Lisbon: I don't know Dewey that well and I'm curious. Why would the Dewey literature arrangement be preferable to faculty? Just because they are used to it?

Alice Allen: It happened before my time at Michigan, but, yes, I think so. The Dewey numbers that Michigan uses are very simple. For instance, English and American literature are all in 828 with a very simple Cutter number for the author and work letters for the title. They can quickly go to the author and see everything by and about him. Part of the problem is perception and not a logical reaction from users about what they want and why they want it. I'm at a library now that is trying to convince users that a COM catalog would be good. A lot of them like 3 x 5 cards and are going to keep on liking them for a long time without a rational explanation for it.

Ms. Ghikas: I think that is true. And I happen to think it is also valid. You deal with what people perceive, not with what they ought to perceive.

Let's turn to another topic. Have any of you had experience with positions split between public services and technical services functions?

Unidentified speaker: We had, and still have, positions split between reference and cataloging. After about two years in split positions, several people moved to one or the other area full-time. In all cases, they made such statements as "I didn't feel that I was learning enough about one area. I got tired of being a generalist. I didn't have a depth of under-standing about either area."

Ms. Ghikas: Do you think that is something that will change again, particularly as reference technologies change? If you are using combi-nations of expert systems, for instance, to handle some not yet defined amount of general reference? If what you are getting as a professional reference specialist are the questions that do not lend themselves to or could not be handled by "do-it-yourself" tools, the user friendly systems, the various expert systems? Does that change that equation if it is really referral reference that you are getting and, assuming that copy cataloging is done by different staff somewhere else, referral cataloging that you are getting?

Karen Muller: I would think that you would become even more frustrated because you would not have the easy standard to compare with or build from with your own knowledge. If you get only referral cataloging you are getting cataloging that is not covered by a national agency or another member of the network. You cannot check for copy cataloging that might be similar to what you are cataloging. I would think the same thing is true in dealing with reference questions.

Ms. Ghikas: So the problem in doing that satisfactorily may be to find some way to package up a context so that you can work in that setting? To find some way to package what has been the cumulative experience within that specific subject area in a way that you can get at it?

Karen Muller: I think things like the *LC Subject Manual* are efforts in that direction. I'm not sure that is working in terms of giving us the same kind of experience that you get from seeing actual cataloging done at LC and seeing what LC is doing in practice with a particular subject heading or kind of subject heading. Seeing all the examples of the actual application give a sense of cumulative experience.

Kathleen Jackson: At Duke, the original catalogers only do materials that have absolutely no copy. So they do not have that experience. Occasionally they will ask the copy catalogers, "What is LC doing?" because they feel they are in complete isolation.

Ms. Ghikas: Isn't that partly a matter of the kinds of tools that we are opting to give people in that setting? What if we gave the original catalogers something that was a regional online catalog, for instance, sitting at their desks? They could look to see what other libraries have done with books of the general variety. That might make a difference.

Alice Allen: I'm not sure I know how successful what Illinois is doing might be. However, I feel very strongly that we are at a point where public service librarians and technical service librarians need to do a lot more talking to each other than they are probably doing right now. We were talking about online systems. Right now, as a cataloger, I would like to know what public service librarians in my library think should be in an online catalog. However, they do not have the language to talk back to me. Ideally, for example, I would like them to understand a little more than they do about what the MARC format is and what kind of information is in it and what the possibilities might be. We are starting from so far apart that it is going to take a while before we are really going down the same track together. I don't know exactly how to do that. It does not always work to just sit people down in a room and say, "Talk to each other." Something has to happen. I'm not sure it has to be as drastic as what Illinois is doing, but I think something has to happen.

Ms. Ghikas: Librarians are talking about things that will force that kind of discussion in certain places. You have, for instance, libraries that are seriously looking at the possibility of integrating online indexing and abstracting with their online catalogs. The online indexing and abstracting services belong to reference and not to cataloging. Suddenly you have two turfs being merged here and questions of who owns portions of the tools that the library uses.

A couple of years ago there was a LITA institute on online catalogs and online reference. One of the most interesting discussions took place during the last ten minutes or so of the last day and concerned what kinds of things should appear in the online catalog. Because of its subject and the line-up of speakers, the preconference included both reference librarians and catalogers. The public services people said they want some value judgments, or quality judgments, in cataloging records. They want to know from the catalog record that *this* is a fundamental basic book on this subject and that *that* one is not. This was a philosophical discussion of significant proportions, but even in those ten minutes librarians were dealing jointly with differing perceptions of what the catalog ought to be doing.

Unidentified speaker: But isn't that paradoxical? Doesn't it take us back to pre-machine, pre-automation kinds of things and argue again for the separation of reference and technical services? Because the quality judgments, unless you can imagine some fantastic online system, are the prerogatives of the bibliographer or the reader's advisor. It is the literature or subject specialist who can say that in reviews this book is the one cited as the most valuable contribution to this topic.

Ms. Ghikas: However, in some cases, the information, or value judgments, already exist. Some people are saying perhaps we just need to add it to our catalogs.

Let's just look at a commercial example. IAC's *Magazine Index* indexes book, movie, and restaurant reviews in mainstream journals. Grades appear in the index. A citation for a book review or restaurant review will have an A, B, or C which is the indexer's translation of how the reviewer graded the movie or restaurant. If you watch library patrons using the tools, you see that they like the grades. Many of them never bother to look up the reviews. They just use the index as a reference tool. They assume that if all the reviews have A's on them, the item reviewed must be good. They will go right out and see the movie or read the book.

Some people have felt very strongly that the creation of things like the subject guide that I described earlier reflect, first, a failure of the catalog, and, second, a kind of distraction. They suggested energies were siphoned off that might have been better utilized in improving the important tool itself, the catalog. I agree that the catalog is a very fundamental tool. It is the basis for a lot of other tools that we create.

You reach a point, however, when you must look at the way real users want to get at information and the way people want to use the library and then you must try to facilitate that use. On that basis, I'm not sure if public services people are wrong in saying that it would be very helpful to have something in the cataloging record on an online public access catalog that gave you some clue as to whether this title is worth filling out a stack call slip for. That is the kind of discussion, however, that needs to go on between catalogers and reference librarians and the managers who make dollar decisions. It's going to be in part up to the catalogers to be educators and advocates.

10

Implementing Classification Policy

Liz Bishoff

This chapter is not intended to be a theoretical discussion of classification policy. Instead, it will touch on most of the major issues that may arise for middle-level administrators—those who can make some decisions on their own, but who may need to get approval to do something drastic. Although my jobs have been in Dewey libraries, most of the issues in implementing classification policy are generic to the process of classification, and transcend the differences between the classification schemes used.

CLASSIFICATION POLICY

What is a classification policy anyway? There may be a lot of libraries where the last major classification policy decision made was whether to use Dewey or LC, or whether to *switch* from Dewey to LC. And while there are few decisions that can compare in importance to those, other big decisions do need to be made from time to time, such as whether to adopt a new edition of Dewey, or whether to retrospectively revise numbers to reflect changes in the schedule.

Less momentous decisions include whether to classify some new format of material, such as videocassettes or microcomputer software, or whether merely to provide some arbitrary shelf-order number. Libraries may have been able to make decisions such as these independently in the past, but with the advent of online union catalogs, managers are having to realize that their libraries will not have totally separate catalogs any more, and that decisions about classification practices have to take this "connectedness" into account.

Classification issues can also be very narrow. One of the instances I remember best happened when I was in my first professional position. A library administrator brought me a stack of books about UFOs and said, "Don't you think that these should be in 629 along with the other books about airplanes?" After I got over being flabbergasted I managed to say, "You may think that UFOs are aircraft, and there may be many people who would agree with you, but I think most of the scientific community would be unhappy to have UFOs classed in with the practical sciences." If I had not persuaded him otherwise, we would have been setting a classification policy that moved the UFO books from 001.942, next to Big Foot, and into 629 along with dirigibles and helicopters.

The strength of my conviction must have made an impression on that administrator, because not long after that, the same person found a book called *So You Want to Be a Ham* (about amateur radio operators) classed in 641.3 with the cookbooks. He almost apologized for asking if it really belonged there. I had to tell him that this time he had not come upon a problem with the classification policy, but, was instead dealing with a simple typographical error.

Even little things like these represent classification policy issues, but their impact on operations and service is limited. Even if you have made a mistake, you can correct it easily. And while these little issues may be fun to talk about, it is the big decisions that affect a great many titles, where a mistake can be extremely expensive, and may seem nearly impossible to fix.

SPECIAL CLASSIFICATION NUMBERS

One common decision of this sort is making up a special classification number to meet some perceived local need. At Pasadena Public Library for instance, we have about 6,000 titles about Pasadena, and they are very heavily used. Once upon a time, presumably to gather the materials together in one location, someone created a special number for Pasadena and decreed that the library would use that number for everything about Pasadena from then on. The library now has 6,000 books classified in that number. By itself this would not be so bad, but at the same time the library has a policy of not providing Cutter numbers on materials. As a result 6,000 books on Pasadena sit together on the shelves in no particular order. The history of Pasadena sits next to a book about Pasadena athletes, which is next to something on the economy of Pasadena, which may be next to a book on Pasadena artists. Users cannot find a thing by browsing the shelves. What we have created, instead of a convenience to our users, is a marvelous example of the dangers of having someone make classification policy decisions without looking at the long-term implications.

There is another local decision that is going to cause a lot of trouble when we begin using the new Dewey schedule for data processing numbers. In Pasadena, all the computer books for adults are classed in 651.8, which is the business data processing number. Books on Pascal,

Vic 20 computer games, artificial intelligence, and business data processing are all in the same number. In the children's collection, however, all the computer books are classed in 510.78. Apparently someone decided that children look at computers from a mathematical viewpoint while adults only think about computers in terms of business. Someone thought he or she was making a sound decision at the time, that users would be pleased to find all the computer books in one location, and that it would be easy to classify materials. The explosion in microcomputer literature simply was not anticipated. Instead of providing a significant service to users, the library has an illogical arrangement of materials on the shelves, which has brought confusion to users. To make matters worse, because our numbers were so far removed from the norm, when we decided to reclassify materials using the new data processing numbers, all the items had to be originally classified, and we were unable to assign the task to technicians.

SPECIAL CLASSIFICATION SCHEMES

Even more important than the decision to use a special number is deciding whether to design a home-grown classification system for all or part of your collection. There are many good reasons for creating a special scheme, but it is getting more and more expensive to keep on using one. It is no longer possible to consider only what impact such a scheme may have at your own library. If you participate in a network of any sort, you also have to think about the impact your special scheme may have on network users. For example, a particularly creative classification technique that may have solved one library's problem could make trouble for others. A library that uses Dewey wanted to classify its Shakespeare collection more finely than Dewey provides for, but they did not want to create and maintain a scheme of their own, so they decided to use the Dewey root number, 822, and follow it with the numeric part of the LC classification number, 2750-3112, as they find it printed on LC cards. Imagine those records going into OCLC, and imagine what might happen when a copy cataloger in another library finds what seems to be matching member copy, and uses the classification number in the record. Then imagine what the impact is on the shelves and shelflist in the second library.

It is perhaps not as remote a possibility as might be thought; something similar actually happened to me. When the Decimal Classification Office began using Dewey 19, the MARC record did not leave a space between the class number and the indicator that shows the edition of Dewey used. Instead of reading class number, space, 2, space, 19, for example, a MARC record would read class number .219. We could not locate 219 in the schedules, but used it anyway because the Library of

Congress had used it. It was not until we had been using the schedules several months that we discovered our error, and by then we could not locate the items that were improperly classified.

COPY CATALOGING

Copy cataloging demands that several big policy decisions be made, the first and most important being: do you simply use the number you find on the copy? Catalogers all know that the Library of Congress makes an occasional error in classification or input, but many administrators want catalogers to take class numbers exactly as they find them on copy, without question. The novel *World War Three* provides a classic illustration of why this may be a bad idea. The Library of Congress had inadvertently classed it in Military History, 355, and the copy cataloger who got the book followed directions and used what she saw. After we had the book for some time, a patron brought it to the reference desk and in a confused manner asked, "This seems to be an historical account of World War III. We haven't had that one yet, have we?" We assured her that there had been no such war, and reclassified the book in fiction. The Library of Congress followed suit later. There may be few enough cases of egregious mistakes that you can still afford to follow a policy of using LC numbers as they come, but part of your classification policy implementation process must include informing the library staff of the potential complications and developing a plan for dealing with the problems when they arise.

Another issue is the allowable length of call numbers. Of course, your automated system may make this decision for you. But even if your system imposes a limit, you still have to implement that limit intelligently, and remember not just to cut the number off at a specified number of digits, but instead to cut if off at a logical, meaningful point. If copy catalogers are going to be responsible for shortening numbers, they must check the schedules to see what the logical break points would be. Failure to do so can result in dangling zeros, duplicate numbers, and other sorts of problems.

One thing that leads many libraries to use the numbers supplied by LC is that in that way they can avoid local inputting errors. But local input is not necessarily sloppy (and LC input is not necessarily perfect). If you expect your staff to be accurate, chances are they will be. In those cases where we check all the input, we find only a small percentage of error. Northwestern University recently had the same experience. In barcoding their collections they found that the error rate in spine typing and call number input was very low, but because even a low error rate in a large collection adds up to a lot of books, they modified their use of an automated system to produce spine labels from the records. That way, even if there is a mistake in input, at least the number in the catalog will match the number on the spine, and users will be able to find the pieces. And since catalogers there edit the input of their own cataloging, the responsibility for proofreading call numbers, and by extension the spine labels produced from the numbers, is placed on the people who are most likely to notice an illogical number.

RECLASSIFYING TO REFLECT REVISED CLASS NUMBERS

The ideal would be to reclassify older materials when the class numbers are revised, but that is frequently not affordable. Even with catalogs that allow subject searching it is hard to tell how confused users may be if they search a subject and retrieve materials classed in two or more different call numbers. In catalogs that allow class number searching, patrons may or may not be confused when they are not able to find everything under one number. It may be that either they do not realize they are not getting everything on one subject under one call number, or possibly they may be so used to the problem that they have no expectation of finding all material that's relevant to their search under the same call number. In general, users are probably more likely to think they ought to find everything they want under the same *subject heading*. For libraries with open stacks, one low-tech solution to the problem of materials split by a change in call number may be to put dummy blocks on the shelves to show the split and tell where the rest of the books on that subject can be found.

Of course it is one thing to have different materials split in a single library because of a single policy, and another thing to have the *same* item classed differently in different libraries that share a union catalog. This is a problem that rarely mattered before widespread use of library automation, but because online catalogs are often union catalogs, they bring with them a whole new range of classification policy problems. For example, I am presently working with a GEAC system that is shared by two libraries with a combined total of 15 branches and 405,000 bibliographic records representing 1.2 million items. We are using the 19th edition of Dewey as applied by the Library of Congress, while our companion library is using an earlier edition. Neither of us is likely to change the edition we use (except *we* will adopt the 20th edition when it is issued), so we have a real problem with patrons not knowing what number is used by which library. At the bibliographic level the system does not indicate which number is associated with which library, so we have to specify that the copy-specific call number had to be the number that was indexed in the local online catalog.

Most libraries do not maintain public shelflists, but an online catalog that offers call number access essentially makes shelflists available to the public. Perhaps it will be necessary to devise the machine equivalent of the dummy on the shelf, to put in online databases to indicate a split file, or else develop an authority structure for classification numbers that will provide guidance between parts of a split subject file.

CLASSIFICATION POLICY AND THE ONLINE CATALOG

There are many other issues relating to classification that need to be taken into account in the design of an online catalog. One old policy that many are going to pay for is a policy of changing call numbers on cards and books, but not in OCLC or RLIN records. When libraries that follow this practice load their archival tapes into an online catalog, or utilize the tapes to generate a library holdings tape, the classification number that is loaded will be the last one that was entered into the database. If numbers are not updated on the network, the numbers that appear in the catalog will be the old numbers, and may not match the books on the shelves.

The Pasadena Public Library currently has the reverse situation. The library undertook a major reclassification project to upgrade the entire collection to Dewey 19. The numbers in the database and on the spines of affected books were changed, but we were so certain that we would soon be implementing an online catalog that we decided not to change the cards. That project was started in 1981, and it will be at least three more years before we have enough terminals to accommodate the needs of our users so that we can remove the card catalogs. Now, because so many items are not accessible through the card catalog, some librarians are threatening to put up signs at the catalogs that say, "This catalog lies. Check the computer catalog." This situation arises from making a classification policy and then only implementing it part way.

After you have a machine-readable database, it has to be maintained just as the card catalog needed to be maintained, but the procedures to be followed are definitely different, and different things may matter. Unless you have an integrated automation system, you may have more than one place to keep the call number current. You will have to maintain your archival files, be they local or part of a bibliographic utility. And you will still have to change the spine labels.

IMPLEMENTING CLASSIFICATION POLICY

Assuming you have taken into account all the issues you need to consider when setting a classification policy, how do you implement it? The first step is planning, but this does not mean deciding what to do and writing the procedures. Planning needs to start much earlier. One responsibility we have as practitioners in classification is to monitor current developments in classification. One way to keep current on classification issues is to attend meetings of the Association for Library Collections and Technical Services (ALCTS) Subject Analysis Committee, which makes recommendations that will affect how materials will be classified in the future. You should also try to go to programs on classification. Read the literature. Be aware that online catalogs have opened up a whole new world of information retrieval. You are then less likely to make a decision that almost immediately turns out to be wrong because of some external development.

Besides informing yourself of what is happening in the profession, you also need to review your own library's past practices. Become familiar with what used to be done at your library—not just what you *say* you did, but what you *actually* did. Analyze what effect a proposed new policy will have on the old one and vice-versa. Think about what you are doing. Think about all the decisions made by your predecessors that make you scream. Before you deviate from any national or network standard, think about what your successor is going to say about you, think twice about what you are going to be doing to a national database, and think again about what the people who will use your records are going to say.

In developing local policy, it is critical to have catalogers and classifiers actively involved. The classifiers should not have the only say in a decision, but if technical service personnel are not given an active role in determining classification policy, a plan developed may turn out to be unworkable. If technical services librarians do not take an active role in setting policy, administrators will continue to believe that the call number is only a shelf location device, and that decisions about classification can be made without paying careful attention to all possible ramifications.

Just as classifiers should not make policy to suit just themselves, public services staff should also not be allowed to set policy without consultation and support from technical services. I am certain, for instance, that the decision to gather all the Pasadena materials together in one number was made in response to what someone thought was user need. I am just as certain that the decision on how to accomplish it was not made by a cataloger. Make certain that other ways of gathering materials are considered. And most certainly consider the long-term implications—collection growth, changing user needs, the evolution of the classification system, and technological changes.

An example of a classification decision that was made by non-catalogers where long-range impact was not considered is haunting the Pasadena Library right now. The library has a genealogy collection of approximately 4,000 titles, and a very active group of genealogists who are not at all reluctant to tell the library what they think needs to be done with these materials. Until recently rather short numbers were used on everything in the collections, and the genealogical materials on individual families and histories were classed in 929.2. In our desire to keep the numbers short, a geographic area number was not added to 929.2, which resulted in materials on Ireland sitting next to materials on South Carolina, next to books on particular families, and so forth. The genealogists did not like this (and who could blame them?), so they suggested that we put the histories of genealogy of specific locations in the respective history numbers, leaving only genealogy of families in 929.2. We went along with this suggestion and have lived to regret it, because now a search of the online catalog for materials on the history of a state or country also yields the genealogy materials for that state or country. This would not be so bad, except that as new materials are added, the suggested Dewey number from LC copy is used, which is usually not all to the genealogists' liking, and much to our horror we have discovered that some of the genealogy enthusiasts are changing the numbers on the books. The catalog is not changed, the database is not changed, and OCLC is not changed. The only place the number changes is on the spine. As you might guess, it is impossible to find any of these materials through the usual methods.

Assuming that you can get all the right people involved in any classification decision, you need next to determine the scope of the project, and its priority as compared to other work that must be done. Further, you should set priorities within the proposal, since you might not be able to afford to do everything you want within the project. For instance, if you are contemplating conversion to new numbers, is there some part of the collection that is heavily weeded? If so, it may not be worth spending the time changing numbers there, since the items will be withdrawn from the collection before long. For example, we have a collection of travel books, where we do not keep anything more than two years. There is no reason to change those call numbers, since the books will be withdrawn shortly. In contrast, a sociology collection classified in Dewey, which is heavily used and is constantly being added to, would probably need to be converted, unless a split collection is acceptable. In determining if there are areas where your users can deal with a split collection, consider how heavily the collection is used, how close the new number is to the old number, and how many books are affected. If you cannot or do not think you have to reclassify the whole collection, you might consider reclassifying titles as new editions become available. Right now, for instance, whenever we get a new edition of some work we apply the new number to the new piece, and reclassify all its previous editions. A major advantage to working piecemeal like this is that it does not have a major staffing impact. You can also reclassify on request; even if you do not usually reclassify materials to reflect new numbers, you can let it be known that you welcome suggestions for particular numbers or areas that would benefit by reclassing. Of course, you have to rely on some restraint on the part of recommenders, and occasionally you have to turn someone down, but it can work.

CONCLUSION

After you have made your plans, it is time to make recommendations for policy decisions. Make certain that what you are proposing balances the needs of public and technical services and is planned within the resources and capabilities of your organization. Not every recommendation succeeds, but if you put together a well reasoned, specific proposal that stresses the positive impact on users, is clear about costs, and includes a number of options, there is a good chance of getting agreement to your proposal. If you are not well prepared, and you simply go to your administrator and announce that you are going to reclassify everything and you need six additional staff to do it, the answer you are likely to get is, "Forget it."

Administrators receiving a classification policy proposal may be too far removed from the battle lines to be aware immediately of all the things that will be affected by the change, so you will have to supply that information to them. It is always desirable to have public services support for what you want to do, which means you will have to talk to the reference librarians, find out how the users are using the catalog, and find out what the reference staff thinks the user wants. In the end, you may have to educate both the public service people and the administrators about the problems encountered and the long term implications.

Your plan should also include a cost analysis, and if possible, some estimation of the costs of *not* following your recommendation, as well as a rough timetable.

If all this seems daunting, remember that you are the expert in these matters. Presumably you were put in your position because someone thought you could handle it, and your proposals and objectives will be listened to accordingly. One thing seems clear: if the knowledgeable technical services librarians do not make decisions about classification, someone else will, and he or she may well be wrong, but *you* will have to live with the decision. Sound classification policy serves users and in the long run saves money, time, and aggravation. But sound classification policy does not just happen. It needs to be thought about, thought out, investigated, planned, followed, and supported. It is up to you to see that that happens.

11

Classification Decision-Making In California Libraries

Elizabeth Dickinson Nichols

In June 1986 Elizabeth Nichols and Jennifer Younger surveyed 356 California libraries to determine classification usage and decision-making patterns in these libraries in preparation for a plenary session paper to be given at the ALA Resources and Technical Services Division Classification Institutes (1986–87).

The questionnaires were addressed to individuals who directly supervise technical services or cataloging in each library. The list was drawn from the RLIN SPIRES name/address database supplemented by some California entries from the *American Library Directory*.[1] A copy of the questionnaire appears as Appendix 11-A.

There were 205 usable questionnaire responses returned, for a good response rate of 57.6 percent. Most California academic and public libraries were polled, along with some cooperative agencies, the State Library, and several special purpose libraries.

One caveat should be noted in analyzing the questionnaire responses. The universe in this case is California libraries. Comparative studies on libraries indicate that California libraries have larger collections and budgets than libraries in other states. For instance, the average expenditure for books in California public libraries in 1986–87 was $181,127. For U.S public libraries as a whole the average book expenditure that year was $46,147. For academic libraries in the same year the average California book expenditure was $151,178, while for U. S. academic libraries as a whole it was $102,555.[2] Library size does influence library materials classification decision-making in some respects.

Special acknowledgement is due to Carl Cousineau, Oakland Public Library, for data preparation and statistical analysis.

RELATED SURVEYS

Little exists in the literature to serve as a pattern for this survey. Two studies, however, did significantly influence the questions posed to the respondents.

In 1969 Richard Hyman polled authorities on library classification from throughout the United States and Canada and received 152 responses on questions concerning the role of classification in influencing the direct shelf approach and browsing.[3] A number of Hyman's extensive questions and responses are relevant to the present survey. For example, Hyman's respondents agreed that shelf classification is necessary to facilitate browsing (78.4 percent agreed). Browsing was seen as a valuable learning tool by 81.2 percent.[4] Respondents also gave quite positive responses (59 percent) to the statement that shelf classification is of much greater value as a locational device than as a systematic subject approach.[5]

While some specific questions asked in the present survey were similar to those posed by Hyman, the purpose of this questionnaire was broader and the universe of respondents was slightly different. This survey was directed to cataloging practitioners while Hyman concentrated his attention on experts in library shelf classification. The objective of this study was to determine how shelf classification is used in library decision-making, while Hyman was particularly interested in the relationship between open shelves, browsing, and shelf classification.

Sanford Berman reported upon another survey by Michael Klossner that influenced a portion of our questionnaire. Klossner conducted a brief poll of Wisconsin libraries using the Dewey Decimal Classification to elicit opinions concerning the justifiability of certain DDC changes, including such massive Phoenix dislocations as those in 301–309 and in 001.6 to 004-006. While two-thirds of Klossner's respondents agreed that substantial revisions of DDC are justified because of the dynamics of knowledge, many found it impossible administratively to cope with the work necessary to make major DDC changes.[6]

The present survey was also intended, in part, to determine cataloger reaction in libraries using the Dewey Decimal Classification system to Phoenix schedules and other major revisions to the DDC scheme, and the practical implementation of such changes. This, however, was just one area of concern addressed by the surveyers.

INTRODUCTORY QUESTIONS

The first question of the present survey (see Appendix 11-A at the end of this chapter) asked the "number of years you have been a head or supervisor responsible for technical services or cataloging in this and other libraries." Respondents were, on average, quite experienced, with an average of 9.2 years in the cataloging or technical services field.

The next three questions elicited demographic information. Figures 11-1, 11-2, and 11-3 show, respectively, the number and percentage of responding libraries by type, size (in book volumes), and type of classification scheme used.

FIGURE 11-1   Responses by Type of Library

Library Type	Number Responding	Percentage Responding
College	69	33.66%
University	29	14.15%
Total Academic	98	47.80%
Public	93	45.37%
Special ([1])	11	5.37%
State or Cooperative	3	1.46%
TOTAL	205	100.00%

1. Special included single subject academic libraries, e.g., theological, law, military

FIGURE 11-2   Responses by Size of Library (book Volumes)

Library Size by Book Volumes	Number Responding	Percentage Responding
Fewer than 10,000	1	.49%
10,001 to 100,000	91	44.39%
100,001 to 500,000	78	38.05%
500,001 to 1,000,000	21	10.24%
More than 1,000,000	13	6.34%
Not available ([1])	1	.49%
TOTAL	205	100.00%

1. Non-profit cooperative responded N.A.

FIGURE 11-3 Responses by Type of Classification

Classification Scheme	Number Responding	Percentage Responding
LC Classification	80	39.02%
Dewey Classification	124	60.49%
Other ([1])	1	.49%
TOTAL	205	100.00%

1. A health sciences library using NLM classification.

The questionnaire asked whether the collection was primarily in open stack or closed stack shelving (question 5). Since 201 of 205 responded open stack, results were not significant enough to be used to determine differences between classification policy and practice by this factor.

GENERAL CATALOGING RESPONSES

Respondents were asked to list their sources for cataloging copy (question 6). More than one response could be listed per questionnaire. The results are shown in Figure 11-4. Bibliographic utilities come out at the top of the list of cataloging copy sources, followed by Library of Congress-provided manual tools—Cataloging in Publication, LC cards, *National Union Catalog*, and vendor/book jobber sources.

FIGURE 11-4 Sources for Cataloging Copy

Source	Number of Responses	Percentage of Responses
Bibliographic utility	142	39.44%
CIP/NUC/LC cards	113	31.39%
Vendor or Book jobber	75	20.83%
Other computerized	13	3.62%
Processing center	12	3.33%
BPR/Reviewing source	5	1.39%
TOTAL	360 ([1])	100.00%

1. More than one answer per respondent.

Of libraries with collections over 100,000 book volumes, only 5 (4.5 percent of such libraries) had no access to automated means for cataloging. All others in this size range employed a bibliographic utility, had a local computer system, maintained cataloging through a computer-output-microform supplier, utilized a processing center with access to an online system, or some combination of the above.

Of the 91 small libraries surveyed (collections under 100,000 book volumes) responses on cataloging copy source were quite different. Of these libraries 42 (46 percent) used only manual sources for cataloging.

Clearly, the bulk of California academic and public libraries, however, have access to some labor-saving technology to assist in the cataloging and classification process, or have delegated this activity to a processing center.

Question 7 asked about staffing patterns. According to the results, the average number of staff performing cataloging and classification in responding libraries is 4.52 full-time equivalents (FTE), comprised of 1.76 FTE professionals, 1.96 FTE paraprofessionals, and .79 FTE clerical staff. The average number of titles cataloged by this staff is 1,447.4 per FTE annually.

Figure 11-5 delineates titles cataloged per FTE by type of library, library collection size and by the classification scheme that is primarily used. The work output varies markedly when broken out by these variables.

FIGURE 11-5   Average Titles Cataloged Per FTE by Library Type, Collection Size and Classification Scheme

Type	Titles Cataloged Per FTE
College	1120
University	1609
Special	1526
Public	1410
State/Coop.	1268
Size (Bk. Vol.)	
10,000-100,000	633
100,001-500,000	1942
500,001-1 m.	2088
1,000,001+	1427
Classification	
LCC	1529
DDC	1369

Caution should be exercised in using these averages to compare with specific institutions. The collection being cataloged, the type of cataloging tools, the level of staff available, administrative policies, other projects utilizing cataloging staff, and a host of other factors affect the results. There was, therefore, little consistency in the responses by libraries of the same type or size, or by those reporting the same number of titles cataloged per year.

In an effort to find greater comparability, however, the author recalculated titles cataloged per FTE for California public library respondents who use bibliographic utilities. The resulting averages by size of library are detailed in Figure 11-6.

FIGURE 11-6 Titles Cataloged Per FTE in California Public Libraries Using Bibliographic Utilities

Library Size by Book Volumes	Number Respondents	Titles Cataloged Per FTE
10,001 - 100,000	14	1772
100,001 - 500,000	30	3084
500,000 - 1,000,000	9	3001
More than 1,000,000	5	2653

Clearly, use of bibliographic utilities greatly improves cataloging productivity.

Further research is needed to pinpoint the impact of other types of cataloging tools on productivity. In addition, without further research the reasons for differences in cataloging output by size, type of library, and classification scheme used can only be speculated upon.

The author suspects that cataloging productivity in smaller libraries is affected negatively by the lack of automated cataloging resources and by the lack of cataloging specialists to do this work. Larger libraries are hindered somewhat in productivity by the need to devote more staff time to original cataloging and classification. Economies of scale, on the other hand, may offset some of the productivity loss of larger libraries as staff develop higher quantitative standards through specialization.

Dewey libraries find lower percentages of acceptable classification copy, as will be discussed later in the survey. This may account, in part, for lower productivity figures among libraries using DDC.

Nearly 81 percent of the responding libraries require professionals on the cataloging staff to have formal cataloging and classification training (question 7a). The formal training requirement, understandably, was reported less frequently for paraprofessionals (12.7 percent) or clericals (1.5 percent).

CLASSIFICATION RESPONSES

Staffing

There are few set patterns among California libraries as to the level of staff assigned to classify library materials, with the exception of those cataloged without the benefit of copy (question 8d). Of those who responded to the question, 87.6 percent use professional staff to do original cataloging and classification, while 7.2 percent responded that both professional and paraprofessional staff assign call numbers on original cataloging.

There is evidence that availability of cataloging copy has not eliminated professionals from making classification decisions. Professional catalogers in California, at least, are quite heavily involved in classifying materials with LC copy. In 59.9 percent of responding libraries, professionals, or a combination of professionals and paraprofessionals, assign call numbers to items with LC copy. On the other hand, 87.6 percent of responding libraries use only professionals to assign classification numbers to original cataloging. Another 7.2 percent of respondents use both professionals and paraprofessionals, while only 4.6 percent use only paraprofessionals to assign classification numbers to items with no cataloging source copy.

The respondents were asked to list exceptions to normal staffing levels for particular types of materials. The most frequently mentioned exceptions were for AV materials and fiction, which are more typically handled by paraprofessionals in these libraries. Other types of exceptions were foreign language materials, biographies, bibliographies, documents, serials, juvenile titles, curriculum materials, mass market paperbacks, accession only items, and new editions or added copies of existing titles. These were not always listed by respondents according to staff level assigned to do the classification.

Call Number Acceptance on Cataloging Copy

Of respondents to 8a, "Do you accept call numbers on cataloging copy," 86.8 percent answered "Yes" or "Most" for materials with Library of Congress copy, while 56.4 percent responded affirmatively with non-LC contributed copy.

The majority of responding California libraries (65 percent) will sometimes make minor call number adjustments from that found on cataloging copy, while 34.8 percent make such minor changes often, and only 1 percent admitted to no change (question 8b).

The reasons for making minor adjustments to call numbers on cataloging copy were quite evenly divided. Of 197 who make minor call number adjustments, 76.1 percent match a local variation, 71.1 percent match to earlier editions, and 53.3 percent shorten the number (the latter primarily among Dewey libraries). A large number of other reasons for making small call number adjustments were noted, including:

- to meet the special needs of a given segment of the collection;
- to add Cutters or prefixes;
- to avoid shelflist conflicts;
- to bring like subjects together;
- to make the copy fit the latest edition of LCC or DDC;
- to fix errors on the copy; and
- to use a number that may be equally correct, according to the classification scheme, but fits the local collection better.

The respondents were asked to estimate the percentage of cataloging copy with no usable call number (question 8c). Of 171 responses, the average for unusable LC copy was 11.1 percent. Of 153 answering the question with regard to non-LC contributed copy, the average was 24 percent. The responses were much different when analyzed by type of classification used. Dewey libraries found many fewer usable call numbers as shown in Figure 11-7.

FIGURE 11-7 Percent of Copy Without Usable Call Number

	LC Classification	Dewey Classification
LC copy	5.2%	13.95%
Contributed copy	14.5%	29.96%

The degree to which Dewey libraries find that they must originally classify or considerably alter class numbers even on LC copy has administrative implications for these libraries. More staff time may be necessary to classify by Dewey because of the more limited acceptable copy. This hypothesis may be borne out by the lower than average number of titles cataloged by Dewey libraries per FTE (see Figure 11-5).

RECLASSIFICATION

A surprising result of the survey (see question 9) was the high number of libraries in California that have undertaken reclassification projects. Fifty-eight libraries reported that reclassification projects were completed, or were presently underway. Twenty-one of these were begun in the 1960s, 18 in the 1970s, 14 in the 1980s, two prior to the 1960s, and three were in planning.

Most reclass projects (71.9 percent) were from Dewey to LC classification schemes. One respondent reported a change from modified LC to standard, three from a local system to LC, four from another scheme to

LC, six from modified Dewey to standard DDC, and two from a local system to DDC.

Thirty-six (62.1 percent) reclassified the entire collection, while 14 responding libraries reclassed a special collection only, seven changed a part of the collection (unspecified which), and one reclassed new materials only.

The majority of reclass libraries (43 of 58) were academic. Ten were public, and five were special.

California libraries did not list any one primary reason for the reclassification decision (question 9e). The reason given most weight as either a primary or contributing factor was growth in collection size. Respondents from several libraries believed that their collections had outgrown the ability of the old class scheme to organize materials with sufficient specificity. Other frequently mentioned reasons included timing in relation to an automation project, greater availability of LC classification numbers on cataloging copy, and, as a contributing factor especially, requirements of public service or administrative staff.

Reclass libraries agreed, however, on a predominant outcome of the reclassification project (question 9f). Reclassification caused at least moderate confusion and inconvenience for patrons and/or staff, according to 25 of the 58 responding reclass libraries. Another 13 reported that the project triggered weeding of the collection, while 8 mentioned that it had improved workflow. Other possible effects were mentioned less frequently.

ONLINE IMPACT ON CLASSIFICATION

It is equally surprising how few respondents believe the online catalog has, or will have, any relevancy to classification policy. Only 57, or 27.8 percent, of those answering the question, believed there is a connection, while the rest either responded "No" or "Not applicable." Of those who anticipated an impact, 25 believed the effect to be primarily that "more types of materials will be classified to provide more complete online access through call number searches." Another 17 felt the primary result of the online catalog is that "closer classification (e.g., more complete enumeration) of items will be practiced." Some of the other impacts or observations enumerated were:

- improved call number accuracy;
- more uniform product will be created for a regional catalog;
- local practice will be minimized;
- the paper shelflist will be discontinued; and
- classification is a less rigid tool for browsing in the online catalog than subject headings.

One might hypothesize that the low positive response rate concerning online catalog impact results from several factors. The date of the survey, 1986, was relatively early in the implementation process for online catalogs in California libraries. A more serious speculation might be that few cataloging librarians have been involved in the planning process for online catalogs. Possibly, few respondents had read recent research reports on the link between the online catalog and classification.

Cataloging expertise in planning for an online public access catalog is *vital* to the successful implementation of such a catalog. Further research is needed to determine the degree to which catalogers were involved in the online catalog process and to further delineate the areas of impact on cataloging and classification practice as the catalog format is altered from manual or computer-output-microform to online.

CLASSIFICATION ASSUMPTIONS

Respondents were asked to mark the relative importance of a number of assumptions, or principles, which underpin their classification decisions. Other assumptions could be added, if desired.

Results were analyzed by type and size of library and classification scheme used. A chi-square test was applied to determine which of the assumptions were answered with significant difference for various sizes and types of libraries.

The survey asked cataloging administrators to indicate how important classification is in general, and to their libraries in particular. Their responses provide evidence that cataloging administrators continue to believe that classification should serve the purposes stated in the survey questionnaire.

The 13 assumptions are listed below. For purposes of identification on related tables, each has been given a convenient "handle" in quotation marks. In addition, the average response of all survey participants on a scale of 1 (lowest) to 10 (highest) is recorded following the assumptions. A score of between 9 and 10 means that the respondents, on average, believed the assumption to be very important to classification decision making. A score in the range of 7 or 8 might be considered an indication of a quite important assumption. Those in a middling range of 5 or 6 are somewhat important, while those at the bottom of the ranking were seen as unimportant to the decision process in their particular library.

A. Classification is primarily important in this library as a shelf location device ("Location device"). Average score: 8.0
B. Classification is primarily important in this library as a mechanism for bringing together like materials ("Collocation"). Average score: 9.0

C. The classification number determined by our source for cataloging copy is accepted without regard to where other materials are in our collection ("Blind acceptance"). Average score: 2.9

D. Browser expectations with regard to where to find the item is an important consideration in our classification policy ("Browser expectation"). Average score: 6.9

E. It is important to carry the classification number out to its fullest extent in order to keep masses of materials from building up under one number ("Close classification"). Average score: 4.0

F. It is important to truncate classification numbers at some point in order to make numbers easier to remember ("Truncate as memory jog"). Average score: 4.7

G. It is important to truncate classification numbers at some point in order to keep materials from getting too scattered on the shelves ("Truncate for collocation"). Average score: 5.0

H. The latest classification schedules must be accepted for the sake of efficiency and cost savings ("Efficiency/cost concern"). Average score: 6.7

I. Older editions and/or translations should be reclassified to current classification numbers in order to prevent dislocations of material when we are cataloging the latest editions into updated classification numbers ("Reclass to avoid dislocation"). Average score: 5.6

J. In our closed shelf library the exact classification number used makes little difference ("Closed stack: classification irrelevant"). Average score: 2.6

K. In our open stack library shelf location is very important to user retrieval of specific material ("Open stack: class for known item retrieval"). Average score: 8.7

L. In our open stack library the retrieval by users of related materials, and thus the logic of where each item is put, is very important ("Open stack: class for collocation"). Average score: 8.3

M. In our open stack library users should be able to find materials by going directly to the shelves once they have determined the general subject location ("Open stack: Class for subject access"). Average score: 7.7

Statements A and B (that classification serves as a locational device and that it brings like materials together) represent the primary theoretical roles served by shelf classification. The other assumptions express various practical implications that may enter into decision-making in specific library settings. Items C and H imply cost and efficiency concerns. Item D considers the needs of browsers. Assumptions E, F, and G relate to the degree of enumeration practiced by respondents' libraries. Statement I relates to the importance of reclassification to keep materials together. Assumptions J, K, L, and M elicit opinions concerning the impact of classification on closed and open stack collections.

Questions relating to the two fundamental principles, classification use as locational device and as a means for collocation by subject, received the highest rankings. Of greatest concern is the subject collocation aspect of classification. Interestingly, regard for the browser played a fairly significant role in determining classification policy in the minds of respondents, as did concern for efficiency and cost. The respondents were quite negative about the suggestion that classification on cataloging copy be accepted without regard to past practice at the specific library. Scores on the assumption that a closed stack library might not need to be concerned with classification were particularly negative. Apparently classification serves an important function in the minds of cataloging administrators, despite the type of shelf access.

Each of three variables that might influence how libraries approach the importance of classifying library collections were analyzed specifically. These variables are library size, library type, and the shelf classification scheme used.

Figures 11-8, 11-9, and 11-10 show the total number of respondents who gave a 1 to 10 ranking, and their average rankings broken out by library size, type, and classification scheme. Chi-square test results for each assumption are also listed. Asterisks denote significant differences in responses by size, type of library, or class scheme.

Assumptions by Size

For assumptions A and B the average responses for size indicate that use of classification as a shelf location and shelf collocation tool is important in all libraries with only slight variation in responses. However, when the aspect of open stack access is introduced, the smaller libraries show a significantly stronger sense of the importance of classification for purposes of subject retrieval and collocation of like materials than did those libraries with collections over 500,000 book volumes. On the other hand, smaller libraries are significantly more negative concerning the idea of blindly accepting classification given on cataloging copy.

Assumptions by Library Type

The assumptions that differ significantly in response by type of library include the three that relate to enumeration and the assumption that covers browser concern. While all respondents believe classification assists the browser, the role of classification in public libraries is significantly more directed to browser needs than in academic libraries. Public libraries are much more likely to truncate call numbers than are academic libraries.

FIGURE 11-8 Classification Assumption Importance by Library Size (Volumes)

ASSUMPTIONS	10,000 - 100,000 VOLS.		100,001 - 500,000 VOLS.		500,001 - 1 MILLION VOLS.		OVER 1 MILLION VOLS.		CHI-SQ. (1)
	NUMBER RESPONDENTS	AVERAGE RESPONSE	NUMBER RESPONDENTS	AVERAGE RESPONSE	NUMBER RESPONDENTS	AVERAGE RESPONSE	NUMBER RESPONDENTS	AVERAGE RESPONSE	* = SIGNIFICANT
A	78	8.2	72	7.8	18	8.1	12	7.5	20.80
B	84	8.9	76	9.3	19	8.1	12	8.5	28.60
C	76	2.9	73	2.4	19	4.8	12	3.8	55.60*
D	82	6.8	71	7.2	18	5.7	12	6.7	26.30
E	68	4.3	65	3.8	14	3.0	9	4.4	33.90
F	66	4.6	53	4.8	11	4.3	11	5.0	17.30
G	68	5.0	58	5.1	12	4.7	7	4.7	27.10
H	67	6.3	68	6.6	17	8.2	12	8.0	40.90
I	78	6.3	69	5.7	18	3.0	13	4.9	37.40
J	16	2.9	13	1.5	3	5.0	7	2.8	35.90
K	86	8.7	73	8.9	19	7.7	13	8.2	43.40
L	86	8.4	75	8.6	17	7.0	13	7.8	53.20*
M	84	8.0	72	7.8	19	6.3	12	6.5	50.20*

(1) Degrees of freedom= 30
Chi-square is significant at: 43.773 for .05
46.979 for .025
50.892 for .01
53.672 for .005

A= LOCATION DEVICE
B= COLLOCATION
C= BLIND ACCEPTANCE
D= BROWSER EXPECTATION
E= CLOSE CLASSIFICATION
F= TRUNCATION AS MEMORY JOG
G= TRUNCATION FOR COLLOCATION

H= EFFICIENCY/COST CONCERN
I= RECLASS TO AVOID DISLOCATION
J= CLOSED STACK: CLASSIF. IRRELEVANT
K= OPEN STACK: CLASS FOR KNOWN ITEMS
L= OPEN STACK: CLASS FOR COLLOCATION
M= OPEN STACK: CLASS FOR SUBJECT ACCESS

FIGURE 11-9 Classification Assumption Importance by Library Type

Assumptions	Academic		Public		Chi-sq. Contingency (1) Asterisk = Significant
	Number Respondents	Average Response	Number Respondents	Average Response	
A	85	7.9	84	8.2	9.79
B	94	8.9	86	9.0	6.23
C	86	3.7	84	2.1	17.60
D	92	6.5	80	7.4	20.60*
E	68	4.8	78	2.9	25.20*
F	63	3.6	68	6.0	28.20*
G	67	3.8	69	6.4	33.00*
H	78	6.7	76	6.4	9.29
I	84	6.3	83	4.8	15.30
J	21	2.4	16	2.6	4.78
K	93	8.7	89	8.7	12.40
L	93	8.4	87	8.4	9.85
M	90	7.5	88	8.0	15.10

(1) Degrees of freedom = 10
Chi-square is significant at: 18.307 for .05
20.483 for .025
23.209 for .01
25.183 for .005

A= Location Device
B = Collocation
C = Blind Acceptance
D = Browser Expectation
E = Close Classification
F = Truncation as Memory Jog
G = Truncation for Collocation

H = Efficiency/cost Concern
I = Reclass to Avoid Dislocation
J = Closed Stack: Classif. Irrelevant
K = Open Stack: Class for Known Items
L = Open Stack: Class for Collocation
M = Open Stack: Class for Subject Access

FIGURE 11-10   Classification Assumption Importance by Classification Scheme

	Library of Congress		Dewey Decimal Class		
Assumptions	Number Respondents	Average Response	Number Respondents	Average Response	Chi-sq. Contingency (1) Asterisk = significant
A	69	7.7	112	8.1	6.34
B	77	8.9	116	9.0	6.04
C	72	4.1	108	2.1	30.10*
D	75	6.2	110	7.3	19.80*
E	55	5.5	103	3.1	33.30*
F	47	2.8	94	5.6	46.80*
G	49	2.8	97	6.1	65.10*
H	63	7.4	102	6.2	16.50
I	69	6.4	109	5.2	13.80
J	15	2.9	24	2.4	4.50
K	75	8.5	117	8.8	9.43
L	75	8.0	116	8.5	15.10
M	71	7.2	117	7.9	14.50

(1) Degrees of freedom = 10
Chi-square is significant at: 18.307 for .05
                             20.483 for .025
                             23.209 for .01
                             25.183 for .005

A = Location Device
B = Collocation
C = Blind Acceptance
D = Browser Expectation
E = Close Classification
F = Truncation as Memory Jog
G = Truncation for Collocation

H = Efficiency/cost Concern
I = Reclass to Avoid Dislocation
J = Closed Stack: Classif. Irrelevant
K = Open Stack: Class for Known Items
L = Open Stack: Class for Collocation
M = Open Stack: Class for Subject Access

Assumptions by Classification Scheme

The reason for the difference in importance of complete classification enumeration between academic and public libraries is probably corrolated directly with the fact that public libraries tend to use Dewey Decimal Classification, while at least larger academic libraries are in the Library of Congress Classification camp.

In fact, the three enumeration questions also show significant differences in response by classification scheme used. Dewey libraries are more likely to truncate, while LC libraries are more likely to completely enumerate the classification for each title.

Dewey libraries reject the notion of blind acceptance, while the catalog administrators of LC libraries give at least begrudging acknowledgement to the possibility that LCC on cataloging copy may be accepted without regard to what is already on the shelf. By the same token, Dewey libraries are somewhat more likely to consider the browser, perhaps because DDC is traditionally considered more "user friendly" to the serendipitous library patron.

There were a large number of other classification assumptions listed. However, most just clarified assumptions given on the form. For example, four individuals mentioned that reclassification is important, but that there is no time, nor staff, to do it. Another four gave specific types of material that are particularly important to keep together (e.g., sets, series) as per assumptions B ("Collocation") and L ("Open stack: class for collocation"). Six believed particularly in minimizing costs while getting materials to the shelves as quickly as possible. Three mentioned that the spine label must be easy to read, which is related, perhaps, to assumption F ("Truncation as memory jog").

There were also some unique insights. Two mentioned that automation and/or spine label programs have contributed to the need to truncate call numbers. One respondent each mentioned that classification must be tailored to patron requests, that classification is a tool for weeding, and that the call number is important in online catalog searching.

SPECIAL MATERIAL TYPES

Figure 11-11 gives the frequency by which various methods of materials organization (question 12 in Appendix 11-A) are used. All responses are tallied. The data can also be analyzed by type, size, and classification scheme of responding libraries.

Type of Library

According to survey results, academic libraries are more likely to classify (using LCC in particular) all of the formats listed. There are only a few exceptions. Most notably, periodicals are more often organized alphabetically, or unclassed. State and federal documents are also frequently separated from the LC or Dewey collection by Superintendant of Documents or state document number (for Depository collections, at least).

FIGURE 11-11 Classification Schemes for Special Materials

TYPE OF MATERIAL	FREQUENCY		DISTRIBUTION						
	DDC	LCC	ACCESSION NUMBER	ANSCR	ALPHA/ UNCLASSED	DOC #	LOCAL	NA	TOTAL
MASS MARKET PB'S	53	44	6	0	29	0	4	32	168
SOUND RECORDINGS	15	9	56	33	5	0	19	28	165
VIDEO/FILMS, ETC.	10	15	60	1	15	0	15	50	166
MICROFORMS	17	24	20	0	39	1	6	42	149
RARE BOOKS/MSS	58	46	5	0	3	0	5	78	195
FEDERAL DOCUMENTS	48	41	1	0	9	35	2	50	186
STATE DOCUMENTS	48	40	0	0	10	22	9	50	179
LOCAL DOCUMENTS	58	43	4	0	10	4	12	44	175
MAPS	11	26	12	0	36	0	9	58	152
PERIODICALS	3	19	3	0	86	0	6	24	141
ROMAN. FOR. LANG.	85	59	1	0	2	0	2	52	201
NON-ROM. FOR. LANG.	62	50	3	0	3	0	3	73	194
MUSIC & SCORES	56	44	4	0	4	0	4	77	189

NA = Not Applicable

Public libraries also classify (primarily by Dewey classification) many of the special formats. Exceptions include sound recordings (often classed by ANSCR), microforms (unclassified), state and federal documents (in document number order), and maps and periodicals (unclassed or treated alphabetically).

Library Size

Not surprisingly, the smaller libraries did not report that they collect many of the formats listed, particularly microforms, rare books, maps, non-Roman language materials, music, and scores. Those that do collect tend to classify by their primary scheme mass market paperbacks, rare books, documents of all types, foreign language material, music and scores. Microforms and periodicals are generally arranged alpha/unclassed, while video and sound recordings are accessioned.

Medium and large libraries are much more likely to collect a broad spectrum of material. Among the larger libraries the categories most likely to be classed according to a scheme other than LCC or DDC are state and federal documents, while videos, film, and sound recordings are frequently merely accessioned.

Classification

Libraries that use LCC are very likely to classify according to their main scheme when collecting the various formats. Exceptions include sound recordings, video/film (accessioned), and periodicals (alpha/unclassed).

There is a much more pronounced scatter of materials handling practice among Dewey libraries. Besides "normal" book materials, only paperbacks, rare books, documents of all types, foreign language material, and music and scores are likely to be classed in DDC. Sound recordings are most commonly classed by ANSCR or accessioned; video/films are accessioned; microforms, maps, and periodicals are shelved alphabetically or otherwise left unclassed.

Primary reasons for use of alternate materials handling for the following types of material included:

- Mass market nonfiction paper-backs   Too time-consuming and too costly to catalog and classify.
- Sound recordings   Alternate schedule is more appropriate for the format.
- Video/Film   Special collection material.
- Microforms   Special collection material.
- Federal and state documents   Alternate schedule is more appropriate for the format.

- Local documents   Special collection material.
- Maps   Administrative or public service pref-
                             erence; too costly to catalog and clas-
                             sify.
- Magazines   Special collection material.
- Music and scores   Special collection material.

The libraries were asked if all materials are intershelved (question 12b). The 15 libraries responding "Yes" included eight academic, four special, and three public. Eight are libraries in the 10,000 to 100,000 volume range. These smaller libraries might find it easier to house varying media types together than the larger libraries. The inter-shelvers are also overwhelmingly LCC institutions (11 of 15).

DEWEY USE

Dewey libraries were asked whether the latest edition of DDC is accepted (see question 13 in Appendix A). Responses were received from 122 of 124 possible Dewey libraries. Of these, 76.2 percent listed an unqualified "Yes," 7.4 percent reported "No," and 16.4 percent use DDC latest edition "Partly."

Most use the phoenix schedules, most notably, the completely revised segments for 301–307 and 004–006. However, of those that have not accepted one or more phoenix schedules, the primary reason is that respondents feel they do not have the staff to do reclassifications.

Of those that have rejected all, or some, complete Dewey revisions, the second most common reason is that these major tinkerings with the schedules have dislocated materials from like items on the shelves. From this standpoint, rejection of Dewey phoenix schedules may be seen as consistent with high scores on assumptions B and L (dealing with the importance of keeping like materials together).

Respondents sometimes commented on their exceptions to Dewey. The most common areas given were the changes in the 300s, the 800s, and Indians of North America (970). In general, these libraries liked to keep new editions, or new material on a subject already in the collection next to the older material without reclassifying to the newer number.

Most California Dewey libraries (81.1 percent) shorten call numbers. The most popular method of truncation is to cut the number off at a prime mark. This relates to highly favorable responses among Dewey libraries to assumptions F and G concerning call number truncation.

LIBRARY OF CONGRESS CLASSIFICATION

As was the case in other responses, the LC libraries were much more unified in their answers to questions on acceptance of latest class schedules (see questions 14 and 15 in Appendix 11-A). With 77 of a possible 80 libraries responding, 72 (93.5 percent) accept the latest LC class schedules, while one (1.3 percent) does not, and four (5.2 percent) do in part. Almost as many, 71, accept the latest literature, language and geographic tables, while six partly accept. For most (90.8 percent) answers to the latest edition question applied to both copy and original cataloging.

Exceptions to most recent edition usage were noted, however, particularly for Z (Bibliography), which received 31 responses; PZ (Fiction and Juvenile Literature—30 responses); and for K (Law—4 responses). It is interesting to note the high number of exceptions listed, even though many of these libraries also categorized themselves as accepting the latest editions without qualification.

SUMMARY

The survey affords some insight into the behavior, and the reasons behind the practices, of California catalogers and classifiers.

For the most part, the most current editions of Dewey or LC classification schedules are used, but not with blind acceptance. Classifying without regard to the materials currently on the shelves or without regard to how the material will be used would run counter to deeply held conviction.

Catalogers in Dewey libraries, and those working in smaller libraries where sheer volume of material is less likely to dictate factory-like production, seem most likely to follow through on classification review and revision. Perhaps, also, Dewey libraries and smaller libraries have fewer resources available for cataloging copy, and thus there is more original work to do to put materials on the shelves where they are likely to be found.

Administrators responsible for cataloging policy must particularly take note of the conditions inherent in our library's size, type and classification scheme used, as well as the basic assumptions concerning the importance of classification to the organization of library materials, in order to effectively manage this essential function. They need to ask:

- What makes classification so important in theory?
- In practice, which classification considerations are most important in *this* library? The response will be somewhat different depending on the library size, type, classification scheme used, and a host of other variables, which must be identified and understood.

- Do our current policies and procedures correspond with what we have identified as important in theory and practice? If not, what can be done about it; how can change be best implemented?

This should be a sufficient battery of questions to keep the cataloging or technical services administrator busy for a while!

REFERENCES

1. *American Library Directory*, vol. 1, 39th ed. (New York: R. R. Bowker, 1986), 69–204.
2. *The Bowker Annual of Library and Book Trade Information,* 33d ed. (New York: R. R. Bowker, 1988), 348, 351. Averaged from book acquisition expenditure totals for California and for U. S. libraries as a whole in Tables 1 and 2.
3. Richard Joseph Hyman, *Access to Library Collections* (Metuchen, N.J.: The Scarecrow Press, 1972), 230–3.
4. Ibid., 325–7.
5. Ibid., 266–7.
6. Sanford Berman, "Consumer Beware," *Technicalities* 5 (June 1985): 14–15. This is part of a four-part series on this survey. The other sections of the report are included in Berman's "Consumer Beware" columns in *Technicalities* 5 (August 1985): 7–9; October 1985: 13–15; (December 1985): 9–11.

Appendix

LIBRARY MATERIALS CLASSIFICATION DECISION-MAKING SURVEY

A Study Being Prepared for the ALA/RTSD Classification Institutes

Name of respondent_____

Position_____

Library name_____

Phone_____

Check here to receive a summary of survey results_____

1. Number of years you have been a head or supervisor responsible for technical services or cataloging in this and other libraries _____

2. Your present library type:

_____College   _____Public
_____University   _____State or Cooperative System
_____School   _____Other
_____Special

3. Please indicate the range your library falls within in number of monographs (book volumes) in the total library collection.

_____Fewer than 10,000   _____500,001 to 1,000,000
_____10,001 to 100,000   _____More than 1,000,000
_____100,001 to 500,000   _____Not available

4. Our library catalogs its main collections using:

_____Library of Congress Classification
_____Dewey Decimal Classification
_____Other--Please list_____

5. We have primarily an

_____Open stack collection   _____Closed stack collection

6. Our library uses the following sources for cataloging copy (check any that apply):

_____Bibliographic utility (OCLC/RLIN)   _____LC cards/NUC
_____COM vendor   _____CIP
_____Mini- or microcomputer local   _____Processing center
       system
_____MARCFICHE or similar service   _____Book jobber kits
_____None
_____Other--Specify:_____

LIBRARY MATERIALS CLASSIFICATION DECISION-MAKING SURVEY

7a. Cataloging and classification is performed in this library by
the following numbers and level(s) of staff (including
supervisory and administrative staff involved to some degree with
this activity):

	Number Full Time Equivalents	Formal Cataloging Training Required (Other than On-the Job) Yes No
Professional (Librarian, Media Specialist, etc.)	_____	_____ _____
Paraprofessional (Lib. Asst., Lib. Technical Asst., Lib. Assoc., etc.)	_____	_____ _____
Clerical (Typist Clerk, Clerk, Lib.Services Asst., Lib. Aide, Student Asst.,etc.)	_____	_____ _____

b. Number of titles cataloged in most recent complete fiscal
year by the above staff_____.

8a. Do you accept call numbers on cataloging copy?

	Yes	Most	Some	No
On Library of Congress copy	____	____	____	____
On non-LC cataloging copy	____	____	____	____

b. Do you make minor adjustments?

Often_____   Sometimes_____   Never_____

If Often or Sometimes, why? (Mark any that apply.)

_____To match numbers on earlier editions
_____To match a local variation
_____To shorten number
_____Other reasons (please list):_____

_____

_____

8c. What percent of copy has no usable call number for your
library? (Estimate if not readily known.)

Percent of Copy
With No Usable
Call Number

LC copy   _____%

Contributed copy   _____%

LIBRARY MATERIALS CLASSIFICATION DECISION-MAKING SURVEY

8d. What level of staff (professional, paraprofessional, clerical) generally assigns call numbers for:

                              Staff Level

    LC copy cataloging   _____

    Contributed copy   _____

    Original cataloging   _____

    List major exceptions, e.g., for AV materials, accession type materials, etc._____

    _____

9. Our library has undergone/is undergoing a reclassification project:

a. _____Yes   _____No   IF NO, SKIP TO # 10

b. Reclassification began approximately:

_____Pre 1950s   _____1970s
_____1950s   _____1980s
_____1960s   _____Currently under consideration/
                                in planning

c. The change in classification schemes is from:

_____Dewey to LC   _____LC to Dewey
_____Modified LC to standard, _____Modified DDC to std.,
       current LC   current DDC
_____Local system to LC   _____Local system to DDC
_____Other system to LC   _____Other system to DDC
(Which:_____) (Which:_____)

_____Other--Specify:_____

d. Reclassification affects/will affect:

_____Total collection   _____Part of the collection
                           _____Certain special collections
                           _____New materials only

LIBRARY MATERIALS CLASSIFICATION DECISION-MAKING SURVEY

9e. Please mark with X the ONE PRIMARY reason for the reclassification, and check mark (✓) any other contributory factors:

_____1) Collection size outgrew ability to provide needed
           specificity of old classification system.
_____2) Timing was right for reclassification due to current or
           anticipated automation within this library.
_____3) Public Service or Administration required the change.
_____4) There were public complaints about the old system.
_____5) It was determined the new system would reduce costs in
           the longrun.
_____6) More class numbers on copy available in the new scheme.
_____7) New system fits our workflow patterns and available
           staffing better.
_____8) We felt it would gain better acceptance from our public
_____9) It is important to reflect changes and additions to
           subject areas as they are specified by the classifi-
           cation schedules.
_____10) It is important to keep like materials together on the
            shelves.
_____11) We physically reorganized all or part of collection.
_____12) Other--Specify:_____
           _____
_____13) I don't know.

f. Please indicate with an X which of the following impacts of
reclassification have actually occurred:

_____1) Reclassification has caused at least moderate confusion
           and inconvenience for patrons and/or staff.
_____2) Triggered a thorough weeding of the collection.
_____3) Contributed to a growing cataloging backlog problem.
_____4) Improved cataloging workflow and staff allocation.
_____5) Made public service staff/administration happy.
_____6) Saved money, in the longrun.
_____7) Improved findability of materials on the shelves.
_____8) Improved collocation of materials on same subject.
_____9) No discernable negative effects.
_____10) No discernable positive effects.
_____11) I don't know.
_____12) Other--Specify:_____
           _____

10. Has/will online access to the catalog influenced your
approach to classification of materials?

a. _____Yes   _____No   _____Not applicable

b.   If yes, how? Mark X by the ONE PRIMARY REASON and checkmark
(✓) all others that also contribute.
_____1) More types of materials will be classified to provide
           more complete online access through call number
           searches.
_____2) "Closer" classification (e.g., more complete enumera-
           tion) of items will be practiced.
_____3) Other--Specify:_____

LIBRARY MATERIALS CLASSIFICATION DECISION-MAKING SURVEY

11. **Classification assumptions:** Mark the relative importance of the following possible assumptions, or principles, which underpin the decisions YOU make with regard to library materials classification policy IN YOUR LIBRARY. Grade the following possible assumptions on a scale of 0 to 10, with 10 being most central to your classification policy decision-making, 0 being neutral/no effect/no opinion, and 1 being completely opposite from your underlying classification principles.

a. _____ Classification is primarily important in this library as a shelf location device.

b. _____ Classification is primarily important in this library as a mechanism for bringing together like materials.

c. _____ The classification number determined by our source for cataloging copy is accepted without regard to where other materials are in our collection.

d. _____ Browser expectations with regard to where to find the item is an important consideration in our classification policy.

e. _____ It is important to carry the classification number out to its fullest extent in order to keep masses of materials from building up under one number.

f. _____ It is important to truncate classification numbers at some point in order to make numbers easier to remember.

g. _____ It is important to truncate classification numbers at some point in order to keep materials from getting too scattered on the shelves.

h. _____ The latest classification schedules must be accepted for the sake of efficiency and cost savings.

i. _____ Older editions and/or translations should be reclassified to current classification numbers in order to prevent dislocations of material when we are cataloging the latest editions into updated classification numbers.

j. _____ In our closed shelf library the exact classification number used makes little difference.

k. _____ In our open stack library shelf location is very important to user retrieval of specific material.

l. _____ In our open stack library the retrieval by users of related materials, and thus the logic of where each item is put, is very important.

m. _____ In our open stack library users should be able to find materials by going directly to the shelves once they have determined the general subject location.

Provide other assumptions or principles you ascribe to, and their relative weight, 1 to 10:

_____

_____

_____

LIBRARY MATERIALS CLASSIFICATION DECISION-MAKING SURVEY

12a. Which of the following types of material or collections are classified in your library by the main scheme indicated in Question 4 (e.g., Dewey, LC) or by some other classification scheme? Also, when the decision has been made not to classify or not to use the library's primary classification scheme, please indicate in the space provided ALL APPLICABLE REASONS (a.-k.) for that decision:

a. Special collection storage or shelving requirements.
b. Classification scheme inadequate for this type of material.
c. Closed stacks--no need to classify.
d. Classifying would take too much time.
e. Insufficient or not adequately trained cataloging staff to classify in this area.
f. Administrative or public service staff decision.
g. Alternate schedule used is more appropriate to this type of material.
h. Classification too costly.
i. No particular reason.
j. I don't know the reason.
k. Other--Specify:_____

	Type of Class Scheme: LCC, DCC, Supt. Doc., Accession No., Etc.	Applicable Reasons (If not main scheme)
Mass market paper-back nonfiction	_____	_____
Sound recordings	_____	_____
Video/Films/ Filmstrips	_____	_____
Microforms	_____	_____
Rare books/mss	_____	_____
Federal docs.	_____	_____
State docs.	_____	_____
Local docs.	_____	_____
Maps	_____	_____
Periodicals	_____	_____
Romanized foreign lang. non-fiction	_____	_____
Non-romanized for. lang. nonfic.	_____	_____
Scores & Music	_____	_____

b. Are all classified materials intershelved, e.g., books, microforms, records, cassettes, etc.?
   Yes_____   No_____

13. Dewey Decimal Classification Use. (FOR DEWEY LIBRARIES ONLY; LCC USERS GO TO # 14)

a. The latest edition is accepted
_____Yes   _____No Edition used: _____
_____Partly Examples: _____

LIBRARY MATERIALS CLASSIFICATION DECISION-MAKING SURVEY

13b. If phoenix schedules are not used, or partly used, please
mark X by the ONE PRIMARY REASON and checkmark (✓) all other
contributing reasons.

_____1) Causes too much dislocation from other materials on
            subject.
_____2) Overlaps with other materials on different subjects.
_____3) We don't have staff/time to do necessary reclassifi-
            cations.
_____4) We object to Dewey Office's choice of numbers for this
            area/feel they are inadequate for our needs.
_____5) The old numbers do us just fine.
_____6) Public Service or Administration staff insisted.
_____7) No particular reason.
_____8) I don't know.
_____9) Other--Specify:_____

_____

c. This library generally, or often, shortens call numbers:

_____Yes   _____No
      _____At a prime mark
      _____Other

14. Library of Congress Classification Use. (LIBRARY OF CONGRESS
CLASSIFICATION USERS ONLY TO COMPLETE 14 AND 15.)

a. The latest edition of any class schedule is accepted.

_____Yes   _____No   _____Partly

b. The latest versions of literature, language, geographic
tables are generally accepted.

_____Yes   _____No   _____Partly

c. Do answers to 14a and b apply to copy, original cataloging,
or both?

_____Copy only   _____Original Only   _____Both

15. What class numbers assigned by LC are not used/accepted in
your library? Examples: U.S. Literature, Subject Bibliography
numbers in Z, etc.?_____

_____

AGAIN, THANKS FOR YOUR ASSISTANCE IN COMPLETING THIS
QUESTIONNAIRE.   PLEASE RETURN IN THE ENVELOPE PROVIDED TO:
ELIZABETH NICHOLS, STOCKTON PUBLIC LIBRARY, 605 NO. EL DORADO
ST., STOCKTON, CA 95202.

12

Classification and the Library User

Jennifer Younger

The question whether to classify library collections is a perennial one. While for the majority of libraries, the decision to classify books by subject has never been seriously questioned, administrative decision makers continue to ask the pragmatic questions, "To what extent is classification useful for this library?" and "To what extent is it more useful than other tasks?"

Classification has a specific purpose—to create order out of chaos. So when administrators look at the usefulness of classification to a library, they are really asking, "Why bring order out of chaos?" To date, administrators have been convinced that it is more worthwhile to classify library materials than to leave them unclassified. Of course, administrative willingness to classify rests on the fact that classification promotes use of the collection by library staff and users by organizing material by subject, thereby making it possible for library users to locate specific topics as well as specific items within the collection. Additionally, subject classification makes it possible to use different library collections in much the same way. In this way, classification is a key aspect of service to library users.

TWO APPROACHES BY LIBRARY USERS

The answer to the question, "Just how useful is classification for this library?" can be pursued by examining how the library patrons use the collection. What patterns do library patrons follow with regard to finding books or other materials at the shelves? According to Richard Hyman, "Very little research has been done on patron behavior in shelf-classified collections or on how the commonly applied classifications affect that behavior".[1] However, the observations of librarians and research studies have identified two basic approaches. First, there is the scenario in which a user searches the catalog under the author, title, or subject heading. He or she finds the exact call number of a particular book or books, which he or she wants to use, and goes to the shelves hoping to retrieve it.

In 1960 a pilot study, conducted by Saul Herner on the use of the Library of Congress book stacks, investigated the importance of marking the subject classification numbers on the books.[2] Through a questionnaire and interviews with patrons in the stacks, Herner found that most of the people were looking for specific books for which they had already identified the call numbers. Unfortunately, methodological problems and the fact that the Library of Congress may well be a unique library do not allow us to draw any firm conclusions from this study as to any generalized use of the method.

This approach can be labelled the "known-item" approach. Through the use of a finding tool such as the library catalog, the library patron finds a particular item of interest, copies down the call number, and goes to the shelves to retrieve it.

The second approach is one in which the user goes to the shelves looking for something but not necessarily with the thought of retrieving any particular book. This approach falls under the general term "browsing," here defined as the informed use of materials at the library shelves. Browsing is a possibility only when the materials have been arranged so that books and other materials on a particular topic are shelved in close proximity. Arranging literature and periodicals alphabetically by the author and title, respectively, also works to provide browsable collections. However, a shelf arrangement based on a meaningless characteristic, such as the date of acquisition, hardly lends itself to browsing.

A general class number may be known by the patron from repeated visits, through the explicit use of the classification schedules, or through searching a subject in the catalog. Karen Markey's recent research has revealed that one primary objective of subject searching at the catalog is to identify one or more call numbers for that subject.[3] These numbers are used not to find the specific titles, but rather they are used to pinpoint an area on the shelves where groups of related books are likely to be found.

STUDIES ON BROWSING

Because subject classification is a prerequisite for successful browsing, it is important to know how widespread shelf browsing is. Two studies on the general use of books investigated how much browsing is done in relationship to the number of books circulated. Herman Fussler and Julian Simon determined that there may be three to nine browsing uses for every circulated use of an item.[4] In a separate and later study, Joanna Ross determined that between five and six browsing uses occur for every circulated use.[5] Thus she adds supporting data to the statement that the ratio of books used at the shelf—or at least within the library—to books circulated is much greater than a one-to-one ratio.

The ability to explore a number of books and/or journals at the shelf represents a library service and convenience to users in several ways. A user can examine several books before deciding which, if any, fills his or her needs. A user who needs a book immediately can make a choice from the available books. Those who want several books on a topic may be able to find them in the same place, thereby making only one stop instead of several.

Patricia Willard and Viva Teece, in their investigation of browsers in libraries, asked two questions: "How often do public library users come to the library to browse?" and "How often do users select materials via the browsing strategy?"[6] They also define browsers as people who want books without having any specific books in mind. The researchers interviewed a random sample of 229 adult patrons as they left a suburban library in Sydney, Australia. Forty-eight percent of the patrons said they came to browse (in this order) in a specific area, a general area, or a particular author. Only 18 percent came to borrow a specific item or to find particular information.

Willard and Teece thereby confirmed their hypothesis that many people come to the library simply to browse. Yet, they wanted to prove not only the existence of the library browser, but also the importance of taking the browser's needs into consideration. What is the importance? In stating their conclusions another way, they found that three times as many people came to the library to browse as came to find specific items or specific information. If this is true, and clearly, replication of the study is in order for both academic and public libraries in this country, then a subject classification and shelf arrangement play a critical role in promoting use of a collection.

William Aguilar also found that shelf browsing accounts for books circulated.[7] At the Allerton Public Library in Monticello, Illinois, he selected 198 books randomly from the non-juvenile collection. The circulation for each title for a 14-week period was ascertained. The books were then divided into two groups. Group A had all related catalog entries withdrawn from the card catalog while the cards for Group B were left in the catalog. The circulation of books in the two groups was again recorded, and it was determined that the removal of the cards had no statistically significant influence on circulation.

A recent study, done in a medium-sized research library, examined the relationship between the number of access points in a catalog record, especially the number of subject headings, and the number of times an item circulated in a year.[8] Gunnar Knutson studied four subject areas within the LC classification. He examined the average number of LC subject headings per record and the rate of circulation for that item. He determined there was no significant association between the average number of LC subject headings per record and higher circulation. Further, he found that there was a negative correlation between subject headings and circulation for materials on criminology in HV (LC classification). Yet, the circulation figures indicated that, for the category of undergraduate library users, the circulation rate was exceptionally high. Together with the fact there was no significant correlation found between subject headings and circulation, the results suggest that browsing may play a larger role in high circulation areas than does use of the catalog to find specific items. The catalog may serve as a guide to the general classification number rather than to specific items.

BROWSING AND RETRIEVAL

Nonetheless, the effectiveness of shelf browsing as a retrieval device in libraries has been questioned as well as championed. According to John Boll shelf browsing as an approach to finding suitable materials is useful only in those situations when the search can be satisfied with the readily available items.[9] In his view, retrieval for research purposes requires both specific titles (because the text is unique) as well as comprehensive and systematic subject reviews. Therefore, for research purposes, shelf browsing alone results in insufficient retrieval.

There are several reasons shelf browsing alone results in limited, not comprehensive, retrieval. There is first the obvious reason that not all books are on the shelves at any given time. Some are circulating to other library users, some are at the bindery, and some are misshelved.

Second, ambiguities that result from shelf classification also work to prevent the user from finding everything on one subject while browsing at the shelves. A linear classified arrangement scatters related, but perhaps mutually useful, materials throughout the classification schedules. In U.S. libraries the general practice is to assign only one classification number, thus omitting designation of any minor topics treated in the book and reflecting only the perspective of the classification scheme, not necessarily that of the browser. What Robert Fairthorne dubbed as the mark-and-park approach, one that employs a single classification number primarily to "mark" the content of the item on the piece and to "park" the item on the shelf in the correct order among other similar items, adds to the limitations of browsing.[10] However efficient this is as a mechanism for retrieving documents from the shelves, it does not take full advantage of the subject revelatory aspects of classification.

Yet the need for systematic retrieval addressed by Boll must be placed in perspective with the findings mentioned earlier—that many people come to the library primarily to browse. Even for research purposes, there is one aspect of shelf browsing that is helpful to the research process, and that is the serendipitous discovery of titles on the shelf, which were not known to the researcher. Clearly, the two major patterns for using the library collections rest on different needs. One approach is based on the need for information or knowledge, which can be satisfied through the use of any one of several items. The second, however, requires specific titles to satisfy the demand. The value of browsing to a particular library will depend, therefore, on which of these two approaches predominates in that library.

BROWSING AND ONLINE CATALOGS

So far, we have been discussing classification as it is used to find related items on the shelf. However, online catalogs are provoking a renewed interest in call number browsing in the catalog. Currently, in most academic libraries, library patrons can make arrangements to "browse" the shelflist or to have shelflist cards pulled and copied for systematic retrieval in a subject area. A few libraries actually place the shelflist in an area where the public can use it at will.

Karen Markey and Anh Demeyer's experimental research demonstrated new search strategies not previously exploited in our present, limited use classification.[11] For their research, they constructed an experimental catalog, which contained bibliographic records together with the DDC classification schedules and the Relative Index to the schedules. Catalog users were able to conduct a subject search using keyword access to the first subject heading in the bibliographic records, to entries and captions in the DDC schedules and terms in the Relative Index. The resulting screen display showed the relevant portion of the classification schedules and allowed the user to browse via classification. Browsing through a subject outline, i.e., the classification schedules, presented in an online catalog offers the same potential for orienting searchers to the topic and assisting them in finding material as does browsing among items on the shelves. While reminiscent of classed catalogs, the use of classification numbers independently of the shelf location is an exciting new concept in providing access to library materials.

The concept of browsing in the online catalog may also change how we expect people to select nonbook materials. Nonbook formats, such as microforms, have usually been thought of as unbrowsable because they cannot be read except at a microform reader. Likewise, a cassette tape cannot be heard except at a listening station. Therefore librarians are able to justify unclassified arrangements because users will have little interest in browsing through title headers on the items. Such rationalizations, made primarily for reasons of cost and secondarily justified by the seeming impossibility of browsing, will be more difficult in the future should patrons adapt their searching strategies to browsing through classification numbers in the online catalog. Classifying all formats of materials is not a new idea. *Nonbook Materials: The Organization of Integrated Collections* suggests that the benefits of subject classification be extended to materials usually given accession numbers.[12]

A survey of academic and public libraries in California showed that for five types of materials—sound recordings, video/films, microforms, maps and periodicals—over half of the libraries use alphabetical or accession number arrangements.[13] In addition, 24.1 percent of the libraries with sound recording collections use the Alphanumeric Classification for Sound Recordings (ANCSR). Only 25 of the 205 libraries responding to the survey anticipated a push from online catalogs for the classification of more types of materials.

BROWSING AND CLASSIFICATION POLICY

Given the coexistence of these two approaches to using library collections—known item searching and browsing—the same survey of California libraries asked how important it is that library users be able to find materials by going directly to the shelves once they have determined the general subject location.[14] The answer: moderately important, the average score was 7.7 on a scale of one to ten.

The survey also investigated what browsing means to library classification policy and asked cataloging administrators how important the following statement is to their classification policies: "Browser expectations with regard to where to find the item is an important consideration in our classification policy." This statement received a score of 6.9, which indicates that browser expectations are moderately important to the classification process. Further analysis of the questionnaire data revealed that there are significant differences in the responses of different types of libraries. As already mentioned and reaffirmed in this survey, public libraries considered meeting browsers' expectations through the process of classifying more important than did academic libraries.

CONCLUSION

Several things emerge from this brief discussion of known item searching, shelf browsing, and classification policies. Even though limited in numbers, research studies tell us browsing is an important approach to the use of library materials. Second, cataloging administrators, at least as it can be determined from those in California, believe that users should be able to find materials by going directly to the shelves once they have determined the general subject location. Last, we should continue classifying library materials, that efforts to shortcut this process may be efficient but not necessarily effective.

Still, many questions remain unanswered. How does the size, layout, and materials type composition of the collection affect browsing? Do users expect to browse in all types of libraries? Will classification numbers in the online catalog make actual shelf arrangement less important in terms of users' expectations, access to, and use of the collections? Will browsing in the catalog be a partial substitute for shelf browsing or be used only in addition to shelf browsing? These questions are critical because the expected use of a library collection guides what resources are expended to provide the necessary arrangements.

REFERENCES

1. Richard J. Hyman, *Shelf Classification Research.* Occasional Papers of the University of Illinois Graduate School of Library Science, no. 146. (Champaign/Urbana, IL: University of Illinois, 1980), 3.
2. Ibid, 10.
3. Karen Markey, *Research Report on the Process of Subject Searching in the Library Catalog* (Dublin, OH: OCLC Office of Research, 1983), 20.
4. Herman H. Fussler and Julian L. Simon, *Patterns in the Use of Books in Large Research Libraries* (Chicago: University of Chicago Library, 1969), 115.
5. Joanna Ross, "Observations of Browsing Behavior," *College & Research Libraries* 44 (1983): 269–276.
6. Patricia Willard and Viva Teece, "The Browser and the Library," *Public Library Quarterly* 4 (1983): 55–63.
7. William Aguilar, "Influence of the Card Catalog on Circulation in a Small Public Library," *Library Resources & Technical Services* 28 (1984): 175–84.
8. Gunnar Knutson, "Does the Catalog Record Make a Difference?" *College & Research Libraries* 47 (1986): 460–9.
9. John J. Boll, *Shelf Browsing, Open Access and Storage Capacity in Research Libraries* (Champaign, IL: University of Illinois, Graduate School of Library and Information Science, 1985), 24.
10. Robert A. Fairthorne, "Mathematics of Classification," in his *Towards Information Retrieval* (Hamden, CT: Archon Books, 1968), 86.
11. Karen Markey and Anh Demeyer, *Dewey Decimal Classification Online Project* (Dublin, OH: OCLC, Office of Research, 1986), p. 20.

12. Jean R. Weihs, Shirley Lewis and Janet Macdonald, *Nonbook Materials: The Organization of Integrated Collections*, 2d ed. (Ottawa: Canadian Library Association, 1979), 3–4.
13. Elizabeth D. Nichols, "Classification Decision-making in California Libraries," published as Chapter 11 in this volume.
14. Ibid. p. 156.

13

Summarizing the Preconference

Arnold S. Wajenberg

There are a number of areas connected with classification that do, indeed, seem to recur in many chapters of this book. One of the first that impressed me was the fundamental importance of classification in what we do in libraries, and for the users of libraries. This was either implicit, or often quite explicitly stated throughout this volume.

People really like to browse through library collections, and it is classification that lets people browse perhaps better than anything else. There is no question that this is true of whatever kind of library you are working in. I must admit that I have spent my professional career in academic libraries, but over the years I have met and talked with people who work in public libraries, and people who work in school libraries, and special libraries, and my impression is that all of the users of those libraries really like browsing.

If materials are not grouped meaningfully on the shelves, browsing is virtually impossible. Here I would like to insert a small defense of that disgraceful American preference for marking-and-parking. There's a lot to criticize about it, but on the other hand, if you are using a class number to mark-and-park your material, you are still arranging that material in meaningful groups. Even if the practice does not have all of the advantages of full original classification, it still puts material together with related materials on the shelves, and the person who likes to go and look for himself or herself is served thereby. And users obviously like to do that.

There's a real reason for users' predilection for browsing that lies in the sort of psychological difference between making use of a library and making use of a school or a school environment. The person who goes to any kind of a school, whether it's kindergarten, or a graduate department at a university, or a continuing education function as presented for instance, by ALA and the various state associations, is essentially passive. You are acted on by the agency that you go to. You go to the classroom and you sit. Your activity for the most part consists of listening and taking notes. If you are particularly brave, you may ask a few questions. That's the extent of your action.

In a library, the institution is passive and you are active. You go with your particular needs and interests and requirements and you do not care what anybody else's interests are. You are going for what you want. You act on the institution, and it is by browsing that you can act on the institution in the most immediate and direct way. So the classifier, by grouping materials with other related materials on the shelves, is enabling the most fundamental kind of service that a library provides. Classification allows the library to be used by the patron instead of using the patron. The patrons like that. We all like that. We like to feel that we are in command of what we are using.

John Comaromi in Chapter 5 suggested a perhaps more fundamental reason that the act of classifying is important. He put it this way: "the social role of the library as an organization is the organization of knowledge." Now, in a sense, that statement needs to be interpreted in conjunction with something that Phyllis Richmond said. We have to remember that when we act as classifiers in a library we are not merely classifying the subject. We do not classify physics or philosophy. We classify material about the subjects, and this "aboutness" makes a difference in the way we approach classification.

But what virtually all the chapter authors are saying is that it is important to use classification for information retrieval. That is the basic reason that we classify the materials that come into our libraries. This leads us to another constantly recurring theme in this book, which I am sure surprised no one: the added importance of classification now that we are increasingly using machine systems. I am going to heroically resist the temptation to present you with a comprehensive summary of Karen Markey's chapter. I will point out, however, that the relationship between machine systems and classification is not limited to Karen's presentation of a very specific, very detailed research project involving the use of a classification scheme in an online catalog. Virtually every chapter at some point or another mentions the importance of machine catalogs in information retrieval. This was particularly true in Russell Sweeney's chapter, which is a very interesting and very valuable correction to our rather parochial view of classification in this country.

For decades the British have been using classification in a very real sense for information retrieval and not just as a basis for organizing material on shelves, although they do use classification for that purpose as well. Russell told us in the nicest way possible that it's about time that we caught up with them in this, and the online catalog makes it possible for us to use classification in a meaningful creative way that has never been possible before. That theme recurs over and over again. The things that make classification unique are the things that will help us the most in the online catalog. Russell also said that he thinks the machine catalog will allow British libraries to make greater use of alphabetic subject headings, and that we may be able to correlate the two on both sides of the Atlantic.

The classified approach to retrieval offers its emphasis on relationships, which is especially unique, on what is sometimes called a tree structure, or hierarchical relationships. I was interested therefore in Karen Markey's preliminary finding that one thing users really like is the ability to go from specific to general subjects. While you can do that by using the cross-reference structure in the Library of Congress Subject Heading system, it is certainly much more immediate and direct and obvious to do this through a classification system. A classification system is really designed to help you go from general to specific, or backward from specific to general, or even sideways to things that are related to your topic at the same level of specificity. I think that classification in conjunction with the alphabetical approach to subject retrieval is going to allow us not only to retrieve more, but to refine our searches when we retrieve too much.

Hugh Atkinson mentions that one of the problems we run into so often with our nice new automated catalogs is that when we enter our searches we get more than we can use. Most users of our catalogs do not want to look at 576 bibliographic items that answer their search query. They do not have the time. This problem may often be helped by a classified approach. Classification will be able to help us refine our searches in conjunction with subject headings to get what we really want.

Another advantage to classification is that classification transcends language. Obviously the numbers by themselves are not very meaningful unless you are very familiar with the schedule, so you have to have an index in a natural language that will get you to the number. But once you have the number that embodies the concept, it no longer matters whether you get to it from an index in English, or German, or Swedish, or Russian, or Urdu. The classified approach then, allows you to cross not only geographic borders, but language borders as well. That is going to be increasingly helpful as our computerized systems allow us to bridge the Atlantic gap more and more frequently. We will be able to cooperate not only among ourselves in this country and on the North American continent, but also with our colleagues and libraries in Europe and other parts of the world.

Another frequently recurring theme—a little bit gloomier this time —is the problems we encounter. The one that comes up very, very often is the problem of change. Dewey users are perhaps especially sensitive to change, and it certainly gets a lot of publicity. Change looks more flamboyant and dramatic with Dewey because every few years there is a new edition. Of course, not everything in the old edition is changed, contrary to rumors to that effect, but parts of it are greatly revised.

Topics that used to be in one place are now in another place, and old numbers are sometimes reused with new meanings. This poses a very serious ongoing administrative problem in every library that uses any of these classification schemes.

Library of Congress classification also changes, so if you have been using Library of Congress schedules for a long time and you have not reclassified every time there were revisions, then you will discover that the books on Buddhism that you cataloged a long time ago are off in the BLs somewhere, while the books you are receiving now are in BQ. Library of Congress classification also revised the medicine schedule. And they really did revise it. They used the old numbers with new meanings. It was a Phoenix schedule for medicine. Shocking. But somehow none of the LC users were shocked. I don't know what it is about us Dewey users that makes us so sensitive.

Your choices for dealing with changes in classification schedules are all bad. You can stick with your old numbers and refuse to accept the new ones. You can stick with the 14th edition of Dewey if that is the one you like, or you can stick with the first edition of the medical schedule of the Library of Congress, but in the long run you will find your solution is increasingly unsatisfactory. For one thing, you cannot share cataloging. You cannot use the cataloging the Library of Congress produces because they are not using the 14th edition of Dewey or the unrevised medical classification any more. So if you want to use their numbers, you have to accommodate yourself to the revisions somehow.

But, how can you reclassify? My University Librarian was asked that very question just yesterday. In our library we leave the old things in the old numbers. We know it makes a mess on the shelves and we are sorry. We do not like what we do, but we do it anyway.

Once in a while, though, we are able to do something different. We persuaded the federal government to provide us money through Title IIC to reclassify our mathematics collection according to the Phoenix mathematics schedule. That is the main reason we chose mathematics as the sample catalog for Karen Markey's project. It was the only part of our collection that was "pure"—that is, where it is all classified according to one edition of Dewey. Actually we did not get the money just to reclassify. We got it to do a retrospective conversion into OCLC, converting the old records to AACR2 cataloging and making our math collection available to anyone to borrow, and at the same time reclassifying it to the 19th edition of Dewey. Now we are hoping to do the same thing with agriculture, but at this rate it is going to take us a while to bring the whole collection into line, and then the 20th edition of Dewey will come out and we will have a new set of different numbers to worry about.

On the other hand, you do have to keep up. That is, we make these changes in classification numbers not because we think it is fun, but because the literature changes, new subjects crop up, and old subjects are structured and approached in different ways by the people who write about them and by the people who use them. We really are in a bind. We cannot just say "I like the 14th edition so I'm going to stick with it." It just does not work. There's very little about computer engineering in the 14th edition of Dewey, and you have to have someplace to put the books you are getting.

This problem of change came up in Arlene Taylor's chapter on organizing copy cataloging. If you expect a support staff member to use the bibliographic record that is retrieved just the way it is, you better be careful. Suppose you found an old record with an old number on it. How will it fit into your collection?

That brings us to the final point: Deviating from standards always gets you into trouble. It is very seldom that you can say "always" about anything in cataloging and classification, but I have come to the conclusion that no matter how good the justification for saying, "In this case I don't like what the cataloging rules require, or what the classification schedule requires, or what the standard subject heading is. It is obviously wrong, so I'm going to do the obviously right thing and make my own rule (or number or heading, or whatever), and I'll commit my library to it." If you follow through with that intent, someday someone will curse your name for leaving him or her a mess to cope with. Following standards is more important than ever as libraries become more automated and as they simultaneously decentralize and integrate their operations. More and more often smaller units within our larger umbrella organizations are performing cataloging, and attempting to cooperate not only with each other, but also with other libraries across the state and the nation, and even the world. Whenever any of these units deviates from standards in cataloging or classification, in MARC coding, or in any other aspect of bibliographic control, it makes it harder for those units to use other people's work efficiently, and it also makes it harder for other people to use the deviant institution's work.

Contributors

Hugh C. Atkinson was, at the time of the presentation, University Librarian at the University of Illinois in Urbana-Champaign, a position he held since 1976, following five years as Director of Libraries at Ohio State University. Throughout his library career Mr. Atkinson explored uncharted territory, wrestling with problems such as how to bring a private city university into a state university system, how to design an online circulation system for a large decentralized library system, and how to restructure a library to take advantage of the possibilities and capabilities of automation. He was a frequent speaker on topics as diverse as automation, organizational structures, and interinstitutional cooperation. In addition to a series of columns on "Technology, Change, and People," appearing in *Library Journal*, his more recent publications included contributions to *Austerity Management in Academic Libraries* (1984), the 1984 *Bowker Annual,* and *Journal of Academic Librarianship.*

Lizbeth H. Bishoff was, at the time of the presentation, Principal Librarian for Support Services at the Pasadena Public Library, California. She subsequently joined OCLC as Manager of Cataloging and Database Services. Before moving to California, Ms. Bishoff held a variety of positions in public libraries in the Chicago area. She was active in professional organizations, holding numerous ALA positions, including serving on the Catalog Code Revision and Subject Analysis Committees, and Chair of the Resources and Technical Services Division's Cataloging and Classification Section. In 1984 she received RTSD's Esther J. Piercy Award. She was a member of ALA's Decimal Classification Editorial Policy Committee and Chair of the Planning Committee for the Classification Preconference and for the Regional Institutes that followed.

John P. Comaromi has been Editor and Chief of the Decimal Classification Division of the Library of Congress since 1980. Prior to joining the Library of Congress, he taught in the library schools for the universities of Michigan, Oregon, Western Michigan, Maryland, and California at Los Angeles. Mr. Comaromi is a frequent speaker at classification symposia and has in recent years appeared around the country conducting workshops on application of the Dewey schedules. He has written extensively on classification, including editing *DDC&: Decimal Classification Additions, Notes and Decisions since 1980.* His monographic publications include *Survey of the Use of Dewey Decimal Classification in the U.S. and Canada* (1975), *The Eighteen Editions of the Dewey Decimal Classification* (1976), *Book Numbers* (1981), *Manual on the Use of the Dewey Decimal Classification: Edition 19* (1982), and *Brevity of Notation in the Dewey Decimal Classification* (1983).

Mary W. Ghikas is Marketing Manager for Gaylord Information Systems. At the time of the preconference, she was the Executive Director of the Universal Serials and Book Exchange, before which she headed technical services operations at the Chicago Public Library. She is an active ALA member, serving in various capacities, including a term as an ALA Councilor at Large. In addition to her editing of *Authority Control: The Key to Tomorrow's Catalog* (1982), other publications include contributions to *Online Catalogs, Online Reference* (1984) and *Interlending & Document Supply.*

Karen Markey was, at the time of the preconference, a research scientist in the OCLC Office of Research, where she served as Principal Investigator for the Dewey Decimal Classification Project, in which the efficiency and acceptability of Dewey Classification as a searcher's tool for subject access, browsing, and display in an online public access catalog was tested. She subsequently joined the faculty of the library school of the University of Michigan. She has been an active speaker and publisher in the areas of her research. In addition to contributions to *Online Catalogs, Online Reference* (1984), *Annual Review of Information Science and Technology* (1984), 1983 ASIS conference proceedings, and numerous journal articles, her publications include *ONTAP: Online Training and Practice Manual for ERIC Data Base Searchers* (1978), *Research Report on the Process of Subject Searching in the Library Catalog* (1983), and *Subject Searching in Library Catalogs* (1984).

Elizabeth Dickinson Nichols is Technical Services Coordinator for the Stockton-San Joaquin County Public Library, Calif. Previously, she worked in technical services in public libraries in Florida and Minnesota. Ms. Nichols has organized and moderated workshops on library automation and technical services and has spoken to library and community groups on library automation, cataloging and classification, and affirmative action. She has been active in national and state professional associations, serving on the ALA Council, the RTSD Board, and in numerous other RTSD posts since 1975, as well as in positions in state and regional library associations. Her publications include articles and chapters on cataloging, library automation, and affirmative action. She also served as editor for the monograph, *Libraries and Affirmative Action* (1983).

Mary K. Dewees Pietris is Head of the Subject Cataloging Policy Office at the Library of Congress. Although she has spent most of her professional career at the Library of Congress, first as a Special Recruit and later as a subject Cataloger and Head of LC's Subject Cataloging, Ms. Pietris has also been Head of the Catalog Department at Northwestern University Library, and was a visiting member of the faculty at the University of Washington School of Librarianship. She is an active ALA member, having served on a variety of committees, including the Resources and Technical Services Division's Subject Analysis, and the

Library Administration and Management Association's Statistics for Technical Services Committees. She is presently the LC liaison to the Subject Analysis Committee. She is a sought-after instructor and was a primary member of the faculty of RTSD's Subject Headings Regional Institutes.

Phyllis A. Richmond was a faculty member of the 1966 RTSD Workshop on Classification, speaking on the advantages and disadvantages of the LC Classification system. She started her professional career as a serials cataloger, and after two more jobs and 14 years of practical experience she entered teaching, serving on the faculties of library science at Syracuse University and Case Western Reserve, and as a visiting professor of library science at UCLA. She has been honored repeatedly by her colleagues, receiving the ASIS Award of Merit in 1972, and the ALA/RTSD Margaret Mann Citation in 1977. Included among her publications are a variety of journal articles as well as *Introduction to PRECIS for North American Usage* (1981) and *Index to Scientific Journal Title Abbreviations in the Physical Review* (1964).

Russell Sweeney is Principal Lecturer of the School of Librarianship of Leeds Polytechnic in England. Prior to beginning his teaching career in 1967, Mr. Sweeney held a variety of positions in public libraries, and later in libraries of the United Kingdom Atomic Energy Authority. He has represented the Library Association to ALA's Decimal Classification Editorial Policy Committee, has served as the Library Association's representative to IFLA's Section on Classification and Subject Cataloguing, and to the National Forum on Bibliographic Standards, and has been a member of the British Standards Institution's Universal Decimal Classification Revision Committee. His numerous publications predominantly concern classification, appearing in journals such as *Catalogue & Index, Journal of Documentation, Library Resources & Technical Services* and *Journal of Academic Librarianship.*

Arlene Taylor is Associate Professor at Columbia University's School of Library Science. She began her career as a cataloger at the Library of Congress, after which she continued to catalog at Christopher Newport College and Iowa State University. She taught in the library schools of the University of Illinois at Urbana-Champaign, North Carolina Central University, and the University of North Carolina at Chapel Hill. At the time of the preconference she was on the faculty of the Graduate Library School at the University of Chicago. She has a knack of anticipating issues of emerging concern to librarians, and her investigations into the problems and potential of authority control in an online catalog have excited considerable interest. She has authored articles in journals such as *Library Resources & Technical Services, Cataloging & Classification Quarterly,* and *Library Research*, and made numerous presentations. Her *Cataloging with Copy* is a standard work. Her doctoral dissertation *AACR2 Headings* (1982) was a welcome addition to the literature in the year surrounding Day One. She was also closely involved with the sixth and seventh editions of Wynar's *Introduction to Cataloging and Classification*, and was editor of Frost's *Cataloging Nonbook Materials* (1983).

Arnold S. Wajenberg is Principal Cataloger at the University of Illinois at Urbana-Champaign. Prior to coming to Urbana he held a similar position at the University of Chicago. Mr. Wajenberg has served professional organizations in a number of capacities. He was a member of ALA's Decimal Classification Editorial Policy Committee, the Committee on Cataloging: Description and Access, the ALA/RTSD Cataloging and Classification Section Executive Committee, and ALA's delegate to the IFLA Standing Committee on Descriptive Cataloging. Mr. Wajenberg has been active in a number of continuing education efforts. In addition to being on the Planning Committee for RTSD's Regional Authorities Institutes and conducting OCLC workshops, he had major responsibility for the Illinois Library Association's highly successful AACR2 workshops. He was responsible for the text in the ALA bestseller *Guidelines for Using AACR2 Chapter 9 for Cataloging Microcomputer Software* (1984) and has published articles in such journals as *Information Technology and Libraries, Illinois Libraries,* and *Law Library Journal.*

Nancy J. Williamson is presently working on the creation of a MARC format for the LC Classification Schedule. She has been on the faculty of the School of Library Science, University of Toronto since 1965, but she began her professional career at the Hamilton Public Library in Hamilton, Ontario, where she was first a cataloger, and then head of the catalog department. She has been active in the Canadian, American, and Ontario Library Associations, serving in both appointed and elective capacities. A frequent speaker, she has published in such journals as *Library Resources & Technical Services,* and *International Cataloguing.* She was a member of the Planning Committee for the Classification Preconference and Regional Institutes that followed.

Jennifer A. Younger is Assistant Director for Central Technical Services at the University of Wisconsin-Madison where previously she served as Catalog Editor and as Head of Machine Readable Cataloging. She also has held positions at the U.S. Department of State Library and at Northwestern University Library. She has been an active member of American Library Association and the American Society for Information Science, serving on the RTSD Board of Directors and as Chair of the Council of Regional Group and as Vice-chair of the ASIS Classification Research Section. She presently is a delegate to the OCLC Users Council. She was the author of "Year's Work in Subject Analysis, 1981" appearing in *Library Resources and Technical Services,* vol.26:263-276.

CLASSIFICATION PRECONFERENCE PLANNING COMMITTEE:

Lizbeth J. Bishoff (Chair): Director, OLUC Product Management, OCLC.

Betty G. Bengtson (Co-editor of proceedings): Associate Director for Bibliographic Control and Access Services, Suzzallo Library, University of Washington, Seattle.

Janet Swan Hill (Co-editor of proceedings): Assistant Director for Technical Services, University of Colorado, Boulder.

Karen Muller (Preconference Moderator): Executive Director, ALA Association for Library Collections and Technical Services.

Mary K. Dewees Pietris: Head of the Subject Cataloging Policy Office of the Library of Congress.

Nancy J. Williamson: Professor, School of Library Studies, University of Toronto.

Index